I0212026

Slavery and Abolitionism on Cape Cod

A Massachusetts Incongruity

Michael V. Pregot

LOCAL HISTORY
PRESS
an imprint of Sunbury Press, Inc.
Mechanicsburg, PA USA

LOCAL HISTORY
PRESS

an imprint of Sunbury Press, Inc.
Mechanicsburg, PA USA

Copyright © 2024 by Michael V. Pregot.
Cover Copyright © 2024 by Sunbury Press, Inc.

Sunbury Press supports copyright. Copyright fuels creativity, encourages diverse voices, promotes free speech, and creates a vibrant culture. Thank you for buying an authorized edition of this book and for complying with copyright laws. Except for the quotation of short passages for the purpose of criticism and review, no part of this publication may be reproduced, scanned, or distributed in any form without permission. You are supporting writers and allowing Sunbury Press to continue to publish books for every reader. For information contact Sunbury Press, Inc., Subsidiary Rights Dept., PO Box 548, Boiling Springs, PA 17007 USA or legal@sunburypress.com.

For information about special discounts for bulk purchases, please contact Sunbury Press Orders Dept. at (855) 338-8359 or orders@sunburypress.com.

To request one of our authors for speaking engagements or book signings, please contact Sunbury Press Publicity Dept. at publicity@sunburypress.com.

FIRST LOCAL HISTORY PRESS EDITION: July 2024

Set in Adobe Garamond Pro | Interior design by Crystal Devine | Cover by Lawrence Knorr | Edited by Sarah Peachey.

Publisher's Cataloging-in-Publication Data
Names: Pregot, Michael V., author.
Title: Slavery and abolitionism on Cape Cod : a Massachusetts incongruity / Michael V. Pregot.
Description: First trade paperback edition. | Mechanicsburg, PA : Local History Press, 2024.
Summary: It is possible that two seemingly diametrically opposing actions can be true simultaneously? Massachusetts was the very heart and soul of the antislavery and abolitionist movement in America while originally serving as an early central hub for the slave trade in New England. To understand the transition, we must look at religious views, political positions, economic factors, and social movements of the day.
Identifiers: ISBN : 979-8-88819-229-0 (softcover) | ISBN : 979-8-88819-230-6 (ePub).
Subjects: HISTORY / United States / State & Local / New England (CT, MA, ME, NH, RI, VT) | HISTORY / African American & Black | SOCIAL SCIENCE / Cultural & Ethnic Studies / American / General.

Product of the United States of America
0 1 1 2 3 5 8 13 21 34 55

Continue the Enlightenment!

This book is dedicated to the true spirit of the words,
"All men are indeed created equal."

Contents

Contents

Acknowledgments

The following people are acknowledged for their assistance in the preparation of this study.

Stephen Allen of the Brewster Ladies Library for his technical assistance.

Rebekah Ambrose Dalton, archivist and reference librarian for The William Brewster Nickerson Cape Cod History Archives, for sharing her materials.

Judith Kuhn Pregot for her constant support and assistance.

Sarah Peachey for her full review of the document.

Lucy Loomis, director of the Sturgis Library, for her help with gathering materials.

Preface

This study of slavery is not an exhaustive exercise apologizing for the evil past deeds committed by immoral people, nor is it a blatant apology of hypocritical people who espouse freedom in their words yet do not hesitate to promote the subjugation of an entire race. This research is merely an attempt to provide deeper context and examine different past events and historic facts found within an emerging country, one searching to define a new governing paradigm. The United States now has centuries of historic occurrences to review. Its stated goal was to treat all men equally in a democratic society, although it seems our country has based its most important actions with our fellow races on dominant political structures more than any moral guidelines. Without a doubt, an analysis of past actions dealing with our understanding of the slave trade is certainly worthy of deeper study.

Since much of the research centers on maritime factors, it is quite understandable how Massachusetts, particularly Cape Cod, played such an important role in these historic developments. America is often viewed as a novel national experiment starting with puritan values, desiring to embrace all forms of freedom in religious and personal expression. Even given this limited definition, it dismisses the presence of our Indigenous people, who were given little voice and were frequently found bound in the shackles of slavery or servitude. The fertile bounty of the sea and the riches connected with deep sea trading were often seen as a prominent key in our colonial development, which connects us directly to slave trading.

Race-based slavery would become a significant factor in our country's history with a long-lasting legacy. It continues with America grappling over nuanced interpretations, even today.

Accepting any form of slavery as a norm coming from the roots of puritan values seems enigmatic and illogical. There is little doubt that slavery, from the very beginning of our nation's origin, was always controversial and highly polarizing. There were only a handful of enlightened men consistently rejecting human slavery, while most ordinary citizens straddled the fence on this issue. From the genesis of American history, people were fully divided into two philosophical camps. Some defended slavery as a political and economic necessity, while others saw it as an unjustifiable and immoral manner in which to treat other human beings.

Can two seemingly diametrically opposing views be true simultaneously? Can we call Boston the very heart and soul of the abolitionist movement while, at the same time, proclaiming it as one of the early central hubs of the slave trade in New England? The response may lie directly in how we pose the question. Can we use past historic events and precedences to better understand our sense of common values held today?

In 1676, an English colonial administrator named Edward Randolph affirmed in his official report to the king that there were under two hundred slaves within the Bay State Colony. By 1860, even though the official federal census data reported zero, researcher Paul Finkelman estimates the number of enslaved people in the state to have been between four thousand to five thousand people.[1] Records on existing slaves can be found in legal wills, estate claims, and handwritten notes coming from legal documents. The growth of this number suggests that the slave population had clearly diminished compated to our overall population percentage; however, it highlights that, for whatever reason, the practice never ended.

As a developing country, taking a firm stand either for or against slavery was consistently argued on moral, legal, religious, financial, political, and even existential grounds. Defining exactly what slavery meant was a complex issue, only tangentially cited in our original Constitution. In fact, the actual term "slavery" was not mentioned. However, the term

---

1. Paul Finkelman, *Slavery in the Courtroom: An Annotated Bibliography of American Cases* (Washington, D.C.: Library of Congress Publication, 1985), 43–44.

"import of persons" was used in Article 1, Section 9, signifying it was a future issue needing attention.

An action approved by Congress defining the very first set of "census" protocols reveals some guiding principles. There is an explanation of how to record representation for whites, others, and slaves in the final count. This decision makes the matter clear. In newly formed states that approved slavery, slaves would be counted as three-fifths of a person for the final determination of acquiring population-based congressional representation. Slavery, as a viable concept and a national practice, existed from our nation's very start. It was granted more than just implicit tacit approval. The concept was used as an obvious strategy, allowing a consensual-based proposal as a vehicle to move acceptance of our first Constitution forward between Northern and Southern states.

This concept appears antithetical to the intentions of our Founding Fathers. The framers of American laws were revolutionary and well-intended thinkers possessing a vision to initiate a country where equity and justice for all could thrive. The founders had a goal of establishing what might become the first successfully functioning representative government in the world, formed by free people, declaring boldly that "all men are created equal." However, seventy years after the original document, a president knew a civil war was inevitable. In his Gettysburg Address on November 19, 1863, Lincoln displayed his admiration for the fallen Civil War soldiers by announcing, "These dead shall not have died in vain—that this nation, under God, shall have a new birth of freedom and that government of the people, by the people, for the people, shall not perish from the earth." A restart of our history was in order.

On external appearance, the Founding Fathers of Benjamin Franklin, Thomas Jefferson, and James Madison took the beliefs of John Locke quite seriously regarding an enlightened view of humanity. Yet, in their private lives, their actions portrayed a different story. As a young man, Franklin held slaves and permitted slave advertisements to run in his paper, the *Pennsylvania Gazette*. Jefferson not only employed enslaved people, but he also raised an entire second family with slavery bloodlines. James Madison owned over one hundred slaves, enabling him to acquire greater wealth. After the United States Constitution was eventually finalized, a change of tone emerged in which Franklin petitioned Congress to end all slavery protocols, and James Madison expressed anti-slavery sentiments even while accepting an inheritance of several new slave families.

While the Age of Enlightenment was a period in which scientific advancements, opposition toward monarchs, and religious freedom flourished, it was also a time concurrent with an increase in the Black slave trade. Hundreds of people were enslaved, forcibly being transported from Africa to the Western Hemisphere.

The unfortunate reality is that slavery flourished due to financial considerations. Plantation owners in the southern United States, the Caribbean, and South America profited from slave labor. The merchants in the shipbuilding industry in the North, who were responsible for constructing and maintaining slave and cargo ships, also benefited financially. Banks and lending institutions that backed the transport of slaves gathered greater wealth.

These initial designs of fairness, justice, and individual personal rights are what many political figures are striving to better clarify and define today. The birth of the United States occurred during a period of profound enlightenment, a refreshing political era with newfound excitement, and an era for revolutionary ideas to arise. Through all this philosophic debate, a person's race would play a significant role, either conscientiously or not, in a person's status within this political experiment of our new nation.

To better understand this issue of preferential racial treatment in Massachusetts, we attempted to analyze it from legal, religious, political, and historic perspectives. One factor that presents itself repeatedly in our review is the crucial role the sea captains played. Mariners were engaged in various aspects and degrees of depth in this nefarious trade. First, there were captains who captured Indigenous people to sell. Later, the West Indies triangular trade route saw boats departing from Boston or Europe, bringing lumber to West Africa, and continuing to acquire enslaved people and bringing them to the West Indies.

The last triangular leg of the trip went from the West Indies to the American colonies, where all trades were finalized. It was not uncommon to see a lower grade of fish, such as alewife, shipped to Southern ports, or to see large cargos of cotton coming from plantations carried up to the North. Either in a direct way or in a related manner of business dealings, many sea captains saw profit from the slave trade.

The last part of this maritime perspective, dealing with the why and how slaves were brought to the New England colonies, is still under current research and analysis. There is little doubt that many slaves were brought to the New England coast by some of our local sea captains. Despite officially citing "zero" in the 1790 Massachusetts census records, historians theorize that the severity of potential legal court consequences after the 1780 Quock Walker case persuaded officials to be surreptitious. The viewpoint was that the estimated true number of 5,300 slaves was so small in comparison to the total free white male number of 95,433 that it was better to approach this number with discretion than admit any true numbers.[2] New York State reported they had 21,324 slaves that year, and Rhode Island proclaimed it had 948 slaves.

As a counterpoint to slavery, there were many captains who became staunch defenders of antislavery movements, wishing to see this injustice end. Many Massachusetts captains were also abolitionists wanting to free slaves, fighting for freedom from bondage. Other captains engaged in the slave trade passively, supporting its promulgation just by carrying certain types of cargo. These mariners may not have directly conveyed slaves from port to port, but they clearly stayed mute about slavery's basic existence or the indignity inherent in the slave trade route. The overall profit margin seemed to be the usual prevailing motivating factor.

Most certainly, there was a perplexing dichotomy on any issue with slavery facing mariners. Immediately after the Revolutionary War, any captain wishing to continue with slave acquisition might face individual state charges based on local court decisions. Other captains who were strongly against the continuation of the slave trade might have considered rescuing slaves who were planning a Northbound freedom run. However, they, too, would then be liable to face charges from federal regulations with the passage of the Fugitive Slave Act. This act made any form of abetting slavery escape a criminal matter. Captains who were

---

2. Joann Pope Melish, *Disowning Slavery: Gradual Emancipation and "Race" in New England, 1780–1860* (Ithaca: Cornell University Press, 2000), 67.

more on the abolition side attempting to take active measures to free Black slaves would be tried in federal courts for violating the Fugitive Slave Laws.

Daniel Webster, a member of the Federalist Party, presents us with an example of his own cognitive dissonance on this issue. The way he felt about slavery differed significantly from the words he would utter.[3] Webster is often quoted as saying that "slavery is more a matter of historical reality rather than a moral principle. It is an established fact." He argued that slavery's existence in the territories had been settled when Congress prohibited slavery in the Northwest Ordinance of 1787. However, he fails to consider how the Union had divided regions into slave and free states in the 1820 Missouri Compromise. If the issue was viewed as being officially settled, it is far from clear. While serving as secretary of state in Washington, he lived an outwardly lavish lifestyle that included the use of personal servants.

However, Webster never possessed sufficient funds to directly purchase freedom for his servants. Instead, he decided to pay them an annual salary that they could personally maintain. These funds could then be used to purchase their own freedom from bondage. Webster spent much time residing in Sandwich on Cape Cod, serving as an attorney in the Barnstable Courts. At the federal level, he promoted the Compromise of 1850, when Congress admitted California as a free state; settled boundaries of Texas and New Mexico; created a territorial government for Utah; upheld the rights of slaveholders over escaped slaves; and banned slave trading in the nation's capital. His future presidential ambitions seemed well aligned with his conciliatory legislation.

One basic factor remains for the slave trade. The sea was the major thoroughfare for its delivery. From the initial travel from Africa, and later to the escape route to freedom from the South, captains carried their cargo over the ocean waves. Evidence suggests that what has been considered for decades to be a land-based operation, the Underground Railroad might be more accurately termed "the Maritime Escape for Slaves." Historical records verify that perhaps more than half of all slave flights to

---

3. Joel Richard Paul, *Indivisible: Daniel Webster and the Birth of American Naturalism* (New York: Riverhead Books, 2022), 168.

the North were accomplished through the first leg of a maritime journey coming in some form of a boat or an ocean vessel.[4]

Colloquially, the term "slavery" typically strikes up a picture of one race enslaving another. In fact, white colonists bought and sold the indentured labor of white, Indigenous, and Black people in the seventeenth-century Americas. The implementation of race-based slavery is a phenomenon with a legacy that flowed seamlessly through the indentured servant system. Trying to conjure up a way to legitimize slave ownership after the Civil War, new terms for contract labor, such as indentured servitude, provided many citizens with the potential to sustain its existence.

---

4. Timothy D. Walker, ed., *Sailing to Freedom: Maritime Dimensions of the Underground Railroad* (Boston and Amherst: University of Massachusetts Press, 2021), 28.

CHAPTER ONE

Early Slave Traders from Massachusetts

To start our study of slavery in Massachusetts, we need only go back to our first governor of the Massachusetts Bay Colony, John Winthrop. A six-hundred-acre estate, eventually named Ten Hills Farm, was founded slightly north of Boston. Winthrop, envious of establishing his "city upon a hill," bought and owned slaves to build and improve his property. He also was responsible for the first set of laws passed in New England, which both permitted and condoned the act of slavery itself. Every successive owner of this property, from the Winthrops to the Usher family, from the Ushers to the Royalls, kept the same legacy intact, engaging in the North Atlantic slave trade. By the 1780s, when Massachusetts legally abolished the slave practice, very little was discussed or even written about it, given this complex history. Nonetheless, many great fortunes were built.

In the first stages of the English colonization of America, land was much more of a valued prize than directly owning people. Finding a large labor source among the Indigenous people to build a new nation was not a vision the puritans had formulated. Nonetheless, if the conquered rebellious people were ever defeated in a justifiable war, the concept of taking long-term hostages was seen as permissible. Now Indigenous people could be used as a spoil of battle. The story of Indigenous slavery directly within the city of Boston was earlier than most people thought yet distinct from chattel slavery.

At first, the Indigenous people of Massachusetts were larger in overall numbers than Europeans and had more mobile populations residing in different geographic areas at various stages of time. The English colonists seemed intent on establishing a "New" England, where a settler colony, preferably of English heritage, would be welcomed. The Indigenous people, under certain conditions, could be captured, enslaved, and made to work the land. Plus, Indigenous people were often seen as a significant barrier to setting up a new colony. It was perhaps an unwritten goal, but their removal could be accomplished by war or by pushing large segments of people to the side. Hence the creation of an accepted Wampanoag jurisdictional land in Mashpee at Cape Cod became a convenient strategy for puritan growth. In addition, many captured Indigenous people were brought by New Englanders to the West Indies to be used in the Atlantic Slave Trade.

One might wonder why the use of Indigenous people was not perceived as a viable labor force, yet Black slaves were more readily seen as being better suited to the task. Indigenous people carried a greater degree of risk with them. It would be much more difficult for African people to rebel when they did not know the local terrain and lacked the potential for any immediate kin to run in for a rescue.

With the establishment of the first New England colonies, slavery and colonization were closely connected. In the preliminary days of the Massachusetts Bay Colony, this new land seemed more experimental. There were no immediate signs of easy wealth to be extracted. The available cash crop of tobacco and produce seemed to be more of a Southern colony opportunity and not, in itself, of great importance. The viability of trade to the West Indies became a known commodity, leading to greater wealth. The English saw the value of sugar, rum, and active slave trading as a foundational way to construct a new colony.

THOMAS DUDLEY (1576–1653)
Governor of the Massachusetts Bay Colony

Thomas Dudley was born in 1576 to a wealthy British family. He started out as a Massachusetts colonial magistrate, eventually rising to oversee several terms as governor of the Massachusetts Bay Colony. Dudley is credited with founding Newtown and then later Cambridge. He built the town's first home. He provided funds to establish the Roxbury Latin School and signed Harvard College's new charter in 1636. During his term as governor, Dudley was always a devout Puritan who opposed any religious views that did not conform to his own. In this regard, he was seen as even more rigid than other early Massachusetts leaders, such as John Winthrop.

There is no direct evidence that he was ever a slave owner, yet he never saw evil in the system. He did own an indentured male servant, passing on the ownership of the servant to his wife. We also know that his son, grandsons, and great-grandsons had enslaved several different families for decades.

Thomas Dudley may never have enslaved Africans or Indigenous people, but he brought with him from England a strong belief in the legacy of multigenerational bondage. Historical records demonstrate that the Dudley family went from a concept of European indentured servitude to adopting a race-based chattel slavery practice within one generational cycle of arrival to the new continent.

What was once called Dudley Square in Roxbury junction has now been renamed Nubian Square. This shift re-centers focus away from a legacy of slavery to honor the Black community who has been living there for decades.[1]

SAM MAVERICK (1602–1670)

As early as 1638, there is evidence of black slaves being brought to New England. An English author and scientist named John Josselyn was commissioned to study what the new colonies contained that might be of future economic value. For example: What types of plants, harvests, animals, or natural products might be available for trade or commerce? While staying at the house of Samuel Maverick in Boston's harbor, Josselyn woke up one morning, hearing a woman screaming out for help. He ran out to see the cause of her distress. The woman responded in a crying voice in a language that he did not recognize.

Josselyn asked the homeowner what the matter was. Maverick responded that he wanted to expand his slave holdings by breeding Black people. He commanded a male slave to "Go to bed to her, willed she, nilled she."[2] In essence, he ordered a sexual assault on a slave, whether she was willing or not, so that his overall number of chattel slaves would

---

1. Brian MacQuarrie, "At Faneuil Hall, A Move to Recognize Slavery," *Boston Globe*, March 6, 2019.
2. Wendy Anne Warren, "'The Cause of her Grief': The Rape of a Slave in Early New England," *The Journal of American History* 93, no. 4 (March 2007): 24-25.

increase. This story confirms the belief that Black slavery occurred in New England much earlier than most historians stated. It was previously thought that the idea of cash crops had generated the concept of family slave ownership. The fact that it occurred in Boston is also noteworthy, in that Boston at that period did not have a cash crop or even a policy on a slave being held as a piece of negotiable ownership. From the very start, a certain group of people had a specific negotiable price placed on their very existence.

In 1631, one of the first ferries in the country ran from Samuel Maverick's farm in Chelsea to Charlestown and then to Boston's North End. Based on his relationships with prominent local officials, he purchased a great deal of Winnisimmet, known as Chelsea today. Seven years later, he sold his land holdings to Richard Bellingham, the deputy governor of Massachusetts. That same year, Maverick sailed to Virginia to buy corn and seed for his farm. Upon returning to the Bay State, he was proud to bring two fully rigged ships and a decent supply of livestock. In 1638, records show that he had acquired several Black slaves, making him one of the first Massachusetts slaveowners.

He saw owning land in Boston as a great investment, securing six hundred acres in Boston and four hundred acres in Braintree. In 1646, along with six other wealthy merchants, he petitioned the Massachusetts General Courts to moderate their local laws to align with the civil and church policies followed in England. This court petition and subsequent essay on the topic was called the Remonstrance. Maverick's sympathies with Great Britain and King Charles led to an appointment to a committee of four men commissioned to arbitrate any grievances in New England on behalf of the crown, and additionally aimed to reduce Dutch influence. Although his political efforts were never realized, the concept of owning slaves and taking them by ship to Boston prevailed for several years. He eventually moved on to live in New York.

As one of Massachusetts' earliest slave traders, he had a land interest in much of New England. A patent under Sir Ferdinando Gorges ceded Maverick land from Boston, Chelsea, Braintree, and Maine. After the Pequot War in 1638, he bought several African slaves who had been traded for Pequot captives. His direct confrontations with the protocol of

Puritan authorities based on his rights as an Anglican caused him several social and political problems. He was even sent to prison for a short time based on his religious beliefs.[3]

Maverick was ridiculed by many and eventually left the colony by 1648. He returned to England after the Restoration and wrote critical assessments of the state of colonial affairs, completing "A Briefe Description of New England and the Several Townes, 1660."

Four years later, Charles II appointed him to a committee authorized to investigate any new complaints to England initiated from New England. After the commission's term expired, Maverick later moved to New York in service to the king.

JOHN USHER (1648–1726)

An Official Sympathizer of Slavery

John Usher was a well-connected appointed official to the Massachusetts Bay Colony. His wealthy British family secured him a post as an English colonial administrator. Born in Boston, he first served as the treasurer of the Dominion of New England until 1686.[4] The Dominion of New England was a structure formed by England to centralize the control of the American colonies, passing laws that denied colonial expansion. Colonists despised this form of rule, as they would lose much of their local control. A Boston Revolt of 1689 overthrew this oppression. While in power, Usher advocated strongly for slavery. His official residence was in Medford on the Ten Hills Farm, where he frequently requested additional slaves be added to his holdings.

After the Boston Revolt of 1689, Usher's position changed. He was twice lieutenant governor of the Province of New Hampshire from 1692 to 1697, and then again from 1702 to 1715. As lieutenant governor, he directly held the reins of power since the appointed governor, Samuel Allen, his father-in-law, was often away from the province. Usher's rule was quite unsupportive of the colonial mission and only added to the importation of slavery. He died a most unpopular figure in Medford,

---

3. Alfred A. Cave, *The Pequot War* (Boston and Amherst: University of Massachusetts Press, 2009), 184-190.
4. Francis Hill Bigelow, *Historic Silver of the Colonies and Its Makers* (New York: Kissinger Publishers, 2005), 80-87.

Massachusetts. Usher's father, Hezekiah, was the first known bookseller in colonial America.

CHARLES APTHORP (1697–1758)
Slave Trader

He emigrated with his parents to New England sometime after 1698. In Boston, he served as a commissary and paymaster for the British Army while establishing his mercantile business. Apthorp was quite a successful, wealthy man with deep trading connections.

Among the goods Apthorp imported and sold on Merchants Row in Boston were Madeira wines, Russian duck, luxurious sorts of European goods, choice good sea coal, secondhand cables, window glass, and anchors of most types containing a parcel of lead shot. Most importantly, he owned a suitable, well-fitted fifty-ton sloop and a ninety-ton brigantine, which was three years old and was waiting at the Long Wharf for his disposal. He used these ships to bring slaves to New England.

By 1746, Charles Apthorp "was called the richest man in Boston,"[5] and much of that was due to the slave trade. Between 1719 and 1781, the *Boston Gazette* ran 2,300 slave advertisements for about 2,000 enslaved individuals.[6] In the 1730s and 1740s, he traded in slaves, posting advertisements in the *Boston Gazette*, with one stating that he had "a parcel of likely healthy negros just imported for purchase."[7]

He was a valued member of King's Chapel, where, still today, an alcove bears his name. King's Chapel is striving to reckon with its complex and nuanced roots. A church-funded research team discovered that at least 219 enslaved people were owned by 55 members.[8] Among its membership, four different ministers held slaves in the eighteenth century. It was during this time, between 1720 and 1750, that enslaved people drove the economy of the still-forming Massachusetts colony. Both enslaved Black as well as Indigenous people were baptized and attended services in the chapel.

---

5. Brian MacQuarrie, "Slave Trading in Boston," *Boston Globe*, March 10, 2023.
6. Vincent Carretta and Philip Gould, eds., *Genius in Bondage: Literature of the Early Black Atlantic* (Lexington: University of Kentucky Press, 201), 89.
7. MacQuarrie, "Slave Trading."
8. MacQuarrie, "Slave Trading."

Enslaved people were never permitted to sit within the general congregation space. They were always directed to the higher rafters of the church to partake in religious services. Indeed, the ministers of the day did not see any moral compromise or feel any type of indignation at the disparate treatment of human beings. Quite to the contrary, many thought that God's will was now being done by the conversation of non-Christian believers to an enlightened perspective on their views of religion and acceptance into polite society.

JOHN AND DAVID DEAS

At one point, the two brothers were among the top three importers of slaves in the country. Their store sold a sundry of items while it was known that connections to slave buying were among the inventories. To promote their business of slave trading, they developed a large wooden board that was displayed in the front of their store as well as images posted in flyers of the day. This advertisement measures 12½ x 8 inches. It would have been an excellent size to post in papers or even to pass out as a pamphlet. The woodcut posts the words "PRIME, HEALTHY NEGROES," and the graphic design is basic yet exceptionally memorable, at least to the sensibility of today's viewers. (See ad on page 8.)

The evocative image of Africans seen only as commodities for trade seems outlandish by today's moral standards, but that would not necessarily have been the case in the 1760s. Colonial consumers would not have been taken aback by this advertisement. People were seen as an accepted potential trade. Accustomed to trade cards and billboards of the day, colonists of the era would not have judged the Deas brothers' advertisement as horrific or even unusual in terms of its bluntness or lack of civility.

Operating from the port of Charleston, South Carolina, David and John Deas's newspaper advertisements for textiles do not indicate any direct involvement with the slave trade. However, it is known that their connections with various shipping captains were substantial. Nonetheless, their trade depicts the moribund aspects and mores of the times. The merchandise mentioned in their advertisements made them a vital part of the transatlantic slave network. Their wealth, gained by the

Charleftown, July 24th, 1769.

TO BE SOLD,

On THURSDAY the third Day
of AUGUST next,

A CARGO

OF

NINETY-FOUR

PRIME, HEALTHY

NEGROES,

CONSISTING OF

Thirty-nine MEN, Fifteen BOYS,
Twenty-four WOMEN, and
Sixteen GIRLS.

JUST ARRIVED,

In the Brigantine DEMBIA, *Francis Bare,* Mafter, from SIERRA-
LEON, by

DAVID & JOHN DEAS.

Slave Auction Ad

consumption of products that depended on human cargo, and their placement of newspaper advertisements offer important insight into the era's advertisement practices. To a small degree, it is evidence of a shopkeeper's, merchant's, or firm's willingness to accept and value slavery to accrue wealth. At their height, the Deas brothers were the third-largest slave traders within the colonies. Their connections to the port of Boston officials and with individual Massachusetts trading giants are not clearly documentable but appear integral to the overall transatlantic slave trade. The brothers operated out of South Carolina but wished to develop deeper relationships with textile and maritime suppliers in the North, particularly in Massachusetts.

PETER FANEUIL (1700–1743)

Peter Faneuil was one of the wealthiest people in Boston during his time. He made his fortune through trade, and his trade was made lucrative through slavery. Although Faneuil was not a major slave trader, his involvement in this system provides insight into the transatlantic economy of 1700s Boston.

Born in New Rochelle, New York, in 1700, Peter Faneuil was among the first in his family to grow up in America. His French Huguenot family fled their native France following the Edict of Nantes in 1685. When his father died in 1719, Faneuil and his younger brother, Benjamin, moved to Boston and became apprentices for their uncle, Andrew Faneuil. Andrew was already a successful merchant in his own right, having built an expansive trade network. Trade was essential to colonial New England's economy since its poor climate and rocky soil prevented potential cash crops. However, Boston's harbor, which offered rich fishing grounds and access to shipbuilding supplies, gave rise to a thriving shipping industry.

With his uncle's guidance, Peter learned to navigate the trade networks, eventually taking over when Andrew fell ill. When Andrew died in 1738, Peter inherited his entire fortune and focused on growing his empire. He traded various goods, including fish, rum, molasses, sugar, manufactured goods, and timber—anything that would net him a profit.

However, Faneuil's financial pursuits came at a human cost. During the late 1730s, slavery permeated every aspect of the transatlantic economy. Many New England merchants imported large quantities of molasses, sugar, and rum, all produced by enslaved labor. In Peter Faneuil's invoice book, entries such as "3 Hogsheads [approximately 189 gallons] of rum" and "77 tierces of molasses, 9 hogshead molasses [totaling approximately 3,800 gallons], 8 tierces sugar [approximately 336 gallons]" were found. These products demonstrate that Faneuil was willing to profit from goods produced by enslaved labor, which shows his acceptance of and complicity in enhancing the institution of slavery.

New England merchants fueled slavery in other ways. One of the most important exports from the region at this time was codfish. Merchants shipped quality cod to southern Europe, which had a high demand for the fish, but lower-grade fish was unmarketable. To get rid of the low-quality fish, New England merchants sold it to the West Indies. There, enslavers readily purchased the "refuse grade" fish to feed the enslaved people on plantations.

TIMOTHY FITCH (1725–1790)
Slave Owner and Trader

Timothy Fitch was a slave trader who resided in Medford.[9] He was a merchant of many wares and conducted business in several New England towns, including Boston, Salem, Nantucket, and Medford. Fitch owned several ships. One of his ships, the schooner *Phillis*, was used in the Atlantic slave trade, also known as the "triangular trade." In fact, the famous poet Phillis Wheatley, who wrote the first volume of poetry ever published by an African American woman, was seized from the Senegambia region. She was taken as a child in the mid-eighteenth century and carried on Fitch's ship, *Phillis*, from which her name was derived. His ships' cargo included slaves, rum, molasses, and various other items. Rum and molasses from Medford were taken to West Africa, where they were used to buy African slaves. The slaves were then transported to the Americas and later sold. The Medford Historical Society has shared a letter sent to Captain Peter Gwinn of Boston, authored by Timothy Fitch, written on November 27, 1769.[10]

Fitch hired several different captains. All received orders to sail from Boston to West Africa carrying goods to exchange for slaves. In many cases, such as the one cited below, rum was often the currency used for exchange.

> *Dear Captain Gwinn:*
>   *My orders are that you Embrace the first favourable opportunity & proceed to the Coast of Affrica, Toutching upon the Windward Coast. where I would have you dispose of your Cargo if Possible & purchase your Slaves, even suppose you to give One Hundred & Fifty Gallons Per head . . . for Prime Slaves . . .*

---

9. Medford Historical Society, "From Africa to Medford: The Untold Story," Medford Historical Society, https://medfordhistorical.orgmedford-history/africa-to-medford/ (accessed December, 14, 2023).
10. "Excerpts from Letters to his Ship Captains," Medford Historical Society, https://www.medfordhistorical.org/medford-history/africa-to-medford/timothy-fitch/ (accessed November 12, 2023).

Make sure you keep them be well tended to keep them in good shape and health. If you have any certainty of a Peace with France and Spain, you may bring home as much Molasses as will Load your Boat with the rest cash. But if you are not certain of a Peace you are then to come directly to Boston with Your Slaves. Lighten your Portage Bill by supplying your People as much as Possible and discharge all the Men you can spare as St Eustatia if you go there.

Your Cargo is one third more in value than the Last Voyage. By a moderate calculation sufficient to Purchase One hundred + twenty Prime Slaves, if well managed. You must be more careful in getting better Slaves than the Last Voyage. Your Wages are three pounds ten Shillings, free stay per Month, Four Slaves Privilege & four percent on the Sales of the Slaves, which is all you are to have. Notwithstanding what is mentioned before, you have Liberty to go to the West Indies in Case the War shall continue. If you think it most advisable to purchase a load of molasses, Coffee, Cocoa, do so.

Endeavor to come off the Coast with Some Ship of Force, if you go to the West Indies. Your Commissions is Six Percent of the Amount of the Neat proceeds of the Sail of the Slaves in the West Indies, which is all the advantage you are to have during the Whole Voyage. Write to me by all opportunities for my government in making Insurance and be very particular. I am wishing you a Good Voyage & a safe return.

Your Friend & Owner, Timothy Fitch

We learn much from the content of this written communique sent to his captain. We see a high priority given to the securement of healthy, younger males compared to elderly ones. Older slaves were only a secondary market, but younger females were most certainly preferred to acquiring any older slaves of either gender.

It is also clear that the wars between France and Spain were frequent, and great care was needed in certain geographic areas to avoid ships being taken as a prize of war. Fitch would have loved to be successful in working with crops such as molasses, coffee, and cocoa, but the inherent value of the slave trade was seen as being much more advantageous. He promised his captains that their salaries would be enhanced with the delivery of any new slaves brought to port in an upgraded, healthy condition. The cargo needed to be fully intact and carefully cared for during the voyage.

CHAPTER TWO

Religious Perspectives

There was a need for a young country to have a master plan to operate in a non-theocratic society. It was evident that even within various religious models, people held conflicting and usually opposing views on the moral standards of slavery. In looking at some early views of Puritan commerce and moral philosophy, we can see several issues of slave trading arise. Governor John Winthrop aspired to see the formation of a "city upon a hill" that would become a haven for all and could be a model for all cities in the world to follow. He also knew that significant industry and commerce must be concurrent to that goal to sustain their effort.

One important viable solution would be ocean trade. A Boston-built ship of two hundred tons, called the *Trial*, was captained by Thomas Coytmore and was the first vessel from New England to initiate deep sea trading from Boston. In 1644, in Winthrop's own words, he remarked:

> *Coytmore sailed first to the Azores where he found an extraordinarily good market for pipe staves and fish. He then took wine and sugan to sail to the West Indies to trade for tobacco, cotton, and iron. By the Lord's blessing, he made a good voyage which did much encourage the merchants, and made wine, sugar, and cotton very plentiful and cheap in the country.*

This quote reflects two salient points about the early commerce of the Bay Colony. First, we can see the products highly valued by the Northern ports, namely tobacco, sugar, and cotton. These items would soon be linked to the triangular trade route. Secondly, we note that the maritime industry was acclaimed as a most appropriate and legal business venture.

The people of Massachusetts took this endeavor seriously, and the seamen of Cape Cod often led the competitive race.

When Captain James Smith sailed the *Rainbow* toward the West African coast in 1644, he unwittingly became enmeshed with unscrupulous English slave traders. The slavers claimed that they took several slaves hostage after the local natives attacked them. When the Africans protested, the English traders used a cannon to destroy a village of almost one hundred people. A complicated series of transactions followed in the West Indies in which Smith remained in Barbados. Keysar, a well-known British slaver, arrived in Boston in May 1645, where he sold two slaves still in his possession. Captain Smith returned two months later to take Keysar to court to settle a complex business deal.

The court decided that the murders in the village were not within their jurisdiction, as different countries were involved. As far as the slaves go, it was ordered that they be returned to Africa, as their capture did not come about because of a just war such as the Pequot War with Indigenous people. It was a case of "manstealing." The court did not condemn the act of slavery itself, yet the process of how slaves were acquired became a stumbling block. The labor shortage in the colonies persisted as a looming issue.

In another case, a Rowley farmer did not have the means to pay the two oxen owed by legal contract to two servants under his agreement. The slaves could work one more year in exchange for the oxen. In court, the farmer asked, "How shall I pay you when all of my Cattel is gone?"

The servant replied, "You can work for me to reclaim them." Winthrop knew that the system of commerce for indentured servants was flawed, and that a new system was needed.

In 1645, two prominent New England families—the Downings and the Winthrops—corresponded about the potential for slavery to remedy the workforce issue. George Downing's son, Emmanuel, was married to John Winthrop's sister, Lucy. On a voyage to England, George wrote a long letter to his cousin, John Winthrop Jr., and suggested the young Winthrop move to Barbados and import indentured servants for a span of six to nine years at a time. The enticement of the puritan colonies to bring slaves to shore to develop wealth was present. George added the sentence, "*You know very well how we shall maintain twenty Moors (blacks) than one English Servant.*"

In straightforward terms, Downing saw a nation where three large groups of people could co-exist. There might be both captive Indigenous people and Black slaves taken from so-called "just wars" along with local whites. Slaves were simply a means to grow the regional economy. The wealthy owners could live in harmony with the subjugated people. This advice was not heeded by the Winthrops.

The primary issue between the Winthrops and Downings was "Should Massachusetts become more like the West Indies, or could they supply much-needed labor in a more racially inclusive manner?" There was always tension when creating a moral subjugation of people. They initially came up with a compromised stance, stating, "the praying indigenous people should have some semblance of dignity."

The Puritan Perspective

The Puritans settling in the Massachusetts Bay Colony were people with strong religious convictions, but nonetheless, like their many colonial equals around the world, they didn't wince to enslave a defeated human group. However, the Puritans believed they were following a practice that predated their arrival. Over the centuries, many New Englanders of Puritan origin grew wealthy in the slave trade, taking advantage before the importation of slaves was deemed illegal.

The Puritans failed to fully separate the religious aspect of humanity from the secular when it came to slavery. Using religious doctrine as an impetus, they were eager to save the souls of Indigenous people and Africans while keeping them in a state of confinement. Many Puritans did not waiver in their opportunity to obtain the servitude of captured white Europeans and Indigenous people.

Puritans also followed the practices of Indigenous people in their views of slaveholding. In fact, an early colonial work of literature delved into this very subject. News stories were written about Mary Rowlandson, a colonial woman who was captured by an Indigenous tribe along with her three children during the King Phillip's War. They were held captive for eleven weeks, and the youngest died of injuries inflicted during captivity. Eventually, Mary was given as a slave to another tribe. On May 2, 1676, the women of Boston raised £20 for Mary's ransom.

Eventually the advent of other religious views in the colonies changed the perception of enslavement. The decline of the Puritans and the rise of Congregational churches brought about practices such as the Half-Way Covenant, eventually leading to the rise of dissenting Baptists, Quakers, Anglicans, and Presbyterians in the late seventeenth and early eighteenth centuries.

The Jewish View

Ancient Israelite society allowed slavery; however, total domination of one human being by another was never allowed. Rather, slavery in antiquity among the Israelites was much closer to what would later be called indentured servitude. Slaves were seen as an essential part of a Hebrew household. Just repayment of a debt allowed for a person to become bound to a series of duties to a family for a specified number of months or years. The Jewish population in Massachusetts was relatively small in the early colonial days but grew steadily over the decades.

Aaron Lopez was the first known person of Jewish heritage in the American colonies. He was a captain and ship owner, arriving in Taunton in 1752. His family and the relatives of Jacob Rodriquez eventually settled in Leicester, founding the first settlement of their religious beliefs near Worcester. This group numbered sixty-one people, staying in Leicester until after the Revolution. The very first Jewish congregation was founded in Boston in the mid-1830s. Many Central European immigrants founded Ohabei Shalom, where they could practice their faith without persecution. This early group of believers never took a firm position on slavery, and at the same time, no records of slave ownership could ever be found by people of the Jewish faith.

The Catholic Perspective

Throughout human history, various forms of slavery were accepted by many cultures and regions where Christianity flourished. Within the Old Testament, temporary, approved slavery was an acceptable way to pay off debts. The Roman use of slavery was typically never criticized by the early Christians.

Once the Romans finally accepted Christian doctrines, there were many examples of mixed messaging. Some argued against all forms of slavery, as it seemed contrary to the concept of moral justice, while others, including the influential Thomas Aquinas, argued the case for slavery, which could be allowed but subject to certain restrictions.[1]

For the most part, a free Christian could not be enslaved, with a large exemption made when a captive was taken in war. However, this was subject to continual interpretation and applied inconsistently throughout history. The Middle Ages also witnessed the emergence of certain orders of monks who were founded for the sole purpose of ransoming Christian slaves. By the end of the medieval period, Christian enslavement was largely abolished throughout Europe, although enslavement of non-Christians was still allowed and had even experienced a resurgence in Spain and Portugal. Slavery's permissibility remained a topic of debate within the Church for centuries, with several Popes issuing bulls on the issue.

The Papal Bull of 1455 justified expanding (Black) African slavery within the early Iberian colonies. This decree allowed for the acquisition of more African captives and land territory. However, the same decree also established a legal framework for sub-Saharan Africans to negotiate with Iberian authorities on equal footing. They could make claims to legalize slavery, thus providing them with a means to protect their rights.

Romanus Pontifex, a papal bull of Pope Nicolas V of Portugal, was written on January 8, 1455. It was disseminated courtesy of the *Arquivo Nacional da Torre*, Portugal. This papal bull legally granted Portugal the right to enslave all people they encountered south of Cape Bojador, on the coast of Western Sahara.

In 1493, Pope Alexander VI issued a papal bull named *Inter Caetera*, which played a major role in the Spanish conquest of the New World. The document supported Spain's plan to secure exclusive rights to the land discovered by Columbus in 1492. It also established a demarcation line one hundred leagues west of the Azores and Cape Verde Islands, giving Spain the sole right to acquire territorial possessions and to trade in all lands west of that line. All others were prohibited from approaching the lands west of the demarcation line without special permission from

---

1. PBS, "This Far by Faith: 1526–1775, from Africa to America," The Faith Project Incorporated, https://www.pbs.org/thisfarbyfaith/journey_1/p_3.html (accessed May 10, 2023).

Spanish rulers. This gave Spain a monopoly on the lands in the New World.

The bull stated that any land not inhabited by Christians could be "discovered," claimed, and exploited by Christian rulers. It also declared that "the Catholic faith and the Christian religion shall be exalted and be everywhere increased and spread, that the health of souls be cared for and that barbarous nations be overthrown and brought to the faith itself."[2] This "Doctrine of Discovery" became the basis of all European claims in the Americas and the foundation for the United States' Western expansion. In the 1823 U.S. Supreme Court case *Johnson v. McIntosh*, Chief Justice John Marshall's opinion in the unanimous decision held "that the principle of discovery gave European nations an absolute right to New World lands."

In essence, Indigenous people on Canadian and American soil had only a right of occupancy, which could be easily abolished in the name of promoting a Christian culture in the new world. As late as 2023, the bull *Inter Caetera* made headlines again. Many Catholics petitioned Pope Francis to formally revoke previous decrees and to recognize the human rights of indigenous "non-Christian peoples in Canada." According to some estimates, there were at most 25,000 total Catholics in a colonial population of about 4,500,000 at the time of the Declaration of Independence in 1776.[3]

The Unitarian Perspective

Clerics and missionaries, such as the Jesuits in North America, were slave owners themselves, as were some Protestant ministers who later tended to become abolitionists. Initially silence about slavery was common, but by the 1830s, condemnation was the norm.

The antislavery movement was, for the most part, an endeavor of Protestants, progressives, and liberals. For all the denominations, however, there were ecclesiastical and moral issues beyond legality, constitutionality, and inequality. Ecclesiastical issues included literal interpretations of

---

2. Cornell Law School, "Doctrine of Discovery," Cornell Law School, https://www.law.cornell.edu/wex/doctrine_of_discovery (accessed April 7, 2023).
3. American Catholic History Classroom, "The Catholic People in American History," The Catholic University of America, https://cuomeka.wrlc.org/exhibits/show/catholic-people/people-background (accessed January 5, 2023).

the Bible in which slavery could be defended as ordained or normal. It was a necessary evil deed vilified as violating the Golden Rule and beliefs about obeying one's conscience to do what is morally right.

For many Universalists, as well as for other denominations, there was also the conflict between antislavery moral stance and a history of financial reliance on members actively participating in or benefiting from the slave trade. Beyond a doubt, most prominent sea captains in Brewster, Massachusetts held Universalist beliefs as their major faith, attended the Universalist Church, and were buried in their cemetery on Lower County Road.

Universalism has more than one interpretation. One basic tenet is that all people will be saved, and God will condemn no one for their religious beliefs. This concept of Christian Universalism dates to the time of Jesus, the apostles, and the early Christian leaders.

As a collective group, Universalist parishioners were certainly opposed to the horrors of chattel slavery, but there were divisions within their ranks as to the best way to terminate this practice. Some early so-called "liberal ministers" engaged in holding slaves as a temporary colonialization technique that would lead to an eventual saving of their souls, while others were firmly in the full and immediate abolitionist camp. An issue of timing became crucial. Should slavery be ended immediately as an immoral concept, as many abolitionists desired, or could it end in a thoughtful, planned, reflective way over time?

William Ellery Channing (1780–1842) was the foremost Unitarian preacher in the United States in the early nineteenth century, and he, along with Andrews Norton (1786–1853), one of Unitarianism's leading theologians, took a gradual reduction stance. Channing deliberately willed not to associate himself with William Lloyd Garrison or David Walker, who wanted nothing less than an immediate end to slavery. Channing might be labeled as a more moderate reformer who wanted the exact same result but approached it in a way viewed as more conciliatory.

Here, we can see a clear difference between Universalists and a Unitarian perspective on Christian thought. The Unitarian belief is that the act of reason itself, and not a specific creed, may define the search for truth, while the Universalist's belief that God embraces all people equally would eventually lead to a Unitarian Universalist tenet that truth and spiritual meaning can be found in all faiths.

This theology became a dividing point in many churches in the early New England Christian churches in the early nineteenth century. Some members wanted to see all forms of slavery dissolved post haste, while others would accept a more lenient view on timing. The controversy and major polarization within the framework of the church itself led to a splintering and loss of church attendance.

The Methodist View

Another example of a Christian church divided in thought on slavery can be found among the Methodists in the Red Top Church in Brewster, Massachusetts. By 1820, there were sufficient members that exceeded the use of private homes for service. Parishioners were intent on building a house of worship. Local people contributed their time, money, and labor to get the job done.

Lumber was delivered to a port in East Dennis and hauled by oxen to a site on Stoney Brook Road in Brewster, Massachusetts. Reverend Elijah Bailey preached at this site for eleven years from a pulpit designed to be three stories in height, surrounded by a gallery and pews. The building itself was called the Red Top Church, and its upper-level roof was painted red to stand out in the community. As a reformed Methodist Church, they opposed slavery but never spoke too loudly about its use. A major split between Northern and Southern factions in the church ensued in the next decade.

A wife of a Southern Methodist bishop held several slaves herself and saw no rationale not to use them. Some congregants in the Brewster church advocated for a more direct return to the principles of John Wesley, a strong advocate for immediate freedom. In 1845, a new church was erected on Center Street in East Dennis. Thus, there was one faction pushing for the immediate release of all slaves, while the Red Top Church members were comfortable disagreeing with those who were immediate abolitionists.

The Quaker Thought

On September 19, 1738, a small man named Benjamin Lay entered a Quaker meetinghouse in Burlington, New Jersey, for the Philadelphia Quaker Yearly Meeting. Wearing a large coat, he hid a military uniform, a sword, and a book containing an animal bladder filled with a bright red mixture.[4]

During this period, the Quaker custom of service was held without the leadership of an announced minister. They strongly believed no formal minister or church was necessary, as all voices were welcomed and invited to participate. Marcus Rediker tells the story of a prophetic event. The ceremony consisted of people speaking out as the spirit motivated them. Lay, a Quaker himself, patiently waited his turn to address the congregation.

When appropriate, he eventually rose to address this gathering of faithful Quaker people. Many Friends in Pennsylvania and New Jersey were becoming successful in Atlantic commerce, and many bought human beings to attend to their labors. In a big booming voice many times larger than his tiny physical frame, Benjamin Lay announced that God Almighty respects all peoples equally, rich or poor, men or women, white or Black.

He said that keeping slaves was the greatest sin in the world. He asked, "How can a people who profess that they adhere to the golden rule possibly maintain slaves?" He then removed his large coat, displaying the military garb, a book, and his sword.

A silence fell over the great hall. He spoke as a prophet yelling out a judgment: "Thus shall God shed the blood of those persons who enslave their fellow creatures." He pulled out the sword and raised a book above his head. He then plunged the sword through its pages. People were astonished as a dark red liquid began running down his arm. Some women even fainted, not knowing exactly what had happened. To the shock of all, he prophesied a dark, violent future. Quakers who failed to listen to the prophet's words must expect physical, moral, and spiritual death. He foretold the horrors that would result for centuries for people who supported slavery in any way.

Lay stood silently for several moments in a statuesque pose. Then several Quakers surrounded the small prophet of God, carrying him from the building. He never resisted. He had made his point perfectly.

Like many religious groups of the day, the Quakers had a divided perspective on the nature of slavery. Benjamin Lay stood out as an

---

4. Marcus Rediker, *The Fearless Benjamin Lay: The Quaker Dwarf Who Became the First Revolutionary Abolitionist* (Pittsburgh: Penguin Books, 2010), 87.

early abolitionist, reminding his flock that the concept was repugnant. In essence, the early Quakers were prominent in accepting slaves as a vehicle to acquire wealth, yet later, they also became one of the most vocal denominations to vehemently protest its existence.

In 1688, a small group of four society members drafted a protest against the trafficking of "men-bodies" at the annual meeting in Germantown. By that time, slavery had been in the colonies for three years. The Society members felt that the general assembly must accept a higher standard. In 1693, a Quaker named George Keith stood before his Society of Friends and declared, "What greater oppression can there be inflicted upon our fellow creature, than is inflicted on the poor Negro, cruel whippings, and other cruel punishments, and by short allowance of food?"[5]

Nonetheless, the 1688 Quaker Meeting avoided this antislavery petition, believing it was too weighty a matter to deal with. In 1776, Quakers became the first religious group to officially prohibit slavery. However, their dictum was never completely embraced by all members or followed by other religious organizations. In 1821, Quaker Benjamin Lundy followed up the discussion of slaveholding with a publication called "The Genius of Universal Emancipation," which elaborated on all the positive reasons for immediately freeing slaves, reinforcing the official Quaker position.

In 1700, prior to the Revolutionary War, Judge Samuel Sewell, in the Province of Massachusetts, authored a pamphlet titled "The Selling of Joseph." It was the first written legal opinion arguing against slavery. His reasoning included the notion that slaves seldom used their freedom well, and different races constituted a basic threat to Puritan culture.

When Quakers such as George Keith and Samuel Sewall were speaking up to end slavery in the country, many Friends remained silent. Sewall never actually advocated ending any form of existing slavery but did not wish to see any new forms of slavery arise.

---

5. George Keith, "An Exhortation and Caution to Friends concerning Buying or Keeping Negroes," *Pennsylvania Magazine of History*, 1889, 14.

CHAPTER THREE

The Enslavement of Indigenous People

Andrés Reséndez offers us a vivid description of early Indigenous slavery. In the 1600s, there were as many as 40,000 people in the sixty-seven villages making up the Wampanoag People, covering the territory along the East Coast.[1] Like many other Indigenous people, the Wampanoag often referred to the earth as Turtle Island. They lived as a nomadic hunting and gathering culture, and their people had been living on this part of Turtle Island for more than 12,000 years. The corn crop was becoming an important staple, as were beans and squash. Together, they were called the three sisters.

Skilled hunters, gatherers, farmers, and fishers during spring and summer, the Wampanoag moved inland to more protected shelters during the colder months of the year. The tribe had a reciprocal relationship with nature and believed that if they gave thanks to the bountiful world, it would reward them.

Even though some indigenous groups adopted the European practice of chattel-type slavery, prior to the Pequot War, there is no record that the Wampanoags followed this belief. However, they certainly knew of this concept, witnessing many of their tribe being captured and enslaved. The Five Civilized Tribes—the Cherokee, Muscogee, Seminole, Chickasaw, and Choctaw nations—all adopted slavery as part of their bellicose principles. If this practice had existed for the Wampanoags, it must have been only an exceptional foray in the aftermath of local attacks and victories between smaller tribal subsets.

---

1. Andrés Reséndez, *The Other Slavery: The Uncovered Story of Indian Enslavement in America* (Boston: Houghton Mifflin, 2016), 93.

Nonetheless, some Europeans had other ideas about the concept of slavery. There are signs that the pilgrims saw the confiscation of people as an act of religious piety. In 1628, a letter written by minister Jonas Johannis Michaelius of the Dutch Reformed Church was preserved in the notes of the *Original Narratives of Early American History*:

> *It would be well to separate the young of the Indian nation while they are still not fully accustomed as their parents to the heathenish tricks and deviltries, which are kneaded deeply into their hearts by habit and obtained deep root. Although it would be hard to achieve this separation, by means of presents and promises, we should obtain some children to place them under the instruction of a godly schoolmaster where they may see examples of virtuous living but must also sometimes speak their own language in order not to forget it and to spread the knowledge of religion through the whole nation.[2]*

This judgmental concept of producing new replicable Christian British (or Dutch) citizens seemed to be not only a worthwhile social construct but a gift to bestow on a heathen people. It became the norm for authorities to adopt and encourage Indigenous youth to be retrained in the aspects of the dominating culture. Some settlers physically kidnapped children for private use, but only because it was a blessing for them to make them civilized. The United States still operates a system like this on Indigenous lands, citing a need to host schools too remote to follow any other type of traditional educational model. The ability to be bilingual in both Indigenous and English languages was never fostered as a vehicle to keep their old culture alive. The loss of one culture must immediately be replaced with another spread of a new wave of dominance and a new language to a whole subset of people.

To better appreciate the American mindset on slavery in seventeenth-century America, we must see what slavery meant and how it was handled centuries ago. Indigenous slave trading was the initial form of enslavement on the North American continent initiated by the British, Spanish, and Portuguese. Columbus's first business venture to the newly explored world consisted of four caravels loaded to capacity, with 550 Indigenous

---

2. Carl Von Clausewitz, "Notes from the Dutch Reformed Church," *Original Narratives of Early American History* (London: Forgotten Books, 2008), 124.

people being brought back to the Mediterranean shores to be auctioned as slaves.[3]

In reviewing his overall accomplishments, Columbus was at once a world visionary and a shrewd businessman. In his negotiated dealings with Ferdinand and Isabella, he insisted a clause be inserted into his new-world travels. He asked that a one-tenth portion of all merchandise, whether pearls, gold, silver, or any other marketable value, be allotted to his credit. He had a triumphal return to Europe in the spring of 1493. When he disembarked in the port of Barcelona, throngs of people offered him high praise. The entire royal court appeared to greet him. Even the high officials within the Catholic Church asked him to sit as an equal on their reviewing stand.

He told the assembled crowds of the marvelous wonders seen and adventures experienced. He then bestowed several token gifts as visual mementos of his travel, which included forty tropical birds of bright plumage, strange jewels made of gold, and six Indigenous people who survived the voyage. These gifts comprised physical man-made articles, specimens of nature, and human beings that he saw as components of financial value.

Landing of Columbus

---

3. Silvio Bendini, *The Christopher Columbus Encyclopedia* (Washington, D.C.: Smithsonian Museum Press, 1991), vol. 2, 204.

Based on Columbus's success, he was now awarded a new contract that went far beyond his first voyage of three smaller ships and an original crew comprised of sailors and convicts. His second commission to the New World came with a fleet of seventeen larger ships manned by professionally trained mariners and some fifteen Iberian men longing for exotic travel and potential colonization in the Americas.

Due to its large numbers of explorers and current densely inhabited colonies, Spain and Portugal were at one time world leaders in slavery transactions. In the early 1500s, the Spanish monarchy saw this trend yet was sympathetic to the slaves held in bondage. By 1542, slavery was banned altogether in Spain, yet a small number of potential exceptions could still be claimed, such as the fruits of "a just war of defense," as was often mentioned in the Bible, or if tribal leaders willingly sold their slaves voluntarily.

One major difference between Black and Indigenous slavery had less to do with the sheer numbers, as these two figures may be somewhat comparable, and more to do with the preference for the captured person. The Black slave trade was more focused on the strong male figure working on a farm, while the Indigenous trade had a stronger tendency to look toward women and children. Women were seen as docile and excellently suited for domestic needs. Children were seen as most adaptable, fully capable of faster language acquisition and modeling new cultural ways. In addition, young people could easily be conditioned to eventually assimilate old habits by weaving themselves into the dominant culture.

Another distinction worthy of note between the general slave trade and Indigenous enslavement is the structure of the institution itself. For Indigenous people, there was a tradition of holding prisoners of war as valuable hostages for a fixed interval. With the arrival of the Europeans in the colonies and their superior military force, a few local Indigenous people occasionally offered their Indigenous captives to the incoming settlers as a gesture of goodwill.

Iroquoian culture was based on a matrilineal system where women held significant value and determined their children's status. Typically, tribes took female and child captives for adoption into their tribe.

In many ways, this system of servitude could be called a form of indentured service. Several tribes held their captives as hostages until receiving payment. Various tribes also practiced debt slavery for limited time periods or imposed slavery on tribal members who had committed crimes. Full tribal status would be restored once the enslaved person worked off their obligations to the tribal society. Obtaining prisoners was a strong interest for Indigenous warriors, as the nomenclature of being considered brave was held as a high social value.

Nonetheless, with the arrival of French and British mariners, European contact greatly influenced the nature, appeal, and look of slavery as it existed in the New World. As some tribes raided other tribes to capture slaves for sale to Europeans, many of the sister tribes fell into destructive wars among themselves, dividing their overall numbers. A sense of hopeless despair settled in as more and more settlers arrived. Their ships regularly disembarked with superior weapons and trained soldiers.

There were other differences between slavery as practiced in the precolonial era among Indigenous people, and the form of slavery practiced by Europeans after colonization. While many Europeans looked upon slaves of African descent as being racially different and of a lower status, Indigenous people took slaves from other tribes and, therefore, viewed them as ethnically inferior or tribally different.[4]

In many cases, Indigenous slaves were allowed to live on the fringe borders of general American society with many positive rights and freedoms allotted to them. The term "slave" here distinctly applies to a brief phase-in period so that the captive people could be slowly integrated into a new, specific tribal set of beliefs and customs.

When the Europeans first contacted Indigenous people, the local tribes began to participate in the slave trade. In their initial encounters with the Europeans, some tribes attempted to use their captives from enemy tribes as a method of playing one tribe against another in a mostly unsuccessful game of divide and conquer.

By the eighteenth century, both Spanish and Mexican authorities voted to officially ban all types of enslaved people. In the United States, the Thirteenth Amendment included the wording "slavery and involuntary servitude," yet the legal interpretation was narrow. In many cases,

---

4. Jill Lepore, *The Name of War: King Philip's War and the Origins of American Identity* (New York: Vintage Books, 1999), 150–51.

Indigenous slavery was seen in a different light. Called by a different name, debt peonage or responsibility to care for enslaved people was often translated as a concept of legitimate, necessary labor.

When we analyze the origins of slavery on today's American soil, we need to look even before the first set of slave voyages started by Spain, and into the role played by the British. In the early sixteenth and seventeenth centuries, English sailors had their eye on seizing some Indigenous people and sending them to London. In 1605, Seaman James Rozier mentions taking five Indigenous men and "pulling them by their hair to bring them on board." Their motives were perhaps to see if these men could be civilized, learn the English language and customs, and share knowledge about their habits as necessary for future intelligence.

In 1614, English sea captain Thomas Hunt captured twenty-four Indigenous people during a voyage to New England with John Smith on board. Governor William Bradford later reported that he intended to sell them into slavery in a Spanish port. This trip turned out to be particularly beneficial to the goal of English colonization, as a specific captive, Tisquantum, came to England and learned a new language. He would eventually return to Massachusetts and assist the Puritans in learning many new survival strategies.

The Virginia Company of London was a joint-stock company chartered by King James I in 1606 for local colonialists wishing to establish trade in North America. This venture allowed the British Crown to collect the benefits of any new world colonization, such as natural resources and new markets for English goods, and build up leverage against any opposing nations without the responsibility of incurring any significant costs. One of its primary directives was to establish representative English colonies as a model of excellence. The rules, protocols, and agreements were based on the British culture that existed in that century. Its rules, particularly on indentured slavery, became a basic framework for the approval of the acquisition of enslaved people of various types, including white, Indigenous, and Black, as an economic staple. Their protocols quickly became a standard that swept across all colonial territories, instilling a belief that normalized slavery.

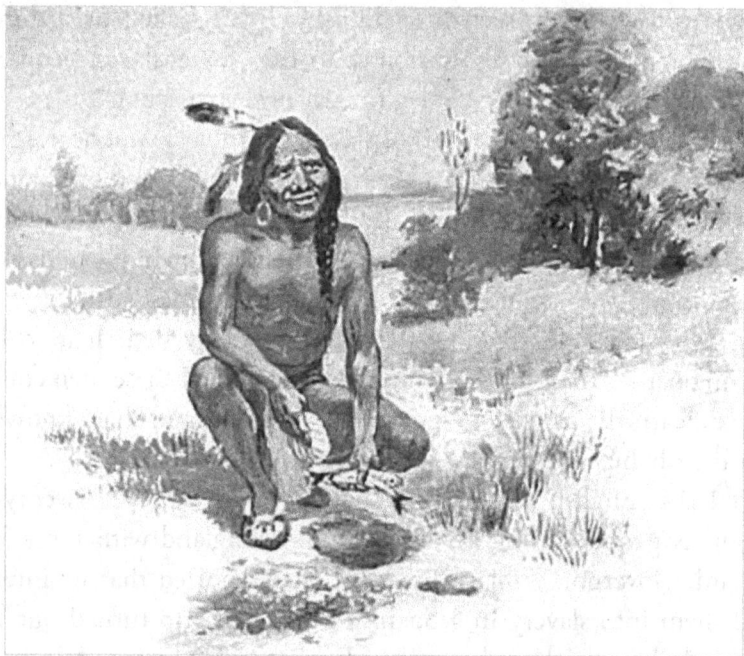

Illustration of Tisquantum (Squanto) teaching the Puritans how to plant corn

Once the Massachusetts Bay Colony was established in 1630, it was a fairly common practice to detain Indigenous people or take them as captives in a war.[5] The Pequot War of 1636–1638 was a prime example and motivator for significant enslavement. Once this war between Indigenous tribes and the colonists ended, over seven hundred captured Pequot were dispersed as slaves to New England colonies. Other tribes engaged in the fight received the same fate, while others were sent to the West Indies to help with local colonization efforts. For the sake of safety and self-preservation, the strong goal of the colonists was to erase the Pequots as a people. For many centuries, even before the English came to America, it was an accepted tribal concept that any enemies taken in a defensive war could be held and traded as enslaved people.

Initially, British entrepreneurs saw value in dealing with the Indigenous trade. In 1636, a Massachusetts General Court even endorsed the concept of legalizing slavery, stating that "a Pequot taken in war can be kept as a slave for life." This finding paved the way for the routine capture

5. Margaret Ellen Newell, *Brethren by Nature: New England Indians, Colonists, and the Origins of American Slavery* (Ithaca: Cornell University Press, 2016), 26.

of human beings. Since there were no specific legal guidelines adopted by the British courts prior to 1641, captured Pequots were seen as fair game.[6]

Even within the British court system of case law, a strong argument was made that the colonists only acted in their own best interests, drawing on the long-standing European tradition of "just war theory." In fact, there were even biblical references to slaves allowed to be taken in a just war. Now we can see that both the Indigenous people themselves and the new colonists believed that slavery was both permissible and acceptable in certain situations. As stated by historian Wendy Warren, "the movement of enslaved and captured people around the world was an accepted reality by the seventeenth century."[7]

The enslavement of the Pequot tribe reached its highest point in 1637.[8] It was at this point that the Narragansetts, with colonial support, engaged in battle, massacring hundreds of Pequots near the Mystic River. Colonial militia took many remaining captives as a form of payment for their military service. Captain Stoughton stated in a letter addressed to John Winthrop, "there is one Pequot that is the largest and fairest that I saw among them. It is my desire to have her for my servant and if it is to your liking, Sosomon, our Indian leader desires a young squaw as well."[9] Any other captives not taken by soldiers were brought to Boston, where they could be seen as useful for trade, local agricultural use, or any type of household help.

The defeated and captured Pequots were divided among the Narragansetts and the English. Captain Stoughton, the principal military authority in this endeavor, contacted the governor of Massachusetts with his recommended allotment of dividing the captives. Massachusetts received forty-eight Indigenous people, eighty went to the Narragansetts, and the rest, about fifty, were given to Connecticut. Massachusetts sent two of the women and fifteen of the boys to be sold as slaves in the West Indies.

---

6. Thrush Coll, *Indigenous London: Native Travelers at the Heart of the Empire* (New Haven: Yale University Press, 2016), 45-46.

7. Wendy Warren, *New England Bound* (New York: Liveright Publishing, 2016), 39.

8. Allen Gallay, ed., *Indian Slavery in Colonial New England* (Lincoln: University of Nebraska Press, 2009), 139.

9. Coll, 51

The business of enslaving Indigenous people in Massachusetts greatly diminished after the Pequot War.[10] However, it reached a new crescendo with King Philip's War in the middle of the 1670s. The Indigenous people mobilized the forces of the Narragansett, Wampanoag, and Nipmuc tribes. The local tribes coalesced to push back against British colonial aggression. The Indigenous men saw a "no-win scenario" confronting them. If they meekly accepted their faith, they feared that future enslavement was certainly imminent. They reasoned that they could either live as free people or die heroically. Nonetheless, if the tribes fought and eventually lost, it would most assuredly lead to complete domination by another culture with irreversible consequences.

The colonial militia felt that they were under direct Indigenous attack and must consolidate to defend their rights. With the colonials being successful, the apprehension of the Indigenous people was realized. In the fall of 1676, the *Seaflower* departed from Boston Harbor with 180 "heathen natives who were sentenced to perpetual servitude and slavery to be sold abroad." Like the case of the Pequot War, any residual captives from this war were either taken as slaves by the militiamen, sold to households, or brought abroad to help pay to subsidize the New England war debt.

By the start of the 1700s, the fear of an Indigenous uprising subsided while the demand for inexpensive labor grew ever more critical. It was not unusual for the local court system to intervene in the lives of Indigenous people, as a greater workforce was needed. More and more, mothers who were deemed unfit or destitute might lose custody of their children. If a petty or even an alleged crime were committed, it may result in a heavy criminal sentence. If an Indigenous person were seen as being "disorderly" in a town, it may lead to a sentence of indentured servitude.

For example, many of the crew members from a Cape Cod whaling ship were Indigenous men induced to serve long periods at sea. It was quite common for a Mashpee family to buy items in a local shop owned by a colonial figure. Blankets, food products, household items, or other necessities were purchased "on credit." Once a sizeable bill was

---

10. Mark A. Nicholas, "Mashpee Wampanoags, Fishery, and the Financial Impact of the Community," *Journal of the American Indian* (Summer 2022): 175.

Lion Gardiner and Pequot War

accumulated, a court could then affirm a legal claim of debt owed by the family. When this debt was duly certified and recognized in court, the family had the unenviable task of paying it within a limited time.

If the funds were not attainable by any other means, the family now had to enter into a written agreement by which the younger son typically served as a whaler fisherman for a period of between five to seven years. This exact fate fell upon Aaron Keeler, who was a seventeen-year-old Mashpee resident when he started his assignment as a non-salaried whaler for many years. Due to a relatively minor family debt that accrued over a year, an agreement was eventually created in which Aaron's parents agreed to let him serve for five years on a ship captained by Freeman Percival. Aaron was a minor in the eyes of the law, so he had to consent to these new rules.

Rather than discussing just one specific whaler from Mashpee, we can also glean a composite view of Indigenous seamen recruitment by analyzing the research of others. A visiting French traveling scholar, Hector St. John de Crevecoeur, visited Mashpee in the 1760s.[11] He recorded

---

11. Hector St. John de Crevecoeur, *Letters of an American Farmer: A View of Early America* (New Haven, Avalon Project Press, 1792), 141.

several direct interviews with Wampanoag families. Piecing together his written notes makes it possible to gain a clearer picture of how whaling was organized in the 1700s and even in the 1600s. We see three concrete operations that, when bound together, provide a better understanding of the whole whaling process:

> At first, a crew needs to be secured. His notes reflect that the natives were every bit as capable as the European descendants in terms of their overall skills, abilities, and courage. Three out of every five men would be of native heritage in a typical ship. The vessels most appropriate would be a brig of about 150 tons in size, particularly used for longer ocean hunts. A minimum of two smaller boats would be on board with a crew of six men. Four men would man the oars while one standing on the bow as the harpooner and a second man at the helm supplied verbal instructions.
>
> Two boats were necessary if the first attack boat was overturned, and the men needed rescue. Most of these initial boats carried Native men. The crew has no direct wages. Each man draws a share as per their written sailing contract. These men never exceeded the age of forty as strength, agility, and unquestionable loyalty must be present.
>
> As soon as the ship enters an area where whales might be sighted, a man is sent up to sit near the tip of the mast head. If one is seen, he cries out, "Awaite Pawana" (Here is a whale said in a native dialect). in less than six minutes, two boats are lowered with all equipment at the ready. They begin rowing towards the whale. Natives typically performed this dangerous part of the hunt.

It is certainly possible that some of the Indigenous crew may have been recruited in a way that was a fully honest proposition, but even so, their individual contract would have been much less lucrative in nature. The indentured whalers served at the criteria of their written contract, which usually had a minimal or limited direct salary, while the free Indigenous people could negotiate a slightly higher recompense. Crevecoeur witnessed that most crewmen on the whaler came from Indigenous backgrounds. However, since the overall tone of his writings, well received in Europe, was focused on the strong work ethic and greater opportunity for the American people, he never made a distinction between the indentured slave versus the free-living Indigenous people serving aboard the whaler.

SAMUEL FULLER
First Slave Holder from the
Mayflower

There is a record of Samuel Fuller bequeathing "Joell" to his son John in his will. This action would not have been a typical thing to do with an indentured servant. There is good reason to believe that the presence of Joell within the family represents a compassionate rescue.

Hector St. John Crevecoeur

In the wake of King Philip's War, several Indigenous children were rescued from the possibility of being orphaned. In 1676, the courts declared that these children should be assigned only to families of high moral character who would raise them appropriately in a good Christian home. It was further expected that, in theory, once reaching the approximate age of twenty-five, the grown child would be released as a fully adult member of society.

Joell was treated with all the legal rights granted to indentured servants attached to a family for an assigned yet limited term of service. This example of passing on the services of one human being to another differed from most indentured agreements as his ownership transitioned from one written agreement of servitude to another relative.

It should also be noted that the relative value of owning an Indigenous slave had less monetary significance than owning a Black slave. In 1690, the going price of an African slave was twenty pounds at auction, while an Indigenous worker only fetched an average of five pounds. The presence of Black slaves in 1680 was relatively meager in scope, estimated to be about 150 people. There was also a prejudice that Indigenous people posed a bigger physical threat to general safety and were more difficult to train. Historian Margaret Newell suggests Indian captives remained far more numerous in New England before 1700. "They offered a cheaper, entry-level investment in long-term bound labor."[12] This status differential between the worth of slaves was exemplified in Connecticut, where we can find some examples of Black slaves able to buy Indigenous people for their personal use.

---

12. Newell, *Brethren by Nature*, 26.

CHAPTER FOUR

The Institution of Voluntary Indentured Servitude Within Massachusetts

Compared to the Middle Colonies of Maryland, New Jersey, and Delaware, there were smaller yet constantly increasing numbers of white servants coming to New England from the very start of the Bay Colony until the Revolutionary War and beyond. Within this population of people, there were distinct classes of servants. Some servants were previously trained for a skill while others were not. Most Caucasian servants were typically never in contract for life but only for a fixed period ranging from one to twelve years.

There were three major distinctions between indentured servitude and veritable enslavement. One basic difference was that any children born from white servants were never classified as servants in their lifetime. The term "servant" never fit the best description of who these people were. Secondly, indentured people could never date or make plans for marriage during their servitude agreement. Finally, the white servants were occasionally promised better clothing, had access to the use of some household goods, and were given better living accommodations than their Black or Indigenous counterparts.[1]

In certain situations where husbands and wives were settled together in the same household or in proximity, Black servants were often allowed and encouraged to bear children. Their offspring increased the relative wealth of the primary owner. Even in cases where the master holder was either the voluntary or unwilling father, the child was still deemed to be forever a slave. This multiplying protocol was never a component of indentured servitude.

---

1. David Galenson, *White Servitude in Colonial America: An Economic Analysis* (London: Cambridge University Press, 1971), 167.

Indigenous people could receive contracts for indentured work. White servants typically came from Europe; free Blacks could come from any local region. Blacks and whites were induced into a form of fixed years of service by local family agreements incentivized by economic promises, use of land for living arrangements, or possible protective services offered by the master family. Of the three groups, Indigenous people frequently had the harshest worded contracts, the most pernicious assigned daily tasks, and the least degree of personal freedom.

The primary incentive for participants behind indentured servitude in Europe was a paid passage to America, a definitive acquisition of a new employment skill, and the chance to start a new independent life, with potentially deferred upward social mobility coming at the end of the arrangement. For the local masters, it provided a new labor source, a way to secure less expensive workers, and even receive a higher perceived social status as witnessed by their upper-level peers.

The need for appropriate labor in the early colonies was of vital concern to the farmer who had to establish a medium-sized functioning farm or a businessman who had much merchandise to move. The concept of using indentured servants toiling on a farm was also known as "husbandry," derived from a long-standing English tradition. Labor was now available for a pre-set number of years for a relatively diminutive fee of seven or eight pounds for a ship passage. In most cases, each geographic area determined the given need, the duties, and the rewards for their indentured servants.

For example, in the Middle Colonies, indentured servants were much more agriculturally based, with mid-sized farms being the norm. Several men were pre-trained for their tasks. Hence, the final financial agreements were more substantial, and correspondingly, the farm work was more demanding. In Massachusetts, farms were typically much smaller, so the demand for larger slave numbers was reduced.

In the Middle Colonies, once a husbandry servant arrived, a colonist would reimburse the contracting company for the individual's voyage expenses and would then put the man (occasionally a woman) to work as per their individual agreement. The servant's master provided food and lodging, as stipulated in the indentured contract. After they had completed their service, the servants usually received items such as three barrels of corn, farming tools to work the land on their own, certain farm animals, and perhaps as much as fifty acres of land. For many, signing on as an indentured servant was seen as a pure godsend, allowing for emigration to a new culture and a viable means to improve their position in life. Husbandry was viewed as a wonderful career potential for a new life.

The core concept of multi-year servitude contracts had more than one defined interpretation and was open to some variance. In specific cases, a young Benjamin Franklin, one of our Founding Fathers, could willingly apprentice or indenture himself to work with his brother to learn the printing trade business at the tender age of twelve. The actual work varied greatly according to individual contracts. An indentured person might be learning a new skilled trade, planting a new crop, learning the art of blacksmithing, cooking, preparing clothes, cleaning the house for a family, or even serving as a mariner searching for the capture of the massive whale.

Their hours might range from daylight hours only, or to twenty-four hours of service with heavy labor involved. In some cases, the work may be seasonal for one given task with a different type of work a few months later.

In some unusual cases, there might even be an additional recompense. In New England, where the farms were smaller, a farmer may be inclined to share a small percent of the total profit when a harvest was plentiful. A store owner might pay a bonus if a task were exceptionally well done. These forms of agreements were the exception. As another example, it was not uncommon for the ironwork servant workers in Lynn or the glassblowers in Sandwich, who needed to possess knowledge of an industrial process and perform exceptionally technical skills, to receive generous salaries for their masterful efforts.

Coming from a puritan perspective, the masters thought of themselves as benefactors or even saviors of the impoverished. This class of indentured servant mastery was known as "redemptioners." Servants from impoverished situations or chaotic families were given the highest priority to work within the home. These poor people needed to be saved on a voluntary basis, so the prospect of traveling to the New World to begin a new life added up to a soul-saving redemption.

In addition, there was a financial aspect to the redemptioner contract. The emigrant signed a contract to pay for their oceanic travel yet could only afford an initial partial payment. Upon arrival, after a brief time, usually two weeks, the reimbursement was expected. If the payment was not possible, the captain had the right to sell the voyager into another form of servitude. The length of time was connected to the size of the incurred debt. This practice was often used with Europeans other than the British or Irish, such as German emigrants. One possible explanation for this kind of arrangement is that the British servants often traveled individually, while Germans traveled by whole families, having potential relations living abroad who would cover their expected travel costs.

On occasion, these indentured servants arrived at the shipping ports, presenting themselves directly to a captain while explaining their dire needs. In turn, a captain either held a pre-set number of available contracts desired by the settlers requesting domestic help or used a negotiation process rendered at the initial port of entry. With pre-set contracts, the settler paid for the ocean voyage and further agreed to provide appropriate clothes, food, and residence. A termination settlement with a fixed ending date was always included with a guarantee of supplemental pay at or near the close of the contract.

It was often the custom in the earlier days of this system to have anywhere between five- to six-year contract terms. However, as the labor shortage increased, the more normal contract was extended to ten or twelve years. These types of contracts could be made with large-scale English companies that held enterprises in the colonies, individual sea captains, or private households. The transfer of these serving contracts depended upon any laws existing within the geographic confines. For example, in some cases the servant was automatically freed if the master died, while in other areas the contract was allowed to be passed on to other relatives.

Looking at the age and gender of these incoming laborers, we can see some marked differences. The share of men aged fifteen to twenty-five was close to 70 percent, considering all males. Based upon labor needs, males displayed a greater potential for growth in a trade even at a younger age. Both genders were perceived as being as popular at a younger age. The younger age group was preferred over the older one. Men and women who may have well-established traits and talents were in greater demand.[2]

2. Galenson, 171.

CHAPTER FIVE

Involuntary Servitude in Massachusetts

There were other creative ways that the Massachusetts Bay Colony courts could find a way to indenture unwilling people without an ocean voyage. The colonists believed that many children, predominantly orphans, delinquents, or the offspring of prisoners, needed custodial placement in a home to save the expenses of governmental orphanages and fill labor needs. Local shopkeepers, farmers, and blacksmiths agreed to pay a small service fee. In exchange, the children could acquire a new trade, be placed in a home, and avoid assignment to institutionalized conditions.

If a man or woman was deemed "idle"—without the means of properly providing for themselves or their families—they, too, could be assigned to various labors as opposed to being sent to a debtor prison. People judged to be immoral, such as thieves or those overly indulgent in alcohol consumption, would need a firm hand to keep them in check. A perfect fit for such a group might be placed in the hands of a firm master who would accept them in exchange for immediate and constant supervision of their individual needs.

Restitution was another typical ploy. If a thief could not pay the full value of a stolen item, a master could assume his debt in exchange for a work assignment. There were even some locals within the colonies deemed to be "fully incorrigible," who were then consigned to slavery duties outside of the confines of the colony.

New England was much less likely to accept convicts and debtors than certain colonies, such as Georgia and Virginia. There was, nonetheless, yet another category of indentured servants that was very much acceptable as a viable population. Some of these groups were opponents of Britain who supported Charles II and were taken in battles such as Dunbar and Worcester. In 1651, one hundred and fifty prisoners of war arrived in Boston on the *Unity*. Eighty other men were put to work in the iron works of Saugus. In 1652, over two hundred lower-class servants were brought to the shipyards of Charlestown to boost the booming maritime industry.

One consistent similarity between the type of transport of slaves brought to the New World with indentured servants can be found in their ship logs. Boats designed to carry a maximum of three hundred passengers were frequently doubled in number to gain a greater profit. The physical space allotted to each traveler was reduced to six feet by two feet per assignment. This trip could last between four to five months.

Changing clothes on the open deck was often not permitted due to modesty as well as the lack of access to their baggage. When a storm arose, the immigrants were ordered to lie flat on their stomachs for hours for so-called "safety" reasons.

During the trip, food was much less than substantial for vitality and frequently unhealthy by any standard. In addition, any rules on sanitization were nonexistent. Medicine was rarely dispensed, and drinking water was rationed by degrees and ounces. Ventilation was often tinged with the rancid scent of illness and death in the air.

If an immigrant became ill once aboard, their life was in grave danger. First, they would typically not receive any special medical attention, and often, dead fellow passengers were left directly on the same deck in obvious proximity. It would not be unheard of to have a mortality rate of 40-50 percent for some voyages.

After reaching the homeport, a major separation occurred. The captains realized that the affirmed and the weak would fetch lower compensation. At times, the ill were sidetracked to another potential entry point if the immigration system was not paying attention. In most situations, the port officials were ordered to be up to the task. The guards were conscious not to let the diseased entrants slip by. If a newcomer was deemed unfit, they were consigned to a quarantine unit as a group. This space, called "the pesthouse," remained their home for months. If the ill did not recover in a reasonable time, they were either sent back home or left to die in their group setting.

If the indentured servants could survive all these challenges and had the proper identification, they were permitted to enter. The wealthiest families willing to pay for the oceanic voyage typically secured two to three servants per home based on social status and fiscal means. The extremely wealthy, who had the good fortune of having a large farm, owning a thriving business, or contracting work for other colonists, were allowed greater numbers.

William Pynchon was originally the treasurer of the Massachusetts Bay Colony in the 1630s. He intuitively realized the potential role that involuntary indentured slaves might make in the development of the new colony. He turned to pelt trading and farming as way to enrich the king's profit. He first settled in Roxbury, observing that the rocky soil was a formidable challenge. In 1636, he turned to officially purchase fertile soil in the western part of the Bay State region that was suitable for farming, then known as "Agawam." He is attributed as being the official founder of Springfield.

To work the land, he was able to entice some tribes along with other Indigenous prisoners of war to cultivate the soil and to hunt beaver pelts. These projects became extremely profitable to the crown. His opposition to Puritan standards led to his book, *The Meritorious Price of Our Redemption*. He believed that "obedience to the master rather than mere punishment"[1] was the better principle to demand. His thoughts led to the first book banning in the Bay Colony.

Pynchon had thirty men and fifteen women assigned to him based on his diverse enterprises in the fur trade, tanning, and construction. Skilled laborers who knew carpentry, cabinet making, or shipbuilding were particularly desirable. Women who were trained and comfortable with weaving, preserving food, or spinning yarn were also most welcomed. Pynchon later retired in England as a very wealthy man.

A normal day for an indentured servant usually exceeded the working time of the master or any other person with similar tasks. The official workday could be from sunrise to sunset for six consecutive days, but in

---

1. Mason Arnold Green, *Springfield, 1636-1886: History of the Town and City* (Sprinfield: C.A. Nichols, 1888), 112.

most cases, the true expectation was that the indentured were "on call" for twenty-four hours as the need arose. Longer hours per day equaled greater productivity and also thwarted the concept of the devil's idleness with the value of hard labor.

A 1696 example of an involuntary servitude contract committing to serve on the privateer vessel *Antegua* can be found in the New York City Historical Records. The *Antegua* was commanded by privateer-turned-pirate William Kidd. Elizabeth Morris, a spinster, was in severe economic straights in England and faced potential civil consequences for her inability to pay debts. She agreed to a work contract of four years in exchange for passage to the colonies. Captain Kidd was responsible for meals, clothing, and employment on his ship. Securing free labor on a pirate ship demanded an extraordinary act of courage. It is unclear if Miss Morris fully understood the type of maritime life that she was about to face. She seemed quite amenable to the terms of the agreement. In all, it is estimated that over 55,000 indentured servants arrived in the New England colonies prior to the American Revolution.[2]

Indentured servants had a lifestyle comparable to that of others living in the master's home. Items such as appropriate new clothing, the quality of the meals consumed, treatment of any medical care concerns, and even the legal rights extended to them matched the level of the other inhabitants.

The basic two obligations owed to them by their master were the assignment of specific work and some formal degree of education. If no formal education was provided, the master would be in noncompliance with the original contract. Two specific activities that were frowned upon were gambling and excessive drinking, as those vices denigrated a person's overall labor productivity. If the servants received any leisure time, it was understood they would spend it in or near the household.

As for any allowable sanctions a master could apply for disobedient acts, there were a wide range of options. In general, most punishments meted out by the master had to be considered fair, with little or no ability to ask for alternative sentences. The most egregious offense of all was to run away from the household. This action always afforded lashings

2. Richard Zacks, *The Pirate Hunter: The True Story of Captain Kidd* (New York: Hyperion, 2002), 72.

inflicted either directly by the master himself or by the local sheriff. In some cases, merely being outside the home without the master's prior consent could warrant the application of the whip.

Other infractions, such as alcohol use, sexual immorality, and theft, were deemed forbidden acts for which the master could punish, either with or without delivering physical blows. To create a consequence against pilfering, the Massachusetts Assembly passed an ordinance that no indentured servant could sell any household item unless they had been granted written permission by the master to do so. Violations of these acts usually were accompanied by lashing.

Masters had the legal right to punish, yet they also had agreed-upon limits as to the severity of their punishments. Inappropriate sanctions inflicted by the master could send him to court, where he was ordered to pay a substantial fine. If a master wished to convey or sell his servant to another person, there were new legal papers to file, additional fees to pay, and other legal obligations to realize. For this reason, in a few unusual cases, direct insolence or defiance was tolerated to a certain degree. The difficulties involved in a legal transfer made the owner think twice about removing his individual problem servant in this manner, as the process was cumbersome.

One particular action taken by the master received great scrutiny. Courts often tended to believe the accusations of sexual mistreatment made by a female servant. If the case went to court and the claims were found valid, a female servant could be transferred immediately to a new household. In severe cases, the female would be directly released to freedom from the master's ownership, and the master was ordered to be lashed for his misdeeds.

If there was clear evidence of physical abuse or cruel beatings by the master, courts could end the contract and place the servants in a new household. The vilest of committable offenses would be if a domestic slave decided to run away. There always had to be a full analysis of the event. If facts pointed to some misuse by the owner, the servant was held in private hands until all the issues of the case were finally resolved.

In comparing indentured servitude in England with the New England model, life was much harsher on the European continent. Life for indentured people was certainly difficult in the colonies, yet there were contrasting benefits, such as gestures for several improved necessities in life, access to a better education, and a defined limit for the length of servitude.

Once the colonial indentured servant was freed in the colony, their prospect of achieving a better life instantly emerged. A social structure that defined expectations for British people in the state of poverty in Europe was harsh yet possibly even removed in the colonies. Eventual assimilation into a new, open, emerging culture of democracy was realistic and attainable. Comparing indentured life with direct chattel slavery is not at all possible. Black slaves never had even a glimmer of hope for freedom from oppression for themselves, their offspring, or their families. Their term of servitude was perpetual.

Germans Emigrate 1874

CHAPTER SIX

Lessons from the British
Slave Trade

Most American colonists came from British ancestry. Our very language, many of our customs, our business principles, our concept of law, and even our founding American values derive from our witness of how our ancestors conducted themselves. The British legacy of obtaining and using slaves as a profitable business commodity set a new standard not only for the world but particularly for a new, emerging nation to follow. It seems strongly ironic that a significant portion of the colonization model can be replicated by a country that wants to shed the title of a colony to become a sovereign entity.

England became one of the most successful slave trading companies in the world.[1] A law in Parliament allowed for the practice of slavery, and the practice continued for many years. Only Portugal/Brazil transported more Africans across the Atlantic than Britain. Until the 1730s, London dominated the British trade of enslaved people. It continued sending ships to West Africa for slaves until 1807, when the British Empire abolished the slave trade.

Early navigators venturing into the Guinea coast realized that human cargo was readily available. By 1502, the first shipload of Africans landed in the West Indies in the mines and fields. English historian George Francis Dow published a book in 1927 detailing how Britain started on the road of colonization using enslaved people.

At first, slave vessels bargained with local natives to trade gold or wax for human slaves. This first process was somewhat slow and inefficient, as much time was needed for a small amount of return, only picking up

---

1. George Francis Dow, *Slave Ships and Slaving* (Cambridge: Cornell Maritime Press, Inc. and Marine Research Society, 1927), 86.

a few Africans at a time. A plan soon ensued with small settlements of Europeans being planted in West Africa at geographic intervals to negotiate for larger numbers of acquired slaves. These new areas were frequently surrounded by a fort for protection and security. These slave factories were now formed in which larger numbers of slaves could aggregate. These factories were placed at the mouth of a river to accommodate easy maritime access. The principal fort of the English was named Cape Coast Castle on the Gold Coast.

In 1562, Sir John Hawkins was the first Englishman to transport slaves from the Guinea coast to America. In 1662, an exclusive charter company for slavery with the king's brother, the Duke of York. Their goal was to supply all the English colonies with three thousand slaves per year. This trading system was replaced with the Royal African Company in 1672, which was also appointed by the royal court and was successful for over a century. The primary feature of the trading operations was the profit margin for selling Black humans to the colonies in America.

In 1790, it had been estimated that the number of slaves sold or kidnapped in that year was over 100,000. It was announced that a small percentage of these newly available slaves were given up in trade by their mother, which lent an air of reasonableness to the perfidy committed. In looking at the British model, American colonists saw that this type of trade was both profitable and sanctioned by most recognized legal societies.

Ship trading on the slave coast most assuredly varied with the locale in which slaves were secured. George Francis Dow relates but one version of a slave trade made in Gambia, opposite James Fort, in 1740. A boat was first sent to the shore with soldiers commissioned to find the nearest local village. The chief was found, and an anchorage fee was paid. The fee, in this case, consisted of ten gallons of liquor for the *alcaide* (or chief), two iron bars, and several cases of wine, beer, and cider for presents. Later, the British ship was supplied with a first and a second linguist. The first linguist served as an interpreter between the broker who sold the slaves, the owner, and the ship master. The second linguist acted as an interpreter for an officer on the ship who oversaw a long-boat delivery of trading items such as gold, provisions, or other goods. Then, slaves could be brought aboard as per agreement.

There were also seamen identified as butlers. The butlers had several tasks, such as cutting wood as needed, bringing water from the local site, and preserving the health of the ship's crew by using damp cloths and physical materials to avoid overexposure.

The linguist would then bring the slave broker on board to inquire about the exact price and desired commission. For the most part, the male slaves were acquired as local prisoners of war. There was also typically a designated medical expert on the British ship who could examine the bartered slaves prior to the final sale being exacted. The broker received his commission, which ended the transaction.

It took the Age of Enlightenment to steer people toward recognizing slavery as an inhumane practice. Initially, American colonists saw that England sponsored and conducted organized slave runs and the highest authorities sanctioned it. It now appears difficult to officially discern the relative breakdown of which slaves were brought to the American colonies by British captains versus the deals made by the American sea captains.

When American colonists saw how Britain approached the slave trade, it must have, at a minimum, made a deep impression on how to think about this operation with fellow humans involved.

CHAPTER SEVEN

The Historic Treatment of Slaves in Colonial America

The first recorded slave trade began in New England with a Salem-based ship named *Desire* in the 1640s. By the mid-1640s, New England ship captains brought slaves to the Boston port with regularity, establishing the great triangle trade. By 1644, New England sea captains were departing either from Boston or Europe with the intention of bringing back gold dust and slaves from Africa. The slave trading aspect was the most profitable cornerstone when captains purchased slaves for four or five pounds in Africa with the promise of a sale price between thirty to eighty pounds based on demand and their physical condition.

On the first leg of the voyage, crews took New World farm products, including corn, lumber, and a sundry of other goods, to the African continent, where the trade for slavery was initiated. The boats were then reloaded with goods, such as slaves, molasses, wine, salt, sugar, and tobacco, due to arrive in the West Indies. The final leg of the transfer was a return call to Boston to supply sugar, rum, and other Caribbean goods. Along the way, slaves were dropped off in South America, and many low-grade fish supplies were brought to the southern region of the Americas, which would eventually become the Southern states, and even a few to New England.

We can learn a bit about the treatment of slaves in Colonial America by examining the life of Ona Judge, who resided in Mount Vernon in 1774 as a personal servant of George Washington. She was often referred to simply as "Oney" by Washington. She was the daughter of an enslaved seamstress and a white English tailor hired by the family. People described her as a light-skinned mulatto with an abundance of freckles on her face. At the age of ten, she served as Martha Custis Washington's personal servant.[1] Her sewing skills were enhanced by the tutelage of her mother. She was deemed the "perfect mistress of the needle." Along with her sister Delphy, Oney was part of the Custis estate, which had the authority to pass heirs on to Washington.

When George was elected president, fifteen-year-old Ona Judge traveled to the various busy cities of New York and Philadelphia. She was among the slaves discreetly removed from Philadelphia to comply with the 1780 Pennsylvania Emancipation Act.

As Washington continued with his presidency, Judge stayed on as Martha's attendant. Some of Judge's duties consisted of mending clothes, organizing personal belongings, bathing, and overseeing household needs. Nonetheless, her life in Pennsylvania differed greatly from her station in Virginia. Slaves were given much more access to societal life in the North. She was awarded a slight monthly stipend and was permitted to see plays and a traveling circus.

She also had access to superior clothing, such as gowns, shoes, bonnets, and stockings. She was also exposed to the city's large free Black community and the concepts expressed in the Quaker neighborhoods. On May 21, 1796, she knew that her master was returning south, so she made her escape. She wrote in her 1846 diary: "Whilst they were packing to return to Mount Vernon, I was packing to go, I did know where. I knew that if I went back to Virginia, I should never get my liberty. I had friends among the colored people of Philadelphia and had let the house know while they were eating dinner."[2]

A few days later, the executive of the White House posted an advertisement in the *Philadelphia Gazette*, declaring that Oney had run off without provocation. In fact, there were two salient reasons. Having had a small taste of freedom was enlightening, and she overheard a conversation in which Martha desired to transfer ownership to her granddaughter, Eliza Parke Custis Law, who was well known to have a fiery temper.

The advertisement offered a ten-dollar reward for Judge's return. It described her as possibly attempting to pass as a white woman with many

---

1. Jessie MacLeod, "Ona Judge: A George Washington Slave," The George Washington Presidential Library, https://www.mountvernon.org/library/digitalhistory/digital-encyclopedia/article/ona-judge/ (accessed June 14, 2023).
2. Jessie MacLeod, "Ona Judge."

types of good clothes into which to change. She was a woman of middle stature, delicately formed, with bushy black hair and very black eyes.

Meanwhile, Washington was becoming quite irritated. Martha's first husband, a member of the Custis family, originally purchased Ona, which meant that George would be personally responsible for payment to that family due to her escape. Beyond the money, he was perplexed at the loss of a maid who was treated more like his own child than a slave. When Oney was one day spotted in Portsmouth, New Hampshire, Washington arranged to send a message to her. She was asked to voluntarily return. Her reply to him infuriated Washington even more. She said she would come back, providing he would fully release her after his death.

Washington's response to her and to the world illuminates the delicacy of the situation. "To enter such a compromise is inadmissible. Even though I am disposed to gradual abolition, it would neither be politic or just to reward unfaithfulness with a premature preference."[3]

Knowing that the federal Fugitive Slave Act, signed in 1793, could be enforced, he understood that taking violent means to secure her release would greatly stir up strong abolitionist feelings. He left word with Joseph Whipple, the Portsmouth custom collector, that if by chance she could be captured in a secretive manner, to do so. No response materialized.

Washington even made a second and third attempt to reclaim her. He knew that Burwell Bassett Jr., a nephew of Martha Custis, was planning a business trip to Portsmouth. Oney once again refused to come willingly. When word got out that Bassett was contemplating a violent recapture, John Langdon, a New Hampshire senator, intervened. He sent a message to Oney to beware while she fled to safety a few miles away.

Ona Judge Staines was interviewed in 1847 by *The Liberator*. Fifty years after leaving the Washington family, she voiced no regret. She said: "No, I am free, and have, I trust, been made a child of God by his means."[4]

Of course, this story is atypical in many ways. Ona was owned by a Founding Father. She most assuredly received preferential treatment both in Virginia and Pennsylvania. She had financial means and received

---

3. Jessie MacLeod, "Ona Judge."
4. Jessie MacLeod, "Ona Judge."

a substantial level of education. She was never physically mistreated or harmed. However, her story shows the tension that existed between Northern and Southern owners. It displays the ferocity that slave owners would take to regain their possessions. If not for the owner's political station in life, the ending of this story most certainly would have been changed.

At the turn of the eighteenth century, there were a minimum of one thousand Black people living in New England, with more than half residing in Massachusetts. The bulk of these people were slaves. There is a record of Captain Samuel Maverick, who was living in the Boston area in 1629, bringing two or three slaves from the West Indies and later bringing them back to Africa.

This action was an exception to the triangle voyage and perhaps marks the very start of a new movement. Just like indentured servants, the transportation of slaves was a messy and unhealthy experience. Originally, slaves were transported between decks three feet wide and ten inches high. This space was occasionally diminished by several inches in height. The slave was never allowed to stand during the long voyage. Laying down in spoon fashion in proximity to each other led to many deleterious issues.

The early New England colonies were fully cognizant of this market. Governor John Winthrop's journal of 1638 tells of Captain William Pierce taking Pequots as slaves after the decimation of a Connecticut village. Initially, the captain felt these slaves were too pernicious a capture to reside in New England, and he transported them to the West Indies to sell in exchange for salt, cotton, and tobacco. By 1652, Rhode Island attempted to pass a law that would limit slavery to ten years.

New England was not particularly well suited agriculturally, theoretically, or economically to expand slavery in its territory. However, there is little doubt that it never turned away vehemently or fully from the concept. Even though New England voices may have cried the loudest against this injustice, some sea captains would not refuse the opportunity to gain a profit in their maritime endeavors while they could.

Historians affirm that between the years of 1755 to 1764, as many as 2.2 percent of the total Massachusetts population was comprised of

African slaves, with much greater numbers brought by other national mariners to South America and the Caribbean Islands.[5] By the middle of the eighteenth century, Boston was the starting hub of slave trading for the Western world. This trade supplied rice and cotton growers in the South with slaves, food, and other essential elements, with close to five thousand slaves per year brought to South America.

Slave traders were never seen as being lower-class scoundrels but rather as acceptable maritime businessmen seeking to achieve a wealthier status and higher social standing. John Hancock was a partner of James Rowe, a well-established trader. Peter Faneuil, the founder of Faneuil Hall in Boston, had a thriving slave enterprise. The founder of Brown University made a fortune in the sale of slaves to the South. Cotton Mather himself believed that slavery was a charitable act, bringing Black Africans out of darkness into a brighter light that would enrich their soul. Many New England clerics were documented slaveholders, with the likes of Reverend Ezra Stiles, Nathaniel Chauncy, Jonathan Todd, Joseph Elliot, Jonathan Edwards, Jared Elliott, William Worthington, Edward Holyoke, Nathaniel Webb, and Samuel Hopkins. The brother-in-law of John Winthrop justified slavery on an economic basis. He reasoned that for every single indentured servant, a person could acquire twenty Black slaves.

At the same time, many puritans strongly disapproved, voicing public push-back. Governor John Winthrop and John Adams often spoke out about slavery's inhumanity and its ultimate result of crushing a man's soul. Overall, puritans generally refrained from owning Black slaves. Governor Winthrop set the example by personally not owning any slaves or servants. Nonetheless, there were still at least over one hundred prominent Massachusetts families who held both indentured and Black slaves.

Samuel Sewall wrote and published the very first antislavery argument in the colony. "The Selling of Joseph" was an article published in Boston that attracted many readers. He rejected any biblical references to the acceptance of slavery with the logic that both whites and blacks were descendants of the same father, Adam. Coming from the same father would inspire more of a sense of brotherhood than a right to ownership.

---

5. Claudia Durst Johnson, *Daily Life in Colonial New England,* 2nd ed. (Santa Barbara: Greenwood Press, 2017), 95.

He wrote, "For as much as Liberty is in real value next unto life: None ought to part with themselves, or deprive others of it, but upon most mature Consideration." Sewall was vigorously attacked by Cotton Mather as well as by businessman John Saffin, who published a stinging response to their opposing concept.[6]

Sewell referred to a specific line in the Bible to bolster his own interpretation. In speaking of Joseph, he wrote, "He is no more a slave to his brethren, than they were to him. God says, he that stealeth a Man and Selleth him, or if he be found in his hand, he shall surely be put to death."[7] Based on this selective piece of scripture, he reasoned this law was of "Everlasting Equity," wherein man-stealing must be ranked among the most atrocious of capital crimes. What louder cry can there be made than that of "Celebrated Warning?" This literary work raised eyebrows and invoked debate, yet in total substance was ignored by many.

By 1715, when an early reliable form of census gave us data by race, there were 158,000 whites and 4,150 Blacks in the Massachusetts Bay Colony. By 1776, the number of Blacks increased to 16,034, with most Blacks being attributed to only the wealthiest of families. As many as one-eighth of prominent New England families held slaves within their house right before the American Revolution.

Although most Africans in the early colonies were considered uncivilized and barbaric people, their lot in life depended on where they lived. In the South, there were often no personal rights or many liberties afforded to them. In New England, a feeling of familial closeness and more legal opportunities were open to them, such as possible education and access to court petitions. The nature of their assigned tasks was often more in line with domestic duties, focusing on varying degrees of housing, food provisions, clothing, and personal needs provided by individual contracts with their owners.

Once chattel black slavery started to grow in the early 1700s, distinct geographic differences emerged regarding the concept of slave treatment. The Northern version held more privileges for slaves, such as provisions

---

6. Edmund S. Morgan, *American Heroes: Profiles of Men and Women Who Shaped Early America* (New York: W.W. Norton and Company, 2009), 126-29.
7. Exodus 21:16 (King James Version).

for better food, clothing, and shelter, usually placing them directly in a home. In specific cases, a slave might even have the option to seek judicial redress. If conditions were not totally right, a potential legal advocate could be found.

A classic example of demanding legal rights for slaves occurred in Boston relative to a whaling contract. Prince Boston was born into slavery in Nantucket, Massachusetts, in 1750. His parents, Boston and Maria, were slaves of William Swain, a Nantucket merchant. In 1760, Swain freed Boston and Maria but required that each of their children remain in servitude until age twenty-eight. Prince, the slave's son, was obligated to serve on a whaling ship for multiple years beyond his age of contract.

In 1773, Prince Boston became the first slave in Massachusetts to successfully sue for his freedom in the Massachusetts General Court while also retrieving some back pay for his services rendered on the vessel. It was the legal custom and norm for any slave who received recompense from any maritime work to relinquish these deserved funds back to their owner. In this case, the owner died while the ship was at sea. To a small degree this case opened the door for Black sea captains to flourish. A few years later, Prince's nephew, Absalom Boston, would go on to become the first black whaleship captain to own his own boat and employ an all-black crew with full rights to financial considerations. More details on Boston come later in this study.

Black slaves worked in many possible industries, such as carpentry, tailoring, barrel making, and tanning. The seagoing trade offered immense opportunities to Black slaves and provided upward social mobility. They served on fishing vessels, on coastal trading boats, as rope makers, in anchor manufacturing, and most definitely in whaling.

Before the revolution, some Black mariners were allowed to serve at sea. Southern states attempted to keep slaves away from jobs on the wharves or docks, as this familiarity with nautical men would lead to a higher rate of escape. It was quite common for a few Black New England slaves to escape from an overbearing master and seek refuge on a ship heading out to the ocean.

By the end of the 1700s, it is estimated that perhaps as many as 50 percent of local whaling ships from New Bedford were comprised of a mixture of Black and Indigenous sailors.[8] Ironically, it might be noted that in the 1600s, Blacks could be conscripted into colonial military service. However, by the end of that century, Massachusetts legislators canceled this practice, believing it was far too dangerous to arm or train slaves in any way during a peacetime militia.

There were very distinct differences in the treatment of Northern and Southern Black slaves. In the North, slaves often received the same residence benefits offered to indentured servants, and attempts were made to socially integrate slaves into the mainstream of current life. In the South, separate quarters for the working farmhands became the norm.

Courtship rights also differed. In most Southern circles, requests for marriage were seen as unnecessary, yet the ability to procreate was strongly encouraged within the home property. The addition of children added to the slave owner's wealth. Whereas in New England, if a Black slave wished to officially wed outside the master's house, the two owners would typically agree to write a formal agreement that responded to several pertinent questions. Would there be sufficient and designated time for the two to meet? If any offspring materialized because of their union, to whom would their children be assigned ownership? What amount of common support might be needed? Who would pay for the costs of the wedding ceremony and any other incidentals required for the married couple? The response to these questions had a financial impact on the owners.

Examples of Contradictory Activities Forbidden by Black Slaves in Massachusetts

Adapted from Johnson (2017), *Daily Life in Colonial America*

Slaves were not eligible to vote yet could be called to perform military duty.

Slaves could be taxed if they had any viable income, yet were never considered full citizens with equal rights, such as voting.

---

8. Skip Finley, *Whaling Captains of Color: America's First Meritocracy* (Annapolis: Naval Institute Press, 2020), 167.

Slaves were frequently excluded from living outside of their master's property except for some who lived in ghettos, typically near a coastal port.

Slaves could never ride ferries or linger in harbors, yet they were at times encouraged to work in maritime positions.

Slaves could never buy merchandise directly for themselves but could buy things for their master with a written note.

Slaves could never keep or own their own livestock but were needed to work long hours in all types of husbandry positions on a farm.

Slaves could bring a legal case to a court but could never serve on a jury.

Slaves could walk into town but could never carry a stick or a cane without a note granting medical permission.

Slaves could never be seen walking in the street during church service hours but were encouraged to collectively pray on the master's property.

Some parishes accepted slaves as congregants but required them to sit in the upper balcony areas of the church away from the general congregants.

Free Black slaves could never entertain other blacks or mulattoes in their own homes, but blacks in general were strongly encouraged to have children.

CHAPTER EIGHT

The American Colonization
Society (ACS)

The American Colonization Society believed in eliminating the scourge of slavery by releasing enslaved Blacks to freedom in Sierra Leone, where a new land of freedom could be instituted. American sea captain Robert Finley modeled his theory of ACS on the principles of British Abolitionism. This theory held to a strong undercurrent of thought that Black men were basically inferior to whites and that the two cultures should not be mixed. Finley and others believed that Blacks should not be held in captivity and should not be integrated into the whole society. This theory disregarded the fact that many families had resided in a colonial environment for centuries, forming many mixed racial combinations.

Some religious movements preferred the full manumission of slaves. However, if fully freed, where should they live? The Second Great Religious Revival wanted all slave owners, upon their deaths, to release their slaves. Primarily encouraged by Quakers, Methodists, and Baptists from New England, some owners freed their slaves after the Revolutionary War.

As slavery continued primarily in the South after the Revolution, prominent men, even presidents such as Thomas Jefferson and James Madison, who owned slaves, believed moving free Blacks to colonies within or outside the United States would be the easiest and most pragmatic approach to solving the race problem in America. This opened a lane to provide an alternative route for free Blacks as opposed to simply absorbing a large population of ex-slaves into white communities through emancipation. The abolitionist movement disavowed this concept as radically and morally wrong and would only further complicate matters.

A devout Quaker and black sailor, Paul Cuffee, who is covered in more detail later, was viewed as a man who could see both sides of any issue. In 1813, Cuffee donated half the necessary funds to oversee a new meeting house in Westport, Massachusetts. This group, the ACS, would admit Black members for the first time. He also originally contemplated that a new slave colony be established in Sierra Leone, a country where the British transported more than one thousand former slaves who originally came from the United States.

Thomas Peters, born as "Thomas Potters," also strongly supported the ACS. A veteran of the Black Pioneers who fought for the British during the American Revolutionary War, Peters resettled in Nova Scotia after the war, where he became a politician and then one of the "Founding Fathers" of Sierra Leone in West Africa. At the request of British abolitionists, Paul Cuffee sailed to Sierra Leone to make his personal observations and gain a deeper knowledge of the pragmatics of the concept. He studied the present economic conditions of the colony while also examining the best ways to help slaves.

Cuffee's first recommendation was to increase the local production of imported and exported commodities going to and from Sierra Leone. He also sought to enhance business, building stronger contacts with many African colonies. These actions led to greater shipping options and growing local businesses. He brought these findings to England and discussed them with the African Institution, an agency supported by the British abolitionists. The British liked these ideas so much that they sent Cuffee back to Africa to see if he could engage in some first steps.

During his final voyage to Sierra Leone, Cuffee transported nine free Black families from Massachusetts to work in close concert with the developing nation. When Americans asked Cuffee what the best action for America might be, he gave the matter much contemplation. He held significant discussions and listened intently to the voices of free Blacks in New York City, Philadelphia, and New Bedford. He eventually chose not to support the ACS movement in America. He contended that training black citizens, providing advanced machinery, and supplying ships was much more helpful to America's growth than simply going on with sending some Blacks back to African soil.

A view of Freetown, a Sierra Leone port, home of the American Colonization Society.

In terms of what this movement looked like in Africa, the colonial state was divided into two different portions. One state was designated for the colonial European population, and another state was for the Indigenous population. Colonial power was mainly found within urban towns and cities, where it was served by elected governments.

There were three major reasons this movement finally failed. Free Black people expressed little enthusiasm for venturing to Africa, as some families had been in the United States for centuries. Many abolitionists favored societal integration over basic national separation. Finally, the costs of implementing this program would be staggering, with the over four million Black people freed after the Civil War.

CHAPTER NINE

A Chronology of Ambiguous Laws on Slaves

The original Massachusetts colony laws concerning slavery were filled with conflicting issues, multiple exceptions, and vague wording, leaving the results open to legal interpretation. It could be read as support for endorsing enslavement just as easily as interpreted to mean citizens should curtail its practice.

1641: THE BODY OF LIBERTIES ACT

The Massachusetts Bay Colony passed The Body of Liberties Act of 1641, attempting to define the legality of slavery in its own region:

> It is ordered by this court and the authority thereof: that there shall never be any
> bond slavery, villenage, or captivity amongst us, unless it be captives taken in
> just wars, as willingly sell themselves, or are sold to us, and such shall have the
> liberties and Christian usage which the law of God established in Israel concern-
> ing such persons doth morally require: Provided this exempts none from servitude,
> who shall be judged thereto by authority.[1]

Most historians concur that this law was designed to conclude that slavery was not a condoned or legal action. Yet its interpretation, as well as its enforcement, instantly led to confusion. Various individual acts would be reviewed in the courts as case law over the next several decades, often with little consequence to possibly limiting or ending its practice. In 1648, the *Laws and Liberties* issued a new contradictory ruling on physical punishment, which was allowable at any time as a punishment

---

1. Massachusetts General Court, "The Body of Liberties Act of 1641," *The General Lawes and Libertyes Concerning the Inhabitants of Massachusetts*, 1648.

by the master: "*We allow amongst us no actions that are inhumane, barbarous, or cruel. And no man shall be beaten with above forty stripes for one fact at a time, except he has not yet answered for the crime or unless his crime be very shameful.*"[2] This definition of cruelty was so broad that practically any punishment seemed applicable. If the use of a whip could be invoked forty times for one single act of disobedience, what type of crime could occur that might warrant an even harsher sanction?

1670: RIGHT TO CHATTEL SLAVERY

In 1670, a colonial law was amended to clarify one specific point. An amendment to the law appeared, stating that "all children born of slaves were to continue in the state of slavery." These words surely implied that slavery was to remain a staple of American life for many years to come.

Legal arguments that desired to permit slavery would be based on a justification that a newly emerging country with a severe labor shortage must face basic survival. Hence, economic grounds alone should justify its existence. Any opposing views on an issue like slavery were not apparent at the federal level. The lofty principles of the Founding Fathers were not only debated but heatedly assailed in various ways.

John Adams and Alexander Hamilton were in the Federalist camp, which espoused the belief that a strong national presence was best for our country and that no slavery should be accepted. Meanwhile, the opposing views of slave owners, such as those of Washington, Jefferson, and Madison, felt that individual state rights should not be lessened, and any state that wished to support this type of enterprise had the right to do so. This clash of moral standards versus legal rights would continue in various ways for decades to come in the American interpretation of slavery.

1765: THE FREEDOM SUITS

In 1765, the first fully enslaved person sued to obtain her freedom, forming a new legal standard in Massachusetts. Jenny Slew was essentially kidnapped by a white owner who believed that Jenny could be claimed for slavery. The Massachusetts Attorney General at the time was Benjamin Kent. He realized that Jenny's mother was white, which would preclude

---

2. *General Laws and Libertyes Concerning the Inhabitatns of Massachusetts,* 1648.

Jenny from being enslaved. This kind of formal action of freeing slaves legally is known as manumission.

The legal process of people freeing themselves from slavery appeared in many variations in the latter portion of the 1700s. Prior to this court case, it was extremely rare for a case to be brought up by a woman, and even more rare to have a case come up based on the claims of a Black woman. Nonetheless, Jenny produced enough evidence to validate that she was not the dependent of a Black mother and was herself of mixed blood. Therefore, she could never be claimed for slavery by any party. She was deemed to be freed by the courts.

Several cases of this type arose and collectively were known as "Freedom Suits," which challenged the classification of a person's social status. Many of these cases were brought to the court's attention by a sympathetic figure of the day. Massachusetts Attorney General Kent heard many of these cases, and many of them resulted in full manumission. In fact, there were so many cases that by 1780, the Quock Walker case, a landmark case freeing slaves, was eventually brought to the Massachusetts State Supreme Court.

1775: PROFITABLE TAXES FROM THE SLAVE TRADE

Boston was a major site of trafficking and suffering for slaves, where at least 2,400 kidnapped people arrived directly from Africa.[3] The city's involvement in the transatlantic slave trade peaked between 1760 and 1775, the same period when Bostonians were staging dramatic protests and escalating their own demands for "freedom" and "independence from Britain." In Boston, there were at least ninety-five voyages departing from or disembarking in connection with slavery. Many ships were traveling to or leaving directly from Africa. New England traders imported sugar and molasses, which were produced by slaves in the West Indies and sold to the colonies. In fact, Massachusetts and Rhode Island built the largest distilleries in the Northeast, creating a need for more labor.

Even after gradual abolition in Massachusetts outlawed the enslavement of Black people, Boston shipbuilders, traders, and businessmen continued to grow wealthy from human trafficking to other ports of call.

---

3. Nat Sheidley, *Revolutionary Spaces* (Faneuil Hall: Museum Exhibit, 2020).

Massachusetts and Rhode Island built an infrastructure that stimulated slavery by planning for state-building projects and using the power of enslaved people. For a brief period, the ports of Boston even collected tax revenues for each slave kidnapped and brought back to the colonies.

Legal Cases Involving Slaves

Historians estimate that between 1755 and 1764, the Massachusetts slave population was approximately 2.2 percent of the total population and generally concentrated in industrial and coastal towns.[4] Massachusetts had declared that slaves were allowed full access to the court.

Before the American Revolution, the Massachusetts courts felt that slavery did not exclude the concept of "personage" within slavery. In fact, there were no reasons why slaves could not bring a civil or criminal court case forward. Two examples of slaves successfully bringing state cases are cited here.

THE MUM BETT CASE

Elizabeth Freeman was born circa 1742 to enslaved African parents in Claverack, New York. At the age of six months, she and her sister were purchased by John Ashley of Sheffield, Massachusetts, whom she served for nearly forty years. Most people called her "Mum Bett" due to her kindly spirit. She also had a young daughter known as "Little Bett."

When the mistress of the house tried to hit Mum Bett's sister with a kitchen shovel, Mum Bett intervened and received the blow instead. Furious, the slave ran out of the house and refused to return, but Colonel Ashley appealed to the law to have her returned. She was represented by Theodore Sedgewick, a lawyer from Stockbridge who possessed strong antislavery sentiments.

Mum Bett had listened carefully while the white men conversed about the Bill of Rights and the new state constitution. She decided that if all people were born free and equal, then the laws must apply to her as well.

In *Brom & Bett v. Ashley* the jury ruled in favor of Bett and Brom, making them the first enslaved African Americans to be freed under the

---

4. A. Leon Higginbotham Jr., *In the Matter of Color: Race and the American Legal Process: The Colonial Period* (Oxford: Oxford University Press, 1978), 212.

Massachusetts Constitution of 1780. The court ordered Colonel Ashley to pay them thirty shillings and court costs. This case set a precedent that was affirmed by the state courts in the Quock Walker case and ultimately led to the abolition of slavery in Massachusetts. The famed author W. E. B. Dubois can trace his lineage to Mum Bett, both of whom came from the Great Barrington region.

1780: THE QUOCK WALKER CASES

When the Massachusetts Constitution went into effect in 1780, slavery was legal in the Commonwealth within certain boundaries. However, from 1781 to 1783, in three related cases known today as "the Quock Walker Cases," the Supreme Judicial Court applied the principles of judicial review and firmly agreed to abolish slavery as a matter of constitutional rights.

This completely new legal interpretation of a Massachusetts slave case came in 1781. Quock Walker was a twenty-eight-year-old slave living in Barre, Massachusetts. His master was a brutish man who often administered punishment in the harshest of ways, with a lash and stern fist. One day, Quock had enough of the physical punishment. He decided to run away from the cruelty.

He secured two prominent lawyers who practiced law in Worcester County. Levi Lincoln and Caleb Strong took on the case on a pro bono basis, testing the rights of a slave to live in a safe environment, avoiding bodily assault and battery. The case proceeded to a jury trial, which upheld the rights of the injured slave. Quock not only won his freedom from slavery—he was also awarded a substantive financial compensation of fifty dollars paid to him by his master.

The nature of the case centered mostly on mean and unnecessary physical treatment. The legal trial was given to a Worcester County jury in a Supreme Judicial Court. At the end of the hearing, Chief Justice William Cushing instructed the attendees that perpetual slavery could no longer be tolerated by the government, adding that liberty can only be forfeited by criminal conduct and not relinquished even by personal consent or contract. This case was now viewed as the death knell of personal slavery in the colony. The legal finding was such that slavery itself was not deemed to be illegal, but the rights of the slave owner were so narrowly defined to the point that ownership was not seen as financially feasible. In 1783, a new incident arose in *Commonwealth v. Jennison*, filed before the state supreme court. Chief Justice William Cushing again reinforced his ruling by saying there could be no such thing as a perpetual servitude by a rational creator.

Massachusetts was the first state to legally negate the right to hold slaves. Soon thereafter, other New England territories followed suit. Vermont, not yet an official state, was the next region to adopt similar laws. In Connecticut and Rhode Island, a law was passed in 1783 making slavery illegal. They also included a clause that children of slaves must remain in that state until reaching a certain age. In Connecticut, twenty-five was the finite limit, while in Rhode Island, freedom was gained on the twenty-first birthday. This type of gradual manumission explains why there were still some legally enslaved people in New England as late as the 1840s.

Slaveholders now lost any legal protection from potential legal suits. It raised a red flag among the public that things needed to change quickly. For protection, some landowners initiated an indentured servant clause to keep their slaves. They went from official slave owners to a written agreements fixed for several years with an indentured servant status. Other slaveholders avoided the risk altogether and simply awarded freedom to their slaves. They typically chose to negotiate any previous work completed by their slaves to a small fee awarded for service. It is interesting to note that the 1790 Massachusetts census reported "zero" for slave ownership, meaning all remaining Black residents were officially reported as indentured servants, avoiding legal prosecution.

1787: U.S. CONSTITUTION FAILS TO MENTION SLAVERY

When the original thirteen colonies started to expand, there was a need to have one concrete document that would encapsulate a national set of standards. The divisions were wide, and the issues were complex. Compromise was a necessary ingredient if a struggling new nation was to exist. In the first draft, there was no use of the word slavery. Many opined that slavery was but a passing trend. It would eventually end, and it was an immoral concept to even bring it up for discussion.

However, the founders did include a clause regarding "those bound in service" in the final draft of the Constitution, after varied amounts of debate and compromise during the Constitutional Convention of 1787.

The Three-Fifths Clause

Representatives and direct Taxes shall be apportioned among the several States which may be included within this Union, according to their respective Numbers, which shall be determined by adding to the whole Number of free Persons, including those bound to Service for a Term of Years, and excluding Indians not taxed, three fifths of all other Persons.[5]

In other words, when a state's population is counted for full representation in the federal government to decide on issues such as direct taxation or congressional seats, the enslaved population would only be counted as three-fifths of its overall population. Untaxed Indigenous people were never even considered as being meaningful citizens within this counting. This clause was seen as a temporary solution for a period of twenty years, projected at a time in which new states could possibly pass acceptable new regulations on the concept of slavery as stated in Chapter Nine.

It also followed that any slaveholding states could now count their slaves, boosting their total population. This clause had a direct impact on electors and representation in Congress. Therefore, this decision likely influenced future legislation, presidential elections, and, by extension, Supreme Court appointments. Theoretically, slaveholding states also had to contribute more in direct taxes to maintain this privilege as they gained greater political influence and potentially received enhanced federal funds.

The passage of this legislation was never intended to raise a level of valid humanity or to give voice to the passionate treatment of enslaved people. Instead, it was merely a political compromise to secure the Southern vote for the whole of the Constitution. Southerners wanted to gain greater clout in absolute numbers and have a larger say in national matters.

---

5. U.S. Constitution, art. 1, sec. 2, cl. 3.

States with large slave populations desired to gain more power in Congress and their corresponding court systems. This compromise further reduced the authority of the abolition states and created division. Nonetheless, the cry for compromise grew so loud that it was uncertain if the Southern states would have eventually capitulated to agree to form that "more perfect Union." Many in the North saw this legislation as a necessary evil, a reasonable concession to create forward progress in the new nation.

In its final draft, the U.S. Constitution has a message of inclusivity, establishing "justice" and ensuring "domestic Tranquility" for the people, echoing the Declaration of Independence's standard that "all men are created equal." Yet in the U.S. Constitution's complex wording, an important premise is left open to interpretation. How should the legal system differentiate between people and personal property? Can a slave be considered a proprietary right for some people and not counted as a free human being by others?

The absence of the word slavery in the Constitution is one of the great paradoxes of our Founding Fathers' era. The framers were revolutionary thinkers who created what would become the first successfully functioning representative democratic government by the people. Their ideas of fairness, justice, and individual rights are what many world leaders attempt to emulate today. Why, then, did so many brilliant minds pledge to be champions of individual rights while reducing human beings to mere chattel?

James Madison played a significant role in defining how slavery should be incorporated into federal legislation during the Constitutional Convention of 1787. The moral justification for slavery must be tempered by a necessity for a practical solution. The political split between states was widening, with Northern delegates having distinct and different labor needs than their Southern peers. Starting a new, approvable constitution required a compromise all members could accept. Madison offered a solution that was imperfect but could be considered consensually acceptable by a majority. Having a final agreement for a written framework and guidelines for a young nation was imminently superior to not having any type of agreement at all.

The Constitutional Convention in Philadelphia met between May and September of 1787 to address the problems of a weakly conceived central government under the Articles of Confederation. In May, fifty-five delegates came to Philadelphia, and the Constitutional Convention began. Debates erupted over representation in Congress, slavery, and the new executive branch. The debates continued through four contentious months. Eventually the delegates reached compromises, and on September 17, they produced the U.S. Constitution, replacing the Articles of Confederation with the governing document that has functioned effectively for more than two hundred years.

As part of the compromise, the Constitution prohibited Congress from outlawing the Atlantic slave trade for a period of twenty years. In addition, the Fugitive Slave Clause required the return of runaway slaves to their owners.[6] The Constitution also gave the federal government the authority to put down domestic rebellions, including slave insurrections.

Some founders knowingly compromised their moral standards, as many were on record as being opposed to slavery. As a basic starting point, the central executive power had to be modified to permit slaveholding on a state-by-state basis. These accommodations were vital to the ratification of the Constitution. In essence, the basics of economic growth and political survival prevailed. Slavery, when all was said and done, was both profitable and convenient for many Southern white Americans who held farm slaves as well as for some Northern maritime interests who could profit from larger shipping and crop sales.

Morality may have entered the consciences of our early politicians, but practicality was also part of the equation. The Age of Enlightenment philosophies of natural rights and growing religious convictions stood in stark contrast to the practice of slavery. The contradiction could not be denied. Philosophies that recognized the rights of the individual were assigned against one entire subset of people who were seen as expendable, equal only to a piece of property.

Another way to justify the inequity involved with slavery is to determine who gets to be considered a full person and who does not. Fabricating a subservient rank order for some people allowed our founding

6. U.S. Constitution, art. 4, sec. 2, cl. 3.

generation to define "all full men" and "the people" as "white men." As a result, white men were guaranteed the rights and liberties promised by the Constitution while preserving a thriving economy largely based on racial oppression.

Not everyone agreed with this type of basic definition. Colonial independence was almost immediately apparent when abolitionist groups pointed out the moral contradictions inherent in slavery. As America spread into new territories, regional blocks formed on both sides of the issue. The abolition movement made significant progress in the North, leading to the enactment of new antislavery laws in some states. Vermont was the first state to abolish slavery in 1777, Pennsylvania in 1780, and others followed suit. In 1782, Virginia also allowed slave owners to free their slaves without obtaining permission from the state. However, further south, where African Americans were enslaved and served as a significant workforce, the white ruling class continued to insist on maintaining a racial hierarchy.

1793: THE FUGITIVE ESCAPE FEDERAL ACT OF 1793

On February 12, 1793, the Second Congress passed an act aimed at interfering with assistance given to persons escaping from the service of their masters. It authorized the arrest or seizure of fugitives and empowering any magistrate of any county, city, or ton to rule on the matter.

In Massachusetts, since slavery was already deemed illegal, this act did not convey great importance, yet its enactment carried serious consequences, particularly for sea captains who either were sympathetic to slavery injustice or were casually approached by any Black servant requesting paid or unpaid safe passage on their ship.

The 1793 law enforced Article IV, Section 2, of the U.S. Constitution:

> No Person held to Service or Labour in one State, under the Laws thereof, escaping into another, shall, in Consequence of any Law or Regulation therein, be discharged from such Service of Labour, but shall be delivered up on Claim of the Party to whom such Service or Labour may be due.[7]

---

7. U.S. Constitution, art. 4, sec. 2, cl. 3.

This law authorized any federal district judge, circuit court judge, or any state magistrate to decide finally and without the need for a jury trial as to the status of an alleged fugitive slave. In other words, in the Commonwealth, a judge had a greater scope of authority to determine the legality of holding people as chattel slaves with minimal evidence needed. Case law resulted in even more formally enslaved people still fearing their freedom based on random claims.

Data Report on the United States Census of 1790

State	Free White	Slaves
Vermont	85,268	16
New Hampshire	141,097	158
Maine	96,002	538
Massachusetts	373,324	0
Rhode Island	64,470	948
Connecticut	232,374	2,764

Census.gov / Throughtheages.org.

It is of interest to note that, on a comparative basis, the total percentage of slaves to free whites in the United States in 1790 was 17.8 percent. This ratio represented the highest percentage or ratio of slaves within our country's history. In Vermont, the first state admitted after the thirteen colonies, the census took place in 1791 after its formal statehood adoption. The number of "zero slaves" reported within Massachusetts was deemed suspect due to its potential legal implications for its residents.

In examining the 1800 U.S. census, there was a total of 5,308,483 people, with 893,602 people designated as slaves. By the 1840s, slaves reached a total of two million people. This figure includes both the new arrivals as well as children born into slavery. It was obvious that more slaves kept coming into the country, even with the polarizing legal challenges. The proportionality of slavery continued to grow right until the 1880s. It seems obvious to conclude that the birth of new slaves could never account for this frenetic rise. New slaves were still being brought to the American shores by sea captains.

TEN DOLLARS REWARD.

RUN AWAY on Friday the 26th of August 1774, from the subscriber, living in Middle-patent, North-Castle, Westchester county, and province of New-York, A NEGRO MAN, Named W I L L, about 27 years of age, about five feet six inches high, somewhat of a yellow complexion, a spry lively fellow, very talkative; had on when he went away, a butter-nut coloured coat, felt hat, tow cloth trowsers; he has part of his right ear cut off, and a mark on the backside of his right hand.

Whosoever takes up said Negro and brings him to his master, or secures him in gaol, so that his master may have him again, shall have the above reward and all reasonable charges, paid by JAMES BANKS.

N. B. Masters of vessels are hereby warned not to carry off the above Negro.

History of the Rise and Fall of Slave Power in America

1840: SLAVES CAN BE COUNTED AS A PERCENTAGE OF THE WHOLE FOR VOTING RIGHTS

In 1840, more than fifty years after the Constitution was ratified, John Quincy Adams would refer to the omission of the term "slave" as "the fig-leaves under which the parts of the body politic are decently concealed."[8]

There were many significant pro-slavery voices, and there were also forward-thinking constitutional framers, like Oliver Ellsworth, a senator from Connecticut, who was optimistic that slavery, in time, would not be even a speck in our country. Though some thought the Constitution's power to prohibit the slave trade would lay the foundation for banishing slavery out of this country, as James Wilson said in the Pennsylvania Ratifying Convention in 1787, many political figures were not enthusiastic about having their names attached to any document that mentioned slavery outright. The last legislative action proposed by Benjamin

8. Lindsay Chervinsky, *The Enslaved Household of John Quincy Adams* (Washington, D.C.: Washington Historical Association, 2018), 18.

Franklin was an act to fully abolish slavery as part of the country's laws, but sufficient support was never generated to even bring it up for a vote.

It is a basic misconception to believe that the clause of having slaves counted, even on a partial basis, represents a small degree of humanity the framers were willing to assign to African Americans. More directly, the South was pushing hard to have their enslaved individuals counted in any way possible so that they could achieve a deeper impact within Congress.

1841: SUPREME COURT CASE OF THE *AMISTAD*

In 1839, a ship headed to Cuba with slaves on board experienced a slave revolt. The ship, called the *Amistad*, was captured by the U.S. brig *Washington* off Long Island on August 24, 1839. The ship and its contents were taken to New London, Connecticut, where the plantation owners were released, and the Africans were imprisoned on charges of murder.

Although the murder charges were later dropped, the Africans remained in custody, and the case was taken to trial in the federal district court in Connecticut. The Spanish government, the plantation owners, and the captain of the *Washington* all claimed ownership or compensation for all items on board, including the Africans.

President Van Buren favored extraditing the Africans back to Cuba, but abolitionists opposed this and raised funds to support the Africans' defense. The abolitionists used the incident to expose the evils of slavery and generate opposition on a national scale.

Lieutenant Thomas R. Gedney was the commanding officer of the *Washington*, and he claimed salvage rights for the full value of $65,000. Under maritime law, compensation was allowed to those whose assistance saved a ship or its cargo from impending loss, even if they were officers of the government. In a written statement, Gedney detailed the encounter with the *Amistad* and itemized its cargo, including the value of the Africans as slaves.

Roger S. Baldwin, a New Haven lawyer, and New York attorneys Seth Staples and Theodore Sedgwick represented the Africans as proctors, or legal representatives, in court. The proctors argued, ". . . each of them are natives of Africa and were born free, and ever since have been and still of right are and ought to be free and not slaves . . ."[9] that the Africans were

9. Emma Sterne, *The History of the Amistad* (Garden City: Dover Evergreen Classics, 2021), 28.

born free and had been forcibly kidnapped from the African coast, not taken in the Spanish domestic slave trade. They further contended that the Africans suffered "great cruelty and oppression" on board and were "incited by the love of liberty natural to all men" to take possession of the ship and seek asylum."[10] The U.S. district court ruled that the case fell within federal jurisdiction and that the claims to the Africans as property were illegitimate.

The U.S. district attorney appealed the ruling to the Supreme Court, where former U.S. president John Quincy Adams represented the Africans. For eight-and-one-half hours, Adams passionately defended the Africans' right to freedom on both legal and moral grounds, referencing treaties prohibiting the slave trade and the Declaration of Independence. The Supreme Court in the case of *The United States v. Amistad* ultimately ruled in favor of the Africans, declaring that they were free individuals who had been illegally kidnapped and transported. Senior Justice Joseph authored the decision, stating, ". . . it was the ultimate right of all human beings in extreme cases to resist oppression, and to apply force against ruinous injustice."

The court ordered the immediate release of the *Amistad* Africans, and thirty-five of the survivors were returned to their homeland. The others either died at sea or were imprisoned while awaiting trial.

1850: THE MORE STRINGENT FUGITIVE SLAVE ACT OF 1850

The Fugitive Slave Act of 1850 was passed by Congress on September 18, 1850, as part of the Compromise of 1850. The act required that if slaves were discovered in any state, even a free one, the slaves must be returned to their owners. The act also made the federal government responsible for finding, returning, and trying escaped slaves.

Once again, it's evident that Congress was fully divided on its stance on slavery. The Compromise of 1850 was a series of measures passed by the U.S. Congress to settle regional disagreements over the state of American slavery. The conflict involved admitting new states and territories to the U.S. and, more specifically, whether they should be admitted as either "free" or "slave" states.

---

10. Emma Sterne, 3.

The abolitionist, or free, states desired to declare Washington, D.C., free as well and to accept California on the same basis. The territory of Utah was admitted with a possibility of statehood down the road. To pass this legislation, an agreement was made that all slaves, no matter where they might be located, could now be seized, and it was a federal offense to tamper with their return to their owner.

This attempted to manage two opposing forces: people who worked diligently to move slaves to safer locales, and slave catchers who made their living by finding, capturing, and returning slaves. Slave catchers were visible in Massachusetts throughout the early 1800s, and this new federal law tipped the scale toward the slave catchers who had the full force of the law behind them. In response, The Boston Vigilance Committee was formed in Boston, Massachusetts, and dedicated itself to protecting escaped slaves.

Many abuses were also committed in which even Blacks who were freeborn in the North could be falsely accused of being runaway slaves and spirited away to a life of slavery, as in the infamous case of Solomon Northup. He was freeborn in New York yet kidnapped into slavery in Louisiana. If a slave catcher merely accused a Black person of being a slave, whether they were free or not, they might be drugged or kidnapped for a trip to a slave state. Solomon Northup described his own brutal experiences in his memoir, *Twelve Years a Slave*. Blacks, free or not, were no longer completely free from the threat of false accusations lurking behind them.

1852: *LEMMON v. NEW YORK*

Lemmon v. New York, or *Lemmon v. The People*, was popularly known as the Lemmon Slave Case. It was a freedom suit initiated in 1852 by a petition for a writ of unlawful detention of a person. The petition was granted by the Superior Court in New York City, whose decision was upheld by the New York Court of Appeals. The decision came in 1860 on the eve of the U.S. Civil War.

The court's decision mandated the release of eight slaves, including six children, brought into New York by their Virginia slave owners, Jonathan and Juliet Lemmon, who were in the middle of relocating to Texas. New York had abolished slavery gradually beginning in 1799, freeing all remaining slaves on July 4, 1827. An 1841 state law explicitly prohibited slaveholders from bringing any slaves through the state, liberating any slaves brought in this manner.

Attorney John Jay, a founding member of the Republican Party, represented the state in the 1852 case. Future President Chester A. Arthur represented the state on the appeal by the former slaveowners. His counsels were William Everts, Joseph Blunt, and Erastus Culver.

1857: THE DRED SCOTT DECISION

The Dred Scott decision was formally called the *Dred Scott v. John F.A. Sandford* decision. On March 6, 1857, the U.S. Supreme Court ruled by a vote of 7–2 that a slave named Dred Scott, residing in a free state and territory where slavery was prohibited, was not legally entitled to his freedom. Furthermore, slaves in this region were not nor could ever be considered citizens of the United States. It further stated that the Missouri Compromise of 1820, which had declared all territories to be free of slavery west of Missouri and north of latitude 36°30', was unconstitutional.

According to judicial scholars, *Scott v. Sandford* is widely considered the worst legal decision ever rendered by the Supreme Court. It has often been cited as the most egregious example in the court's history of wrongly imposing a judicial solution on a political problem.[11] A later chief justice, Charles Hughes, famously characterized the decision as the court's greatest "self-inflicted wound" in the history of our country.[12]

Dred Scott was a slave who was owned by John Emerson of Missouri. In 1833, Emerson, who was serving in the U.S. military, moved as part of his service and took Scott from Missouri (a slave state) to Illinois (a free state) and finally into the Wisconsin Territory (a free territory). During this time, Scott met and married Harriet Robinson, who also became part of the Emerson household. Emerson married in 1838, and in the early 1840s, he and his wife returned with the Scotts to Missouri, where Emerson eventually died in 1843.

Scott reportedly attempted to purchase his freedom from Emerson's widow, who refused. In 1846, Harriet and Dred Scott, with the help of

---

11. Earl Maltz, *Dred Scott and the Politics of Slavery* (Lawrence: Kansas University Press, 2007), 37.
12. Earl Maltz, 86.

antislavery lawyers, filed individual lawsuits for their freedom in St. Louis on the grounds that their residence was in a free state and a free territory and freed them from the bonds of slavery. It was later agreed that Dred's case would move forward first, and the decision in that case would then apply to Harriet's case. Although the case was long thought to have been unusual, historians later demonstrated that several hundred similar suits for freedom were filed by or on behalf of slaves in the decades before the Civil War.

The Dred Scott decision fueled the erupting sectional controversy and clearly pushed the entire country much closer to the start of civil disobedience. Civil war seemed inevitable.

Dred Scott and Harriet Scott wood engravings after photographs by Fitzgibbon

1863: THE LEGAL END OF SLAVERY

President Lincoln issued an order, known as the Emancipation Proclamation, which stated that slaves in the Confederates States would be freed starting in 1863. Additionally, he offered the Southern states a chance to rejoin the Union if they, too, outlawed slavery. However, even after the end of the war, the Southern states were reluctant to comply, which made the Reconstruction of the United States more challenging.

In 1864, the Thirteenth Amendment was proposed to make slavery unconstitutional and was passed without the participation of the Southern states. It was debated by Congress until 1865 and was ultimately passed by a narrow majority. The amendment was then slowly ratified by all thirty-six United States over the next few years. The freedom clause of the amendment applied to the Confederate States as the country continued to expand.

The Thirteenth Amendment Text

Section 1. *Neither slavery nor involuntary servitude, except as a punishment for crime whereof the party shall have been duly convicted, shall exist within the United States, or any place subject to their jurisdiction.*

Section 2. *Congress shall have power to enforce this article by appropriate legislation.*

Even though the original constitution never formally addressed slavery, it certainly allowed for involuntary servitude by a select number of people, such as orphanage-placed children and prisoners to be indentured, a form of keeping a person bound to task without complete voluntary acquiescence. One clear exception could be found within the legal system where a convicted felon or even an orphan child could be enticed to perform assigned tasks like prison labor to secure their freedom.

Section 2 of this amendment broadened the congressional scope to deal with the interpretations of what is deemed slavery and enforce any opposing treatment to its continuance. "The badges and incidents of slavery" must be removed. Therefore, new legislation could be enacted that might end racial discrimination or other acts that resemble the injustices of slavery.

1896: *PLESSY v. FERGUSON*

Many related legal cases spun off this decision for years. In 1896, a man who was of seven-eighths European ancestry and one-eighth Black attempted to enter a train car that was marked "whites only." The Supreme Court found that since separate options were available for Blacks and whites, this was not a violation of the law. This interpretation led to decades of legal suppression and double standards of human rights for both whites and Blacks.

Summary of Laws on Slavery

The practice of slavery in Massachusetts evolved gradually through case law interpretations. As an officially sanctioned institution, slavery ended in the late eighteenth century through judicial actions litigated on behalf of slaves seeking their freedom. In some of the legal jurisdictions, enslaved people in Massachusetts occupied a dual legal status of being both personal property and persons before the law, which entitled them to file legal suits in court.

Prominent Massachusetts lawyer Benjamin Kent represented slaves in court against their masters as early as 1752. He won his first "freedom suit" in the American colonies in 1766. The post-revolutionary court cases, starting in 1781, heard arguments maintaining that the practice of slavery was a violation of Christian principles. It was also a violation of the constitution of the Commonwealth. From 1781 to 1783, in three related cases known today as "the Quock Walker case," the Court applied the principle of judicial review to effectively abolish slavery. It was declared incompatible with the newly adopted state constitution in 1783.

A larger legal threat to both present and former slaves and freemen living in Massachusetts was then posed by slave catchers. It was their chosen profession to find and capture slaves who fled from the South, sheltering in the North. Under American law at the time, any individuals who were even accused of being slaves would be subject to detention and return to slavery in any jurisdiction that had not yet ended slavery. Many abuses were also committed in which even Blacks who were freeborn in the North could be falsely accused of being runaway slaves and spirited away to a life of slavery.

This ongoing legal challenge of human rights started the abolition movement in the North. Greedy-spirited people seeking compensation could declare any Black living in a free state to be a runaway, particularly if they had no visible means to prove their free credentials. The cry for justice was declared. Slavery must definitively be ended across the United States. Massachusetts became the leading center for abolitionism in early nineteenth-century America, with individual activists such as William Lloyd Garrison and Frederick Douglass and organizations such as the Boston Vigilance Committee advancing its cause.

CHAPTER TEN

The Impact of Cape Cod Sea Captains on the Slave Trade

There were several identifiable categories of sea captains within the complex business of slavery. There were captains who owned slaves to be used as crew members, original slave traders, captains who began as traders but then transitioned to slave savers, runaway slave advocates, indirect beneficiaries of the slave trade, proslavery catchers, possible slavers but who lacked direct evidence of involvement, and captains of color who commanded ships. Of course, some mariners fit comfortably into more than one of these designated categories. As with most aspects of slavery, a person's moral compass as to the most appropriate way to accept or reject the concept of owning slaves evolved over time, containing subtle or major variations of thought.

Categories of Sea Captains Directly Connected to the Slave Trade

Captains Who Used Slaves on Their Ships

For the first category of ship captains engaged in slavery, we can identify Benjamin Bangs, an early slaveholder of Indigenous servants and Black slaves. His diary has passages in which Black and Indigenous men were ordered to work for his various enterprises. His servants farmed his land, tended to his personal house chores, and assisted him in his whaling supply operations. Several other sea captains experienced similar circumstances, but written records are scarce. Black slaves were smaller in total numbers than the Indigenous population. Anecdotal stories for the first half of the 1700s suggest that Black slaves were best utilized for in-house domestic duties while Indigenous people could handle the rigors of ocean life. Before the American Revolution, there is little evidence of widespread Black slaves on ships.

BENJAMIN BANGS (1721–1769)
Captain and Slave Holder

Lee Roscoe published a story on the life of Captain Bangs in the *Barnstable Patriot* in 2013, which refers to Bangs's personal journal and uses direct quotes. The captain frequently mentioned the satisfaction he felt when his slaves' performance was admirable. In this early period, if slaves worked on a whaler, any profit gained from their employ remained the property of the slave's owner. However, if the vessel was fully under the ownership of the captain, contracts for duties and salary could be individually negotiated. One factor complicating the full count of slave use on ships was defining their actual race. Many Black men intermarried with Indigenous women, so it would be unclear which crewmembers were correctly termed slaves.

Benjamin Bangs lived in Harwich's North Parish, now called Brewster, before it separated from Harwich's South Parish. He was prominent in the whaling industry and became a successful merchant of whaling equipment later in life. He owned several whaling ships, hiring local maritime talent to take command. He ran the largest whale supply shop on Cape Cod. Captain Bangs also invested in other whalers and crews, taking a percentage of their returns. He mentions using both Black and Indigenous slaves for the manual work on his farm and assisting with his boats.

Whenever whale men became sick, incapacitated, or fell into financial trouble, Bangs would take care of them, often lodging them at his house or in town on Stoney Brook Road. Payment would arrive later when the captains returned to sea, giving up a share of their eventual salary to him.

This turned out to be a shrewd business decision because he realized shipping in those days was never a sure thing. As a shipowner, he dealt with herring, sugar, molasses, tea, and carrying passengers to foreign ports. All these options could prove to be risky propositions, so he needed to hedge his bets. He kept seafaring men comfortable in a time of need, providing them with housing and safety, accompanied by a written pay-back plan.

Throughout his life, Bangs was a gracious farmer. His journal describes him plowing, mowing, making hay, keeping livestock, and growing wheat. These crops were typically seen as solid regional investments. He also was the primary supplier of whaling equipment for the local region.

A diary entry dated October 1743 talks of a good corn harvest. "Got 177 bushels corn off 6 acres of land."[1] In December 1745, he describes a snowstorm. "Sheep covered up with abundance."[2] He mentions having to physically dig the animals out of the drifts. On February 24, 1748, he told of "A wild creature in woods and it does much harm to my sheep."[3] Wolves were common in Harwich. In 1759, Bangs recalled many sightings of bears weighing in the 300- to 400-pound range. His belief was that the creatures were forced from their natural habitat by the French and Indian War.

Bangs was occasionally seen as an affectionate man. In his journal, he included his dog as a crew member, noted the birthdays and wedding anniversaries of many of his captain friends, and usually called his wife, Desire Dillingham, his "dearest friend."

He demonstrated a paternal concern that all fathers must have when a child falls ill. On May 31, 1761, he wrote, "overwhelmed with grief for our little daughter who lies in great distress and tears and groans enough to pierce the heart of those unconcerned, or more of tender parents."[4] Luckily, the child recovered within a few weeks. As a celebration, Bangs took his family on one of his schooners for a long pleasure cruise while violinists played a concert.

On September 29, 1760, he recorded weather notes with details: "Wed. Cloudy. Rains. Went to Chatham. Sloop aground on the west side of Quitnesset. The tide fell at sunset as we brought in three wounded men."[5] They had struck a whale at Sandy Point. The whale was hurt and endangered the crew, so they cut it free, leaving her alone. The men were brought to Thomas Mirick's for medical care and a place to rest.

---

1. Benjamin Bangs, November 1763, Massachusetts Historical Record Society, 102.
2. Benjamin Bangs, November 1763, 112.
3. Benjamin Bangs, December 1763, 180.
4. Benjamin Bangs, March 1764, 200.
5. Benjamin Bangs, April 1764, 201.

Bangs was also noted as a well-known negotiator and peacemaker. In October 1762, he noted that "Thomas Mirick and his wife, have at been at odds in the same house, considering divorce." Later, by November of that same year, they were happily back together again due to the efforts of Benjamin Bangs.[6]

Like several affluent eighteenth-century Cape Codders, Bangs kept slaves as household servants. He records selling a slave who did not perform well, saying, "Good riddance to bad rubbage."[7] He also kept indentured servants; some were half-Indigenous and some half-Black, whom Bangs declared were treated like members of his own family. Of the Indigenous people remaining on the Cape, Bangs appeared to have treated them with a degree of reverence, swelling with pride when "his Indian" struck the biggest whale ever sighted. He started mourning when an Indigenous friend, "Jonathan Coshomon, died of sickness."[8]

Bangs was not immune to injury. On one voyage to the Bay of Fundy, he loaded wood to deliver to soldiers at their camp and slipped, injuring his leg. He was shipped back home on another Cape man's sloop, so much in pain that he could barely walk. There were cases of smallpox and possible influenza epidemics, which Bangs also mentions.

A notation from January 1764 states, "News from Nantucket and Martha's Vineyard. Old Indian plague rages. 3/4 Indians and some of their societies have scarce living one left counted. Same as rages before the coming over of the Englishmen. Neither English nor Negro can take it."[9] He then pleaded for inoculations from the local towns to be made available to all residents.

Bangs's journal shows the coming break with England as a prelude to war. He complains that the "colonies are at civil war over the stamp act."[10] He called it "ye slavery act," describing soldiers billeted all over the Cape, which was the result of a despised act by Parliament forcing colonists to house British soldiers.

Benjamin Bangs never lived to see the War of Independence. He died in 1769 at the age of forty-eight, leaving his sons to fight and die for the

6. Benjamin Bangs, May, 1764, 203.
7. Benjamin Bangs, June 1764, 221.
8. Benjamin Bangs, June 1764, 224.
9. Benajmin Bangs, January 1764 , 220.
10. Benjamin Bangs, January 1764, 231.

American cause. Bangs is buried behind the First Parish Church in Brewster. When he conducted his whaling supply business, it was estimated that perhaps half the men on the Cape were connected to the whaling industry in some form. Most whaling captains in the Cape bought their equipment from him.

Direct Slave Trading Captains

Other captains primarily dealt with trading slaves to the North American continent. Of course, they may have brought other cargo with them from the North American shores to Africa, such as lumber, crops, or some commissioned items for barter, but this merchandise was typically used in exchange for slaves.

FRANCIS BOWEN
Often called the Prince of Slavers

The *Nightingale* was a Boston-based shipping vessel of significant size that was constructed in 1851 and mastered by Francis Bowen, a well-known slave trader. On one trip to the West African coast, he was being pursued by Commodore Perkins on the USS *Sumter*. He was strongly suspected of slavery sales but was difficult to catch. A note written by Commodore Perry indicates that Bowen was wily in his affairs. "The clipper ship, the *Nightingale* of Salem, shipped a cargo of 2,000 negroes and has gone clear with thew. She is a powerful clipper and is the personal property of Captain Bowen, called 'the Prince of Slavers.'"

Bowen's capture was described by Captain Taylor, who was commanding the US sloop of war, *Saratoga*. Late in 1860, the *Nightingale*, a clipper of one thousand tons, returned to Africa, believed to be carrying out the trading mission. Taking two smaller boats in the dark, Lieutenant Guthrie entered the vessel on a surprise visit. Guthrie found 961 slaves on board and expected even more to arrive. The United States government immediately seized the ship.

The slaves landed in Liberia, but not before 160 of them died from African fever. The *Nightingale* continued to New York City to allow the court to decide its eventual fate. Guthrie reported that Bowen and a Spaniard named Cortino somehow escaped from captivity. It was later discovered that Guthrie was directly complicit in the whole affair. The court condemned the ship, which the government eventually bought and used as a supply vessel.

JOSHUA VIALL
A Slaver Captain Who Lost Courage Mid-Journey

The ship, *Nancy*, arrived in Senegal in August 1807. Captain Viall had brought lumber and other provisions which he later sold in port. He took the proceeds from the sale to purchase eighty slaves at an average cost of 120 dollars each. The *Nancy* was only sixty-seven feet long, so its total capacity was extremely limited. Once at sea, the male slaves rose in rebellion against him. Viall was able to subdue the mob but still feared for his life.[11]

Being short-handed, Viall first attempted to reach the neutral port of the West Indies, where perhaps more crew might be willing to finish its run to Rhode Island. However, the restlessness and number of slaves continued to frighten him. He felt overmanned by his human cargo. He relinquished his goal by asking the HMS *Venus* to assist him in safe passage. A prized British crew was eventually put on board to run the vessel. The *Nancy* was brought to Tortola and condemned for being a ship hostile to Great Britain. The spoils of war meant the complete loss of ship and cargo.

JAMES TAYLOR
Branded his Slavery Cargo

Captain Taylor was born in Boston. He was the skipper of the brig *Tartar*, sailing out of Charlestown. In 1806, a ship merchant named Frederick Tavell commissioned Taylor to sail in the Pongo River, just north of Sierra Leone, to pick up a cargo of slaves. Tavell's orders strictly stated that securing slaves was Taylor's primary duty. The captain was granted a shore stay of several months to perform his task. If slaves were scarce, a secondary cargo of beeswax would possibly be permitted.

Taylor was ordered to brand or stamp any obtained slaves with the letters "FT" to show the newly obtained slaves were the property of

---

11. George Francis Dow, 299.

Frederick Tavell. His brig could hold 160 tons of cargo. His merchandise for trade consisted of tobacco, brandy, claret, tar, flour, five bales of dry goods, and a box of white hats.

New slaves were indeed scarce in some years, and his brig laid in port for twelve full months for the captain to make his deal. The slaves were natives of the Windward Coast. As required, once secured, the captives were marked with an "O" on the right thigh and a "P" on the right hip. The *Tartar* commenced to return to Charlestown and made it as far as Martinique, where it was captured by the British ship of war *Ulysses*. The British crew claimed that Taylor was holding illegal cargo, which made the ship worthy of forfeit under the United States' new maritime laws passed after January 1, 1808.

The Escaped Slaver Sea Captain of the *Martha*

A story cited in George Francis Dow's book tells a story about a slave ship, the *Martha*, to illustrate how the laws were so lax that slavers could avoid the threat of prison, but Dow does not reveal the captain's name.

In 1850, the *Martha* was one of the largest slave ships, with two tiers of painted ports. Suspecting the ship to be holding slave cargo, the brig USS *Perry* boarded her for direct observational review.

The first act that raised suspicion occurred when the captain hauled down the American colors and replaced them with a Brazilian flag. The captain denied having official papers, yet the *Perry* observed items tossed to the side. These papers were then retrieved, identifying the captain as a New England citizen. When confronted with the evidence, the captain admitted that he was prepared for a slave trade. Below deck were four hundred bowls and spoons. It left little doubt of his obvious future cargo. The captain was expecting a shipment of eighteen hundred slaves, intending to take them at night.

The *Martha* was eventually brought to New York, where it was condemned and seized. The captain's first bail was set at five thousand dollars, then lowered to three thousand. Simply by posting the required fee and then forfeiting it, he was set free and then was never found again.

Captains who Began as Slavers or Witnessed the Slave Trade, Transforming to Abolitionism

The next category of captains is perhaps the most curious to describe. They are those who began their career as either enslavers themselves or directly witnessing the brutality of the slave market in their maritime work, only to become the most ardent supporters of the abolitionist cause.

AUSTIN BEARSE (1808-1881)
An Original Slave Trader

Austin Bearse can be seen as the Cape Cod captain who perhaps best exemplifies the engrained moral and political confusion of his day. For the first two decades of his life, he was an active slaver, delivering slaves for barter up and down the Southern coast. He gave little thought to the unkind business that kept men in shackles and deprived them of any basic rights. Over time, after witnessing many scenes of horror, beatings, and cruelty, he gradually changed his perspective, becoming a champion of human rights and a leader in the Massachusetts abolitionist movement.

His memoir, *Reminiscences of Fugitive-Slave Law Days in Boston*, conjures up an image of brutal savagery perpetrated on human beings. In his own words, he describes why he had a change of heart.

> We separated families and connections with as little concern as calves or pigs are selected out of a lot of domestic animals. We used to allow the relatives of slaves to come on board to stay the night before sailing. In the morning it was my business to pull off the hatches and warn them it was time to separate, and the shrieks and cries at these times to make anybody's heart ache. In my past days, the system of slavery was not much discussed. I saw things as I did without interference. Because I no longer think to see these things in silence, I trade no more south of Mason and Dixon's line.[12]

By the time his writings were published in 1880, Bearse states he had witnessed slave trading in almost every port on the East Coast. Many

---

12. Austin Bearse, *Reminisces of the Fugitive-Slave Law Days in Boston*, (Boston: Warren Richardson, 1880), 88.

times, the images that he recalled from Southern plantations were as fully evil as anything he had ever seen in any place, anywhere in the world, heathen or Christian. He once said that any pleasure cruise taken in the South would surely come across the same picture. Fellow shipmasters saw Bearse as always a friendly face, often entering through the back doors of plantations.

Bearse was born in Barnstable, Massachusetts, and went to sea as a young lad. His first engagement with maritime duties saw him serving on ships that traded off the coasts of New Orleans and South Carolina. Bringing slaves to the auction blocks of New Orleans was a frequent stop on his route. In his assigned role as a slave auctioneer preparer, he finally became ill from the grief of what he had witnessed. His first fugitive slave rescue occurred at the insistence of the Mott sisters.

Bearse writes:

> In the year 1828, while mate of the brig "Milton," of Boston, bound from Charleston, S.C., to New Orleans, the following incident occurred, which I shall never forget. The traders brought on board four quadroon men in handcuffs. An old negro woman, more than eighty years of age, came screaming after them, "My son! Oh, my son!" She seemed almost frantic, and when we had got more than a mile out in the harbor, we heard her screaming yet.[13]

In later years, his maritime goals completely reversed. In the following excerpt from his memoir, Bearse tells us the story of his role in the safe transfer of a young fugitive named Bernardo.

> People used to write to Mr. Phillips from the South, out in those places just before slaves were about to start their voyage. Mr. Phillips received these letters, and so he was on the lookout when the vessels got into Boston harbor. He would know the name of the vessel, and who was on board, and be all ready to help them.[14]

---

13. Austin Bearse, 63.
14. Austin Bearse, 68.

Letter of Mr. Phillips to Captain Bearse

Dear Friend:

When my little colored boy arrives, I wish you to take charge of him, and keep him till you can get some safe way to send him to the Cape. You know it is not safe to have colored children travelling about alone, so be very careful that you get him a safe conveyance. He is to be sent to J.E. Mayo, Harwich, to stop at the Union Store there. If Mr. Mayo is not there, Captain Small will attend to him. You must write to Mr. Mayo two days before he will arrive, telling him when to expect him. Pay postage on your letters. His name is Bernardo. I shall direct the Bath people to have him left at 21 Cornhill. So, tell Wallcutt about him and let him attend to Bernardo till you arrive. Write me of his arrival the moment he comes. Charge expenses to me.

Yours truly, WENDELL PHILLIP

August 18, 1853, P.S. I got the boy safe down to the Cape, as Mr. P. wanted.[15]

Bernardo, the boy in question, stayed for several years with the Harwich ship captain who took him in, but he eventually became ill, probably with tuberculosis. His last few weeks were spent in the care of abolitionist Mrs. Frances H. Drake, of Leominster. Her home was a stop in the Underground Railroad, where she attended to slaves as faithfully as her own family.

In another instance, Bearse undertook a slave rescue in his thirty-six-foot ship, the *Moby Dick*. In one case, the Boston Vigilance Committee hired him to retrieve Sandy Swain, a fugitive slave, from the brig *Florence*. The ship moored at Fort Independence after sailing from North Carolina. Bearse brought with him several white abolitionists and a group of Black dock workers from Long Wharf to persuade the captain of the brig to hand Swain over. As Bearse's crew sailed away, they dressed Swain as a fisherman so he would blend in with all the sailors as they landed at City Point House. From there, Swain was driven to a safehouse in Brookline, and continued the next morning on his way to Canada.

---

15. Austin Bearse, 71.

On another occasion, Bearse was asked to retrieve a fugitive slave from the *Sally Ann*, also from North Carolina. He could not enlist a party of men to go with him on such short notice, so he and his brother decided to try on their own. The captain of the *Sally Ann* threatened Bearse with immediate bodily harm if he did not leave his ship. Being with only two men, he had to think quickly. He departed the boat with a need to devise a new plan.

To intimidate the other captain, Bearse tied blue jackets and hats to the railing of his own ship with brooms and sticks to make it appear as though he had a large crew. He then sent his brother in a rowboat to pick up the stowaway. Apparently fooled, the captain of the *Sally Ann* turned the stowaway over to the Bearse brothers, who brought him to South Boston. The freed slave then continued to the Underground Railroad to Canada.

Bearse had two distinct ways to assist runaway slaves. He commanded the *Moby Dick*, which anchored in Boston Harbor. During the day, the ship could be charted for fishing voyages, but by night, it became a beacon of freedom for those who sought to arrive at a safer vicinity. His position as an assistant with the Port of Boston allowed him to know which boats were in town. Bearse quickly learned the captains' direct attitudes toward slavery, either pro or con. In 1853, Bearse was interviewed by Harriet Beecher Stowe at the office of *The Liberator* as part of her research for the content of *Uncle Tom's Cabin*.

JOSEPH BATES (1792–1872)

From Captain to Devout Minister

Bates held similar sailing experiences to Bearse. Serving aboard boats populated mostly by Black men, he saw the injustice of slaves transported at sea. He, too, witnessed slaves being dragged on and off vessels at many ports and heard the cries and sobs uttered in sheer futile exhaustion by separated families.

Joseph Bates was born in Rochester, Massachusetts, on July 8, 1792. His mother was the daughter of Barnabas Nye of Sandwich, a well-established Quaker sea-faring family from Cape Cod, and his father, also named Joseph, was a soldier in the Revolutionary War. In 1793, the Bates

family moved to the part of New Bedford that would eventually become
the township of Fairhaven in 1812. In June 1807, Bates sailed as a cabin
boy on the new ship commanded by Elias Terry, called the *Fanny*, going
to London via New York City. This was the commencement of Bates's
maritime career.

Experiencing the horrors of the slave trade first-hand, Bates adopted
ardent abolitionist views and went even further into his spiritual beliefs.
He converted from the role of American captain to a new career as a
revivalist preacher. His study of scripture led him to the acceptance of the
Seventh-Day Sabbath movement. In a literal reading of the Old Testament, the true Sabbath started at sundown on Friday night and lasted
until darkness on Saturday.

He became a co-founder and developer of Sabbatarian Adventism,
whose followers would later establish the Seventh-Day Adventist Church,
a Protestant Christian denomination distinguished by its observance of
Saturdays as the seventh day of the week and a dramatic emphasis on the
imminent Second Coming of Jesus Christ at an unknown day when final
judgment would occur for all.

Captains Who Benefited Indirectly from
the Slave Trade

In this next category, we will cite three examples: Captain Sears Crowell,
John Bowles, and Josiah Richardson. In truth, however, countless other
mariners could be added to this list. Any merchant who brought any type
of food or cargo, such as low-grade fish, down South for slave consumption, or any sailors who carried products to the North coming from the
plantations, such as cotton or peanuts, surely took strong advantage of
the slave trade.

Sears Crowell, however, could also be included in the category of captains who transitioned to abolitionism. He was particularly well-known
for transporting cotton from plantations to many ports in the North. He
would change his thoughts later in life by securing and providing major
resources to the abolitionist cause.

PRINCE SEARS CROWELL (1813–1881)

Helped to Move the Cotton Trade

Captain Crowell was born November 13, 1813, to a devout Quaker family. As a youth, Prince Sears attended the Quaker Seminary on Spring Hill in Sandwich, Massachusetts. When he became old enough to go to sea, Crowell served as a director of cargo on the sailing vessels his father captained. As a supercargo overseer, Crowell was in charge of buying and selling the ship's merchandise, most frequently cotton taken from Southern United States ports and brought to Northern factories to produce clothes. It was a fact that bothered him.

Crowell married Polly Dillingham Foster on July 26, 1835, in East Dennis. The couple had eight children: Persis Sears, Prince Freeman, David, Christopher Columbus, Azariah Foster, Emma Lauraetta, Edwin Dillingham, and Evelyn.

Crowell eventually became captain of various vessels trading up and down the coast of the United States, England, and Europe. His experience had taught him how to trade goods effectively in foreign parts. In his early sailing days, he observed the many terrors of family separation at the slavery auction block but said nothing.

Because of his Quaker upbringing, Crowell ultimately did not accept the inhumanity of keeping slaves. After a few years, he converted to strident abolitionism. He then spoke out to his maritime peers as to how carrying certain products promoted slavery. He not only stopped his cotton trade, but he was also seen and known for his strong antislavery stance.

When his shipping business took him to New Orleans, he was in serious mortal danger since he was a known contributor and subscriber to *The Liberator*, an antislavery magazine, and a known acquaintance of many abolitionists. When Methodism swept Cape Cod, the captain's family joined the Red Top Methodist Church in Brewster. However, they found out that this church was not abolitionist to the highest degree. While several members were against slavery, they would not allow a former slave to come to speak as an invited guest. The captain did not agree with this decision. He became upset, removing his pew from the church. He eventually started a new church in East Dennis.

At the age of thirty-three, Captain Crowell made a trading trip to the Far East. He left in February 1846 and returned the following October. Raisins, tobacco, and fish were some of the new goods placed into his cargo. This was a successful trip for the captain. He decided not to go to sea again but continued his association with shipping by holding shares to become the sole owner of many vessels. He fought vigorously against any type of shipping that enhanced slavery. To increase his presence in maritime trade, he became one of the principal backers of the Shiverick Boatyard in Dennis.

After he left the sea, the captain was involved in many ventures outside the shipping business. He started the first salt works in Boston. He was part owner and first president of the Pacific Guano Factory in Woods Hole, Massachusetts. He was instrumental in starting the Old Colony Railroad, which was needed to service the guano factory in Woods Hole.

Crowell also took control of the presidency of the Bank of Cape Cod. His son Azariah moved to Woods Hole in 1867 to work as the chief chemist at the Pacific Guano Factory and held his position as chemist for more than twenty years. In 1874, in addition to his work at the factory, he began Woods Hole's first wholesale retail fish market in partnership with Isaiah Spindell. Azariah was also associated with the Bay and Woods Hole Weir companies, and the Net Fisherman's Association, of which he was treasurer. Along with Spindell, Crowell helped the U.S. Fish Commission, now the National Marine Fisheries Service, obtain land for its laboratory, which would eventually become the world-renowned Woods Hole Oceanographic Institute (WHOI).

Crowell started a tradition in which children and people of all ages collected coins and placed small amounts into a separate box. A local representative would then gather these boxes for abolitionist causes. These boxes became quite popular in Massachusetts and advanced a movement of both financial resources and a new mindset that physical action was needed by many to counteract slavery.

CAPTAIN JOHN BOWLES (1765-1873)

Also known as John Bolles

John was born in Hamilton, Massachusetts, to a long line of sea captains. He started out as a coaster, moving all types of products from Maine to Florida, and specialized in acquiring and delivering agricultural and textile products.

He first brought materials to Boston Harbor, where fruits and vegetables of all types were welcomed. The wharves, with their long row of warehouses, were filled with merchandise. Lines of square-rigged ships discharged their cargo upon the piers. The creaking of hoisting blocks was heard above the shouts of stevedores and the bustle of longshoremen. Sugar and molasses, hogsheads, coffee, and bales of wool and cotton were piled up to be taken to the dock. During the fruit season, oranges, lemons, and raisins were sold at auction.

John became quite friendly with other Portsmouth, New Hampshire, sea captains and took his wares there. Crushed stone, dimension stone, and natural gemstone were building products in demand in the Virginia area. His typical trek became a loop from Portsmouth to Norfolk.

Portsmouth in the 1800s was a hotbed of abolitionist advocates. Dover, New Hampshire, seemed an unlikely place for an antislavery movement. After all, the town had huge mills using millions of bales of cotton produced in the South by slave labor. At that time, Dover was the site of a radical, tenaciously antislavery newspaper produced by Freewill Baptists. Its publishers stuck to their guns despite fierce opposition, even within their own denomination, eventually winning over those who had initially thought that slavery was a subject outside the realm of religious discussion.

This connection to slavery appealed to Bowles, who became involved with the protective passage of runaway slaves to New Hampshire. When Oney Judge, the servant of George Washington, asked for passage to Portsmouth, he agreed to take her on board to gain passage to the North.

JOSIAH RICHARDSON (1808–1853)

A Most Moral Sea Captain of Barnstable County

At the young age of twenty-one, Josiah Richardson became master of the schooner *Hetty Thon*. He made his first deep-sea voyage the following year aboard the *Orbit*, sailing from Boston to Kronstadt, Russia, near St. Petersburg, a major trading center. For the next nine years, he roamed the oceans with his cousin George Richardson of Boston, primarily aboard the brig *Owyhee*. On some trips, he brought lumber from Cuba to Russia, and then returned with Russian fir used to construct elegant American homes.

In 1839, he took command of the *Chatham*. This ship was a favorite of Richardson's, as it carried almost double the weight of his previous vessels. He brought cotton from the Southern United States ports and delivered it to Liverpool or Le Havre, often stopping at Cuba to secure rum. Speaking of rum, in one specific instance, when the remains of a deceased passenger started to decompose without alcohol aboard, he was said to have hailed a passing British vessel to purchase a keg of rum for its use, keeping the decaying body intact for the remainder of the trip.[16]

While in command of the *Walpole*, he took copious notes on various dangers that lurked in front of the sea captains during that era. In 1847, his log recorded, "Heavy gales from N. W. and rough seas. Squalls, snow, and hail. Tried using the pumps without success, the ship laying down so much upon her board side the water would not come to them at all." Despite all the meteorological challenges, he sailed the *Walpole* across the Atlantic in twenty-eight days. Even with an inventory of mostly broken and inoperable nautical instruments, he brought the *Walpole* back to Boston safe and sound. His maritime skills were deemed legendary. When he learned that his next assignment was to go to Manila, he was delighted. Wishing for warmer climates, he looked forward to seeing new tropical ports.

His logbooks reported with great pride:

> *The Walpole arrived at its destination to the straights of Sundra which separates Java from Sumatra in record time. Our passage has been ninety-five days, rather*

---

16. Shrewsbury Historical Society, "Captain Josiah Richardson," Shrewsbury Historical Society, https://www.shrewsburyhistoricalsociety.org/josiah-richardson (accessed December 2, 2022).

short, as the vessels that sailed before us have never noted such a wonderful time.[17]

While in Manila, it took four months to secure all his desired cargo, loading sampan wood, hemp, manila, rope sugar, buffalo hides, and sugar. Securing those items would return a reasonable profit. It was always a carefully considered risky enterprise to buy items on impulse compared to purchasing only from a set menu of heavily demanded items. Sea captains needed to become shrewd entrepreneurs with a keen sense of which exotic items would best appeal to the public.

Between 1812 and 1850, there were four major recognized types of deep-sea captain operations: general trade with Europe, transatlantic passenger travel from Boston or New York to Liverpool, long sea voyages to China and the East Indies, and finally the advent of the clipper trade from local ports from Cape Cod to Boston and beyond. Captain Richardson was one of the few shipmasters who participated in all four types of maritime excursions.

Since his ships would most often carry cargo and passengers, additional challenges were inherent. On one occasion, the voyage between Boston and Liverpool was filled with a crew of "Liverpool Irishmen" notorious for their rum drinking and expert skills with a knife. Keeping the crew in full control and on their best behavior while still making the trip enjoyable for travelers required a delicate reflective balancing act.

The captain needed to be firm with sailors without seeming overbearing. He allowed the consumption of rum but only up to a fixed limit, and he even enjoyed a small libation himself with the crew. His demonstration showed how rum could be enjoyed and consumed in moderation. He exemplified cordiality to both crew and passengers throughout the voyage.

In 1849, many medium-sized clippers traveled the ports around Cape Cod. Master shipbuilder Donald McKay designed the *Staghound*, a ship recognized as a nautical design wonder. Her lines had the maritime world abuzz with envy. She was the largest and most revered ship of that

---

17. Josiah Richardson, "Logbooks of Josiah Richardson, 1847-1852," Shrewsbury Historical Records (accessed December 2, 2023), 41-42.

century. With the appointment of Richardson as its captain, he immediately became the hero of the shipping world.

Before taking command, celebrated underwriter Walter Jones questioned his wisdom. "With such a ship of great weight, so heavily sparred and for so long at sea, are you not nervous?" Richardson responded, "I would never go on any ship at all if I ever for a minute suspected that it would be my coffin."[18]

While on its inaugural launching, the *Staghound*'s main mast broke mid-voyage. Richardson composed a note to his owners: "The ship is yet to be built that would beat the Staghound. I am perfectly in love with her. You have reason to be proud of her. I shall get a new main topmast, take in in my water and leave here for San Francisco."[19] True to his word, a record travel time was recorded even with the time wasted for an emergency repair.

A letter written by the American Ambassador to Russia is proof of the integrity and international respect that people held for Captain Richardson. The congratulatory note memorialized Richardson's heroic efforts of traveling out of his way to save a Russian captain. In all, eleven sailors were stranded on a boat during a storm. Not knowing exactly where to send the letter, the ambassador first sent the note directly to Daniel Webster, the secretary of state. Webster then brought the note to the Customs Office in Boston, which forwarded the laudatory message to the captain.

To further cite the humility of the respected captain, his log for the precise day of the rescue was composed without fanfare. "Came across a small ship of nine Russian men. Took them on board lamenting that one of their men, the ship's carpenter, was lost at sea."[20] In short, the local mariners of his era frequently referred to Richardson as the maritime model, par excellence, suitable to use as a guide for proper behavior for all future sea masters. With his connections to the cotton supplies, the rum trade, and his deep knowledge of other ship captains of the day, he also profited from aspects of the slavery trade.

---

18. Josiah Richardson, 50.
19. Josiah Richardson, 52.
20. Josiah Richardson, 61.

Captains Venturing to West African Ports, Without Any Direct Proof of Slave Trading

Some captains ventured to the west coast of Africa for trade on at least one or two occasions, to ports where previous slavery efforts have been recorded, yet most historical factors are circumstantial. There is no "smoking gun" to verify their veracity. It is possible that these men were engaged in carrying slaves, but the maritime community and financial supporters usually regarded these captains as serious mariners. Based on current data, accusing them of criminal activities would be unjust, for their stories lack any conclusive evidence.

ELIJAH COBB (1768–1848)

A Witness to the French Reign of Terror

Without a doubt, one of the most noted and colorful of the Brewster sea captains was Elijah Cobb. He engaged with Barbary pirates, witnessed the guillotine of a legendary French revolutionary figure, charmed foreign governmental officials into the payments of retribution, and chaired the town's negotiation of paying the British ransom to save Brewster's saltworks. He became a preeminent negotiator for trade with Europe. After these exploits, he served his local town as its state senator and even spent time as Brewster's town clerk.

Born on a small Brewster farm, he was forced to leave home at the age of six due to the death of his father, who perished at sea. Being adopted by another maritime family, his life at sea commenced as a cook and cabin boy. As a responsible and grateful youth, he frequently sent funds back to his mother to provide her with daily sustenance.

As a crew member of early cargo runs to Europe, he understood the *dey* of Algeria was sponsoring pirate attacks on American vessels. The First Parish Church often held special collections to fund the ransom of local sailors. "To the shores of Tripoli" was an early battle cry for the Marines. To avoid the spot of frequent pirate incursions, Cobb once took his ship north of Spain, leading him to another adventure. His was one of a hundred ships gathered by French forces while they quarreled with British forces.

On one trip, the French scuttled his full cargo from the *Jane* in order to feed their army. Being a businessman with panache and extraordinary courage, he boldly ordered his ship to return to homeport with the first mate in command. Meanwhile, he ventured to the interior of Paris to secure payment for his seized ship. Armed with pistols, he carefully scampered through the French countryside to reach a high-ranking Parisian official, who wrote a note to no one less prominent than Robespierre, requesting an official audience. His wish was granted.

The French revolutionary leader was in deep turmoil at the time and reluctantly agreed to pay in the future. Cobb witnessed the very heart of the French Revolution. Finally, he obtained the "paper" commitment for funds and took it to another set of French officials. It is unclear if he was ever officially compensated.

For several subsequent days after this agreement, the Reign of Terror continued throughout France as the stark, steel blade of the guillotine sliced through many an unprotected neck. Within a few days, Robespierre, who had ordered the deaths of so many, was guillotined himself. Cobb's eventual return to his homeport was equal to the welcome of a naval and business hero.

His skill as a navigator through war-torn Europe made him much in demand as a negotiator with foreign nations. Upon taking command of the ship *Monsoon*, he realized that his precious cargo included a large shipment of New England rum. His trading acumen told him that Ireland might be the perfect country to pay top dollar for his cargo. This was a risky proposition at that time. Britain declared that all alcoholic spirits sent to any part of the British Kingdom must come from an approved English plantation.

As the ship landed near Cork, Cobb appeared "aghast" to learn that the locals attached the King's Seal to all spirit consignments. The Irish contingent carried the prized merchandise to shore with a wink and a nod. Captain Cobb acquired a small fortune both through his ingenuity and outright bribery.

His ship, *William Tell*, was seized by the British during the War of 1812, and Cobb was briefly imprisoned. During the war, he stayed at home, bound by great anger and angst that a British navy ship could threaten his country's local sovereignty. In fact, as a town representative, the British demanded a "tribute" of $4,000 and threatened that the sound and fury of cannons would ensue upon the town's saltworks. Since the local citizenry did not have access to accessible funds, the burden of payment fell upon three local merchants who eventually agreed to assist.

After this war, Cobb resumed his maritime adventures along the African coast, and his fortune grew because of these trips. However, his good luck expired when he commissioned Captains Clark, Nickerson, and Mayo to partake in a new expedition to West Africa. The ship *Ten Brothers* was consumed by African fever, leaving seven men and an eleven-year-old cabin boy dead. The entire ship was eventually fumigated, filled with disease, and burned.

In a report mandated by Boston port officials and published in 1819 by the *New England Journal of Medicine*, the *Ten Brothers* was condemned and in need of total fumigation. Upon docking, the ship carried ballast only as well as a deadly yellow fever that eventually led to the death of hundreds. The Boston Board of Health initiated an investigation, asking two basic questions: "Did Cobb knowingly bring yellow fever to Boston and did this ship ever carry slaves as a commodity?"

The board spent several months investigating this issue from medical and political aspects. They reported that in viewing the boat, the interstices of the timber were indeed filled with corn and coffee yet also had a horrific stench. They further stated that there was no evidence that the disease was imported by Cobb's boat or that any connection to slave trading could be ascertained. Of course, Elijah Cobb was an influential and affluent man with connections at many levels of government, so this political factor is acknowledged. Yet this investigative committee found no concrete evidence to substantiate slave trading. The captain himself vehemently denied any dealings of slave transportation.

Captain Cobb wrote to his wife on February 4, 1819, from a region of West Africa where slave trading was known to occur:

> My Dear Friend, We are here; & all well, thanks to the controller of every event,
> but under circumstances, must remain here two months longer, as we have a
> considerable part of our cargo still on hand, business is astonishingly altered since

last voyage, the coast is crowded with vessels & goods of every description, & the
natives have nothing to buy with. This circumstance is owing to the late interior
war, which has recently raged with great violence & prevented the natives from
procuring Gold dust & Ivory as formally—my object for waiting is to git clear
of the Perishable part of my cargo for coffee, when their Crop comes in, which
is now commencing but will not be at its height until the last of march or first
of April—I also calculate to touch at one of the windward W. India Islands (on
my passage horeme) in order to s[ell] my Tobacco, Flour, Tea & salmon; which I
cannot sell here for an[ything]—& some Corn, which I shall receive in barter so
[that] you need not be antious if we don't git home until [the last] of July . . .

Respectfully Yours,
Elijah Cobb[21]

This letter confirms that the principal products of securing gold dust, ivory, and coffee were the official objects of his voyage. His ship charted a route used by some to acquire slaves. This circumstantial event is not connected to any other direct evidence.

There were indirect slavery connections to his profits, as with many sea captains. Cobb was known as a rum trader, a vital vestige of the triangular trade route, and for bringing inexpensive alewife fish to the South for slave consumption. Simultaneously, he brought products coming from plantation crops to be used in New England. He gained a decent profit from all types of trading, which was viewed as entrepreneurial acumen.

Cobb stayed in Brewster and eventually committed to a more genteel life. He established a small farm and concurrently served as an elected official in many capacities, such as senate representative for two years, state representative for eight years, selectman for two years, and town treasurer for ten years. It seems most appropriate that in 2016, his stately residence on Lower Road became the home of the Brewster Historical Society, containing many valuable artifacts of the Brewster sea captains.

The return of the *Ten Brother's* ship to Boston Harbor caused quite a stir, yet Cobb's legacy cannot be directly evidenced to any direct complicity as a slaver. Foreign officials saw him as an able negotiator with skills as a mariner.

---

21. Elijah Cobb, *The Memoirs of a Cape Cod Skipper* (New Haven: Yale University Press, 1925), 116.

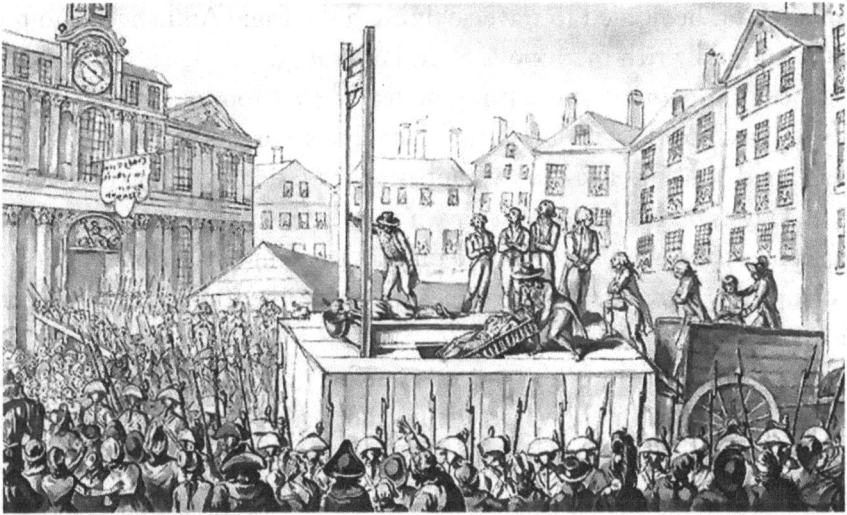

Octobre 1793 supplice de 9 émigrés

Elijah was a member of the First Parish Church in Brewster, Massachusetts. He believed in the Golden Rule: "do unto others as you would have them do unto you." This included loving our neighbors as ourselves, working for a better world, searching for truth with an open mind, using reason to explore religious ideas, and granting everyone the right to choose their own beliefs.

ISAAC CLARK (1761–1819)

Opened Up Travel to the White Sea

Clark was an associate of Elijah Cobb, often sailing one of his ships. Being a thrill-seeker and always searching for new adventures, Captain Clark disregarded the more traditional and established ports of Europe to see what the extreme northern seas might offer. In 1800, he ventured up the Baltic Sea through the Gulf of Finland, facing extreme cold and more artic conditions, and into the Russian port of Kronstadt. This was quite a daring and bold move, as he had yet to receive official permission from any government official to be in that region.

Clark was the first American sea captain to enter the White Sea. Once there, he needed governmental clearance to discharge and take cargo aboard his vessel. Since he needed authorization from the American ambassador, he needed to traverse through the frigid Arkhangelsk to the more culturally rich metropolis of St. Petersburg.

Being impetuous and daring, he feared that too long a wait might freeze his ship, the *California*, in place. He secured a local heavy-duty sleigh and whisked away to the ambassador's residence in St. Petersburg as quickly as possible. He must have indeed been a persuasive and charming spokesperson, as he convinced officials to grant navigational rights to a completely unknown upstart sea captain after the trip had already been made.

His successful meeting and convincing personality opened a new pathway for maritime travel in the northern region. He returned to his ship and loaded it with valuable Russian fir timber. This wood was in high demand in North America due to its unusual color, flexibility, shape, and adaptability for home construction. The captain's former Georgian-style mansion on Stony Brook Road distinctly displays fine Russian fir trim.

Later in his life, the call to the sea, combined with the urging of his life-long friend, Captain Cobb, beckoned him once again to the deep sea. This time, Clark paid dearly, as it claimed his life. He was asked to head along the African Coast, an area that had seen the slave trade, to trade in the highly popular and seductive commodities of oils, palm trees, gold dust, and ivory tusks. Although no definitive evidence exists, his final command of the Cobb ship, the *Ten Brothers*, leaves open a sense of inquiry.

Throughout his many years at sea, Clark had a distinct record of being an honest and able navigator. Nonetheless, his final voyage was undertaken as a favor to Cobb. It turned out to be ill-fated as the sickness of Africa's Black Water Fever was forever present. Like many other Brewster captains before and after him, he never returned. His body was eventually buried on Africa's Prince Island, far from the Cape Cod town he represented for many years. It was said that Captain Cobb, for many years thereafter, felt a deep sense of regret at coaxing this honorable fellow captain to a location that he initially did not want to go with the earnest premonition that so much potential danger existed.

DAVID NICKERSON (1772–1819)

Commander of the *Ten Brothers* and an Associate of Cobb

This description comes from Joan Paine, author of *Cape Cod, Masters of the Sea*. Before we look at Captain Nickerson's West African trip, there is one specific noteworthy yet completely unsubstantiated story of his exploits. Historians are certain he was an American living in France while the French Revolution was in full swing. They are also sure that a royal heir was born of the union of Marie Antoinette and Louis XVI. However, historians are not confident about what truly happened to the dauphin.

One unconfirmed, rumored event circulates that a French woman approached Captain Nickerson and thrust a small baby into his arms while swearing the child was the royal heir to the throne of France. However, the dates of his life seem to conflict with the chronology of events, so the rumor is likely untrue. As the story goes, the woman asked Nickerson to call the child Rene Rousseau, but the captain received no justification for that name. The woman asked Nickerson to deliver the baby safely to the United States, away from the blood-thirsty rabble of the French Revolution.

The woman never said who this child might truly be, and the captain was never certain of the boy's lineage. Nonetheless, he brought the child to Brewster, where he raised him as his own son, teaching him the ways of the sea. Unfortunately, Rene was lost at sea when he was twenty-five, without ever producing any evidence of his actual parents. He is buried in Brewster adjacent to Nickerson's headstone.

Nickerson was known to have operated three different ships. In 1795, in his first captainship, he took command of the *Monsoon*, traveling from Boston to Russia and back. This trade was primarily for fur skins, lumber, and farming implements. He was commended for his fiery spirit and his skill with maritime travel. Initially a first mate under Captain Cobb, Nickerson secured a good profit trading rum with German citizens. Cobb had such confidence that he commanded Nickerson to take the return trip home while he stayed in Europe to negotiate further commercial ventures.

Nickerson was put in charge of the schooner *Hope*. When Cobb provided him with the glowing profit reports of the *Ten Brothers*, Nickerson agreed to take command of that vessel, carrying a cargo of gold, ivory, coconut oil, and coffee. He did contract the West African virus. Captain Cobb sent letters home to Brewster, offering a medical chronology of how that illness attacked Nickerson's body.

February 4, 1819, Cobb wrote "Capt. Nickerson is very sick on shore."[22]

February 7: "Since the above, to the astonishment of all, Capt. Nickerson has so far recovered, we have taken hm on board."[23]

February 14: "Nickerson does not gain strength, wishes to go to sea, and try a change of air, he is seldom himself."[24]

February 18: "Capt. Nickerson is very sick on board this ship, but his fever being turned, it was the advice of everybody to send him to sea, I accordingly did, but I fear he will never reach America."[25] He did indeed die at sea off the coast of Africa.

In 1819, Nickerson contracted African Fever and died aboard his ship. In a cemetery in Brewster, we can see a marker without any mortal remains, bearing his name and that of his son, Rene Rousseau, with salient dates and names. His body was never returned to Brewster, but his family wanted the captain's name memorialized on a gravestone in his hometown. In his honor, a new gravestone was authorized and placed in a spot of prominence in his home cemetery in Brewster.

JEREMIAH MAYO (1786–1867)

Celebrated Captain and Associate of Elijah Cobb

We know much about Jeremiah Mayo as seen through the eyes of his daughter, Sarah Augusta Mayo, as written in her biographic manuscript, *Looking Back*. She was an occasional traveler on his voyages. We know that the women in Brewster were influential in local societal life and in the fortune of families. We have a front-row seat into the lofty economic status of Brewster in the 1840s and a foreshadowing of economic decline in the late 1850s as the ship industry slowed and forced the community to redefine itself.

---

22. Elijah Cobb, 25.
23. Elijah Cobb, 31.
24. Elijah Cobb, 33.
25. Elijah Cobb, 42.

Jeremiah was a huge figure of a man. His physical presence took up 6 feet, 5 inches, and his booming blacksmith-like voice carried through the air with elegance. In his first career, he stayed with his father, forging metal as needed by the local farmers. Starting out a bit later than his contemporaries, his first fishing-related paycheck at sixteen hooked him right into a career at sea. His first turn as captain of the *Sally* brought him a sense of adventure and a feeling of proper placement in life. He acquired a worldwide reputation for sailing the *Sally* and how no ship could ever speed past her. In 1805, as a first mate on the *Industry*, he witnessed the cruelty of pirates. The ship's captain was maimed by North African marauders, which led to his promotion to shipmaster, continuing the perilous voyage to Dublin.

On the brig the *Salem*, it was evident that Mayo could make sagacious decisions. Captain Clark noticed the loaded-down brig becoming unmanageable in the stormy sea, and he relinquished command to the younger Mayo. In his first act as captain, he encouraged the crew to partake of the strong spirits stored in the hold. Then, with renewed vigor, the crew lugged several quintals (100-pound weights) of cod to the deck to toss overboard, lightening the ship and securing better balance. This maneuver worked, and Captain Clark gave him full reins to serve as captain. While Captain Mayo was a close associate of Elijah Cobb, who was allied with other captains of African trading, there remains no direct evidence linking him to any voyage participating in the slavery process.

Since *Salem* was French-owned, Mayo's next mission was to smuggle claret, an embargoed item under British law, into a French harbor. This daring and audacious action forced him to circumvent blockades, and he produced forged papers when necessary. Being a purveyor of strong spirits in those days of war resulted in handsome profits.

In 1815, an event occurred that could have significantly reshaped world events. His ship *Sally* was moored in Le Havre when two of Napoleon Bonaparte's representatives asked Mayo to sneak the military strategist away from lurking danger and deliver him to the United States. The captain accepted this dangerous mission. However, at the last moment, Napoleon decided to flee to exile in Elba, which turned out to be the better alternative, as his loyal forces rescued him, and he reclaimed power in France.

Sarah Mayo stated that her father greatly admired Napoleon and the lives of the French people. He saw Napoleon leading the charges at Bayonne and into Spain, and gave witness to the execution of Marshall Ney in 1815. "Men said the captain was a true man of the world. He had rare conversational powers, and his talk would give word pictures of places and events."

Mayo gave up sailing for a long retirement at Cape Cod. He served as the town's treasurer for four years and then secured a position as selectman for over a decade. He was always interested in town affairs up until the time of his death in 1867.

Mayo's daughter, along with Mary Louise Cobb, demonstrated the influence of women in these times, showing their community that there were finer and more esoteric things in life to benefit the town, such as literature and a public library. The daughters asked their fathers to donate books whenever they returned from their voyages to new foreign ports. Over one thousand books were accumulated over a period of a few years.

The women were so successful that the Brewster's Lady Library came to be in Brewster, first located at 1772 Main Street. Men were allowed to borrow books, but they were charged a slightly higher fee due to their easier access to funds. The site was opened to the general public in 1853 with an initial fee of one dollar. The surcharge for males was eventually dropped. Today, the town is rightfully proud of the modern, popular, attractive facility.

Captains of Color

In this category, we are reporting on the many maritime captains of color. These sailors were mostly free Blacks or of perhaps mixed Black and Indigenous blood. The Cuffee family, being of Black and Indigenous roots themselves, were deeply woven into the whaling and maritime history of the United States. The American Colonization Society, designed to liberate all enslaved people, is deeply linked to Paul Cuffee. The mere fact that these black captains were able to assume a position of local and national prominence in a country torn with deep racial division is particularly noteworthy.

ABSALOM BOSTON (1785–1855)

First Black Captain, Integrated Nantucket Public Schools

Absalom Boston of Nantucket was simultaneously a mariner, an entrepreneur, and a civil leader. He was the well-respected captain of the whaling ship the *Industry*. Using an entire African American crew in 1822, he became full captain of the vessel at the age of thirty-seven. In that era in Nantucket, it was not unusual to see whaling captains rising from within the crew ranks. It was a most profitable yet very perilous pursuit.

That particular year, many ships reported both losing crews and witnessing severely damaged whaling ships while fighting the world's largest mammals. Nonetheless, Boston returned the *Industry* to her home port of Nantucket with a complete, injury-free crew and no ship damage. In addition, Boston achieved his mission of securing seventy barrels of oil. He learned his craft as a free teenage black sailor serving aboard the decks of various whaling ships.

Boston was always known as an ambitious, dedicated worker who would succeed in every assigned task. Whaling voyages, in those days, typically lasted anywhere from six months to a full year. It was a lonely, exciting, but dangerous career. In the mid-1800s, whaling was among the five largest industries in the country. In that decade, over 20 percent of whaling crews were of African descent.

To become a captain of any vessel required significant economic resources. Based on his solid family's lineage on the island and his demonstration of trustworthy behavior, Boston's reputation slowly grew. By the age of twenty, he acquired property on Nantucket. His popularity allowed him to open an inn and a store on the island.

Captain Boston's wealth granted him respect and familiarity with the court system. Boston was incensed when his own daughter, Phebe, was denied admission to enroll in the local public school on Nantucket. He took the case to a local court hearing and eventually won. In 1846, he was seen as an advocate for blacks who should be allowed to integrate into the public schools. The Massachusetts State Legislature supported Boston's position. Phebe and another African American student, Eunice Ross, were both admitted into the school. This case preceded the *Brown v. Board of Education* ruling by the U.S. Supreme Court by a full century.

His popularity also helped him as he ran for a local town election. He was an original founder of the African Baptist Society and the African Meeting House on Nantucket.

When he died in 1855, Boston was a wealthy man. He owned three houses, a store, and several additional lots of land. According to an article published in the *National Sailing Hall of Fame* magazine, authored by Jeb Jobson, "Boston left a legacy of improving lives for mariners and African Americans and is most worthy of induction into the 2022 Sailing Hall of Fame."

PAUL CUFFEE (1759–1817)
A Wealthy Ship Owner and Sailor

Paul Cuffee was the product of a multiracial family. His mother, Ruth Moses, was a Wampanoag from Harwich, and his father was an Ashanti slave from today's region of Ghana. Ashanti slaves differed in many ways from other Blacks in America. These slaves had legal rights under the law, could inherit and own property, and could choose their own spouses. Since his father was released by his Quaker owner at the time of purchase, Paul Cuffee was born a freeman in Cuttyhunk. In fact, the family gladly took on the task of raising sheep and holding the only full-time residence on the island. They lived there for fifteen years.

From there, the family acquired a large one-hundred-acre farm in Westport, where Paul was raised. His father died when Paul was thirteen. Paul signed up as a whaler to learn more about shipbuilding. During the Revolutionary War, Cuffee delivered goods to Nantucket, avoiding the British blockades using a small sailboat. He became a maritime expert and built boats with his brother on his land along the Westport River. Once established, he started a viable coastal route that enabled him to gain significant notoriety with many Eastern cities.

As the offspring of a slave himself, he was always dedicated to assisting the less fortunate. He founded the first fully racially diverse school in his hometown of Westport. He was taken with the Quaker philosophy and often advocated for the manumission of enslaved people. In 1813, he contributed half of the needed funds for a new Quaker meeting house. He oversaw the building's construction and rolled up his sleeves to provide the labor. During this era in history, the Quakers were the first to invite Black members directly into their congregation.

In 1780, at the age of twenty-one, Paul refused to pay his taxes. He did so as a matter of social principle, not legal defiance. In that year, free Blacks did not have the legal right to vote. Since taxation without representation was the battle cry of the American Revolution, Cuffee screamed these same words out loud. He petitioned the council of Bristol County to change their rules without success. Nonetheless, his suit was brought forth to the state legislature three years later. Finally, the legislature granted full voting rights to all free males living in the state.

Cuffee was a shrewd entrepreneur and boat carpenter who built ships for twenty-five years on his property in his own shipyard on the Acoaxet River. His reputation as an honest businessman and trusted captain kept the family name deeply respected throughout the region. It is believed that Cuffee was among the wealthiest African American or Indigenous men in the entire country. He navigated his ship, the *Traveler*, the first deep-sea ship manned by an all-Black crew, to Liverpool. His trading with Sierra Leone eventually led to the founding of the Friendly Society of Mutual Aid, a precursor to the American Colonization Society.

When his ship was confiscated in Newport in 1812 due to an embargo question, Cuffee appealed for its release. He met with Treasury Secretary Gallatin and President Madison. He was warmly welcomed to the White House as a respected businessman and free Black citizen. It was his opinion that the dedication to the ACS movement should not be enacted. In his biography of Cuffee, Henry Sherwood noted: "He realized the mastery of poverty; therefore, he gave pursuit to wealth. He believed in the amelioration of his race; therefore, he consecrated himself to it."[26]

While the legal justification for slavery was basically the law of the land during this era, Cuffee's family never accepted the status quo. The whaling business itself was in sharp decline by the end of the Civil War. The Cuffee clan should be acknowledged for their dedication to improving the lives of Blacks and for being notable historical figures.

---

26. Henry Noble Sherwood, "Paul Cuffee," *The Journal of Negro History* 8, no. 2 (April 1923): 229.

The Cuffee Clan

The maritime exploits of Paul Cuffee were covered above, but his family and related associates played a monumental role in expanding the whaling trade. When New Bedford grew as the hub of the whaling enterprise, Cuffee used nearby Westport as his home base. He acquired whaling and commercial vessels to establish a fleet of sailing ships. He made millions of dollars by continually reinvesting any profits by adding more ships to his personal fleet.

Paul Cuffee from a drawing by John Pole, MD of Bristol, England.

MICHAEL (MICAH) WAINER

Michael was the son of a Black man and an Aquinnah woman. While Blacks were forbidden to marry white women, it was not uncommon in the Massachusetts Bay Colony for Blacks to intermarry with Indigenous people. Michael married Mary Slocum Cuffee, Paul Cuffee's sister, and became a whaling partner in the Cuffee business. Michael's sons, Thomas and Paul, would go on to captain several whaling ships. Together, Paul and Michael purchased their first ship, the *Sunfish*.

THOMAS WAINER

Like his father, Michael, Thomas wed an Indigenous woman named Lydia Pequit. There are records that he assisted in rescuing slaves while serving as captain of the *Ranger*. He would become the third black whaling master in the family. He organized a long line of products sold in a New Bedford general store managed by newly freed slaves. He, too, sailed out of the Westport harbor. Using a mostly Black crew, he saw several surprised faces from dock workers from Wilmington, Delaware, to Kennebec, Maine.

PAUL WAINER

Another relative of the Cuffee family was born in the middle of the American Revolution. He was married to Chloe Dodge Cuff, from Gay Head of the Aquinnah tribe. All the Cuffee relatives modeled their lives on the Quaker beliefs of strong family values and respecting human life in all its forms and variations. Making good business decisions was always a key aspect of success in their lives.

ALAN PHELPS

Alan married Paul Cuffee's daughter Mary. He was a free Black man who displayed many maritime talents. His most frequent voyages included whaling ships going from the Deep South to Northeastern ports. As a well-respected Black captain, he most assuredly came in direct contact with slaves who yearned to arrive at the safety of a Northern harbor. He once commanded a whaler traveling to the mid-Atlantic with a mostly Black crew.

JOHN MASTEN

He was listed as a "malatto" on the national census. He gained access to the Cuffee family through his marriage to Michael Wainer's daughter. He was a Barnstable sailor, rising to fame as a whaler and a deep-sea captain.

PARDON COOK

He was most likely a free Black man who raised a family of nine children in Dartmouth, Massachusetts. He sailed many of the vessels owned by the Cuffee Dynasty, such as the *Elizabeth*, the *Almy*, and the *Juno*. On one trip alone, he returned with 220 barrels of sperm oil. In total, he embarked on six whaling jaunts, securing an equivalent of over two million dollars in today's economy.

Captains Working as Slave Catchers

In another classification of sea captains, a few captains aimed to gather a profit by turning in any runaway slaves who were struggling to earn their freedom and hid or sought refuge in a boat for a fee. These slaves were carried to the North only to be returned to their original masters as the captains claimed a cash reward under the Fugitive Slave Act. These unscrupulous mariners were often a major target of rage for the abolitionists, who saw this behavior as unconscionable.

JAMES HANNAM

Proslavery supporter

Ship captains who traded with the South made every effort to return stowaways, no matter the cost. To illustrate, in September 1846, the crew of the *Ottoman*, a cargo ship hailing from New Orleans, found a stowaway named George in Boston Harbor. Upon discovering him, Captain James Hannum took George into his custody—not for his own protection but rather to claim a reward.

Captain Hannum stopped at one of the island's hotels in Boston Harbor named Spectacle Island for a "small drop of liquid consolation."[27] While the captain grabbed his drink, George made his escape. He stole Hannum's small boat headed for South Boston. Captain Hannum, however, immediately realized what had happened and jumped in another boat to follow. When describing the pursuit, first by boat, then by foot, Hannum wrote, "we took off after him, through cornfields and over

---

27. National Park Service, "Exploits of Captain Drayton in Boston Harbor," National Park Service, https://www.nps.gov/SafeHarbor (accessed January 12, 2023).

fences till finally after a chase of two miles, I secured him just as he reached the bridge."[28]

The news of George's capture spread rapidly throughout Boston's abolitionist community. Hannum was subsequently charged with kidnapping and a warrant was issued for his arrest. Hannum, aware that he needed to take swift action, arranged for George to be transported on the *Niagara*, a ship bound for New Orleans. As Hannum transferred George to the *Niagara*, he realized that abolitionists had obtained a boat and were quickly approaching his ship. Describing the scene, Hannum wrote:

> *No sooner had I left the bark than I discovered a steamer making directly for us. Knowing she could chase but one, I steered a course opposite to the Niagara . . . Bayonets glistened in all parts of the boat; darkies were there of every hue, crying out run him down, fire into him.*[29]

Instead of the *Niagara*, the abolitionists followed Hannum's ship, the *Ottoman*, and were unable to secure George's freedom. In response to the failed attempt, Boston's abolitionists organized a meeting at Faneuil Hall to protest the "shameful outrage upon the sacred rights of humanity." John Quincy Adams, the seventy-nine-year-old former United States president, presided over the meeting. Known for his prestige and acknowledged profound wit, Adams received the authority to speak at the opening of the meeting. "It is not a question whether this Commonwealth is to maintain its independence as a state or not. It is a question whether your and my native commonwealth can protect the men who are under its laws or not."[30]

After speeches from Charles Sumner, Wendell Philips, and Samuel Howe, the attendees resolved to establish a committee of vigilance in 1846, the predecessor of what would later be known as The Boston Vigilance Committee.

---

28. National Park Service, "Exploits of Captain Drayton in Boston Harbor."
29. National Park Service, "Abolitionism in Boston Harbor," *Boston Harbor Exhibit*, 2023, 4.
30. National Park Service, "Safe Harbor: The Maritime Underground Railroad in Boston," National Park Service, https://www.nps.gov/articles/maritime-underground-railroad-in-boston.htm (accessed August 4, 2022).

Courageous Slave Protectors and Active Slave Savers

In still another group of maritime men, we can find other captains who were always dedicated to assisting runaway slaves and were called "slave savers." These men needed to be most careful. The Fugitive Slave Act made it a federal crime to assist runaways. The slave savers needed to work in complete secrecy and took tremendous personal risks to rescue slaves, bringing them to safety from hazardous situations. It was a common practice to see courageous, ardent maritime abolitionists taking their ships and putting actions into their words. They desired to free enslaved people whenever called upon to do so.

JONATHAN WALKER (1799–1878)
"The Man with the Branded Hand"

Jonathan was raised a farmer's son in Harwich, Massachusetts. Farming in this part of Cape Cod was particularly difficult due to its dry soil composition. Unlike many other sea captains, Jonathan was the first in his family to set sail around the globe. He would be the first male Walker from a family of ten males to sail. At the age of seventeen, he left home.

As a youth, he remembers hearing the rhythm of heavy metal chains rattling down in the lower deck. Perhaps he was exposed to serving on a slave ship when he started his maritime career. During his twenties and thirties, Walker's concern for the plight of the American slave deepened.[31] As a sailor, he met and encountered many black men. He later wrote, "I have long since made up my mind that slavery ranked with the highest wrongs and crimes ever invented by man. This system was ingeniously designed to destroy the social and kind feelings that existed from man to man."

Jonathan placed a great deal of confidence in Benjamin Lundy, a wealthy, deaf Quaker and prominent abolitionist. Lundy encouraged Walker and a young ship mechanic to bring a small boat that Walker himself built in Fairhaven to the Gulf of Mexico. Walker believed that a fiery congressman from Tennessee, named Sam Houston, needed help in the Texas adventure of seceding from Mexico. His arrival time closely

---

31. Alvin F. Oickle, *The Man with the Branded Hand: The Life of Jonathan Walker, Abolitionist* (Yardley: Westholme Publications. 2011), 210.

coincided with the Battle of the Alamo. He saw that a free land in the South might just be the perfect spot for the free black slave population to go. He remarked that he found the country to be in a very unsettled state, with strong and growing prejudices displayed by many United States citizens. Jonathan's boat-building skills were much in demand during the war. He had a terrible experience in which some thieves robbed him and his vessel, taking over four thousand dollars in cash. This money was never recovered.

In 1843, Walker had two entries in his journal. "Late in the Fall of 1843, I left my home in Harwich, Massachusetts, and took passage bound for Mobile, where I spent the summer and spring, mostly in working at the shipwright business, which is my trade."[32] His very next sentence was: "I left Mobile on the second of June 1844 for Pensacola, in a boat belonging to myself: chiefly for the purpose of raising a part of the vessel sunk near the latter place, for the sake of getting the copper that was attached to it."[33] Rather than boast about his accomplishments in work, the modest captain went about his trade as a builder. He constructed at least two new boats during this time.

"Soon after meeting with friends in the bay, I learned that there were a group of men who strongly desired to leave an island near the Keys, I gave them to understand if they chose to go to the Bahama Islands with me, I would share the risk with them."[34] This decision would forever change his life. He knew that a trip in any direction, North or South, with runways was fully unlawful. During his time in the South, he noticed that white men were never imprisoned for a crime, even murder. However, a white man assisting a runaway slave was an exception and a daunting task to accept.

He wrote a passage in his diary: "On the evening of 22, seven men came on board, and we left the harbor, following the directions of the coast, traveling eastward."[35] He sailed the seven runaway slaves around the peninsula of Florida in that summer heat. The slaves wished to reach the Bahamas, seeking the freedom of another nation for these African American men. They almost reached their goal but were captured just

32. Oickle, 62.
33. Oickle, 71.
34. Oickle, 74.
35. Oickle, 82.

a half day's journey from their selected port. The slaves were returned to their masters, but not before escaping the whipping of the jailer who imprisoned Walker and the slaves, leaving them on a dirty cell floor. One of the slaves died on this spot.

Jonathan spent a full year in jail, participating in two different trials in the US court system as a slave sympathizer. He was first to be severely fined, locked into a pillory, and eventually ordered by the court to be branded on his hand by a U.S. Marshal. While in prison, he witnessed the marshal's office whipping naked slaves daily in the grime of the front prison courtyard.

In 1846, as a final punishment, the two letters "S S" (slave stealer) were permanently burned into his right palm, irrevocably labeling him an enemy of the state and showing the world that Jonathan was not to be trusted. His punishment was unique in this type of physical sentencing—the first ever and most likely only—administered in the annals of court trials.

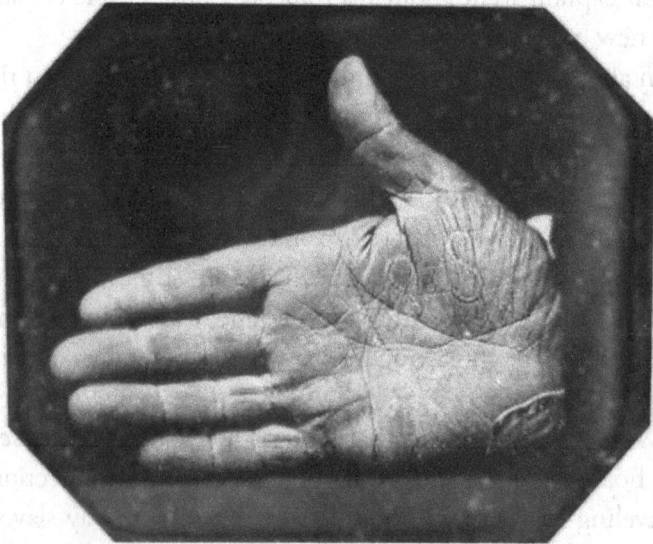

Jonathan Walker's branded hand, 1845

Jonathan was an ardent abolitionist many years before the Civil War. He became a noted and respected speaker against the cause of slavery. His wisdom and personal courage were cited as a vital rationale, fueling the fires of a national reckoning to end this tyrannical treatment of mankind. His deeds became the subject of a poem by John Greenleaf Whittier as his exploits were cited and extolled. "He became the man with a branded hand."

In the mid-1840s, Jonathan Walker began a new career as a spokesperson for the abolitionist movement. Along with Frederick Douglass, Walker toured the nation, condemning the evil perpetrated against a whole race of people. He spoke in town halls from Plymouth to Mattapoisett, explaining his rationale for his actions and the punitive treatment he had received from contrary ideological forces. He authored a book titled *American Chattelized Humanity*. He realized a need to expand beyond the current East Coast base, aiming to preach his antislavery message to the new territories forming in the country. This action led to his relocation to Wisconsin. He eventually moved to Michigan and Wisconsin, on the edge of Northwest expansion.

As he once watched a slave trade in operation in the Midwest, Walker was quoted as saying, "My heart aches to see the slave children being torn away from their family."[36] The concept of separate bidders for slaves within one united family was one specific evil within a complex of other treacherous behaviors by which he could not abide.

A second book he authored was called *A Picture of Slavery, for Youth*. He concluded that the best way to reach the minds of new citizens about the evils of slavery was when minds were young and still in their formative years. He worked diligently to have every schoolhouse pick up this somber message.

In 1845, his final notes were given to Maria Weston Chapman, a famed author of abolitionist causes. Her home in Boston was often rife with sympathizers and antislavery advocates. In her book, *The Anti-Slavery Crusade in America*, she held the calm, patient, devoted demeanor of Jonathan Walker as a perfect guide of what needed to be done.

She wrote:

> *There are those who, while they condemn slavery, at the same time assert that its*
> *extinction may be best promoted by studied silence, and by a quiet waiting for*

---

36. Oickle, 121.

the gradual operation of a moral and religious system which declares that it is not in its nature sinful and justifies it from the scriptures: and of a solemn guaranty in its favor.[37]

She exalted that the example of immediate action followed by an intellectual life dedicated to preaching the need to remove the chains could serve as a reference point for others. She saw in Walker a man who had begun the work of self-sacrificing reform within his own heart by refusing all political and religious barriers that blocked the way.

RUSSELL MARSTON (1816–1907)

Here is indeed another "rags to riches story" of a young lad from Cape Cod. He acquired success both in maritime adventures and in commercial business. As a youth from Centerville, Massachusetts, he had limited prospects at home. He aspired to see the world and learn a trade by signing up as a cabin boy on a coastal vessel. His first salary would be a meager total of three dollars per month.

Yet he would go on to own and command a commercial ship, the *Outvie*, by the age of thirty. He did well for himself as a coastal supplier, bringing wares from New England to as far south as Florida. In 1847, after twenty years as a commercial captain, he saw the writing on the wall in terms of future sailing ventures. He sailed his ship to Boston Harbor and attached a broom with the straw end facing upward, indicating the ship was now for sale.

Using these funds, he bought a food shack on Commercial Wharf. He found a chef with a knack for preparing clam chowder, which became enormously successful and symbolic of Boston. From there, he moved to 13 Brattle Street, setting up a restaurant that became a businessman's delight. In 1854, clients could purchase roast lamb for fifteen cents or sirloin steak for twenty-one cents. Business expanded so quickly, he moved to 27 Brattle Street and opened "Marston's" with a much larger seating capacity. He acquired a row of buildings from 23 to 29 Brattle Street, along with a hotel—the Marston House—nearby. His close friendship with William Lloyd Garrison distinguished him from several ship

---

37. Oickle 145.

captains of his day. He went on the record saying, "slavery was a great and unparalleled wrong, a deep injury to the victim, degrading in its effect upon the oppressor and the community in which it exists."[38]

He even went against the popular feelings in the local churches, suggesting that a quiet, eventual waiting time to end slavery was not the best decision. In his history of Barnstable County, Simeon Deyo described Marston's mindset: "He found that the churches were generally arrayed with the side of the slaveholders as being either champions or apologists which made a lasting impression on his mind."[39] Russell felt that every person was equal in the eyes of the Lord and held in a spiritual sense with each other. He was a man well ahead of his time, wanting to see equal treatment for races, genders, and degrees of affluence.

He frequently returned to Centerville, not far from the residence of William Lloyd Garrison, where Russell established a magnificent home and gardens. He provided funds to the Hampton Institute, a training school for Blacks. In his Marston restaurant, he hired mostly Black staff, afforded Black clients equal treatment to whites, and permitted unescorted women to dine in-house if they chose to do so. A memorial statue can be found on Commonwealth Avenue, not far from the entrance to Boston Common.

In concert with Garrison, Russell arranged to bring many runaway slaves up North on various shipping vessels. He even named his daughter Helen Garrison Marston. Garrison became his direct neighbor by buying a summer residence nearby in Wianno, a section of Osterville. There are records of two former slaves, George and Sarah Washington, living on his estate before being allowed to move further north.

Upon his death, he bequeathed his wealth evenly divided to his son and daughter, contrary to the norm of leaving the larger share of inheritance to the eldest son. Russell was a champion of new societal norms in many respects.

---

38. "Russell Marston Observes his 90th Birthday," *Boson Globe*, October 15, 1906.
39. Simeon L. Deyo, *The History of Barnstable County, Massachusetts* (Barnstable: Higginson Book Company, 1890), 404.

DANIEL DRAYTON

Organized the Largest Maritime Slave Escape

Born in 1802 in southern New Jersey, near Delaware Bay, Daniel Drayton first successfully took a slave family from Washington, D.C., to Frenchtown, New Jersey, in 1847. In April 1848, he planned to take seventy-seven slaves between the same two ports aboard his schooner, the *Pearl*. When Drayton's plot was revealed to several ship owners and eventually foiled on April 15, most of the slaves he intended to save were sold on the New Orleans market, and Drayton was imprisoned. Despite seeking numerous appeals, Drayton and his two assistants spent more than four years in prison.[40] This was the largest recorded attempt by enslaved individuals to escape in U.S. history. It became known as "The *Pearl* Incident."

In 1852, a petition requesting the release of Drayton was presented by Massachusetts Senator Charles Sumner. The petition was initiated by Drayton's wife and signed by twenty-one of the forty-one slave owners whose slaves were involved in the *Pearl* Incident. Sumner successfully persuaded President Millard Fillmore to pardon and release Drayton. On August 12, 1852, Drayton returned to his impoverished wife and children in Philadelphia.

Drayton went to New Bedford three weeks later, on September 9, 1852. He spoke before a crowd, filled with both Blacks and whites, at Sears Hall. According to the *New Bedford Standard*, "it had a marked effect on its audience."[41] Charles Thomas, a man of color who had migrated to New Bedford from Washington with his wife, Hannah, in 1851, supported Drayton's account. When Drayton spoke to the audience, "it was awakened to the inequities of slavery through years of working on coasting vessels running between Savannah at the South and St. John's, New Brunswick."[42] Drayton had many connections with the city of New Bedford, Massachusetts, as a sailor, author, speaker, and abolitionist. It was the city where his life would end at his own hands.

He once wrote, "There is not a waterman who ever sailed in Chesapeake Bay who will not tell you that, so far from the slaves needing any

---

40. Daniel Drayton, *Personal Memoirs of Daniel Drayton* (Ann Arbor: University of Michigan Press, 2005), 109.
41. *New Bedford Standard*, August 26, 2015.
42. Daniel Drayton, 102.

prompting to run away, the difficulty is, when they ask you to assist them, to make them take no for an answer."[43] As a sea captain, Drayton knew of the many slaves living in or near the coastal cities and yearning to escape. Of course, the laws prohibited this option, but the ardent abolitionist paid little heed. He had known instances where men would lay in hiding in the woods for a year or two, hoping for an opportunity to escape on board some vessel. Drayton tried to help them, convinced he needed to help slaves escape, but he failed several times.

While visiting New Bedford in 1857, Drayton went to his room and had not been seen for almost twenty-four hours. When his door was broken open, Drayton was discovered on the floor. The coroner and a jury of inquest returned a verdict of death by suicide. The captain who assisted so many slaves to freedom and willingly faced the probability of imprisonment finally gave in to his fading mental and physical health.

It was during his voyages to and from slave-owning states that Captain Drayton met slaves and formed his views about the practice of slavery. He saw it on a first-hand basis and was struck by its inhumanity. He could never grasp the logic of treating Blacks and whites as unequal, and he personally felt the human pain of slavery culture.

In his memoir, Captain Drayton wrote:

> *The idea of having first one child and then another taken from me, as fast as they grew large enough, and handed over to the slave traders, to be carried I knew not where, and sold, if they are girls, I knew not for what purposes, would have been horrible enough; and, from instances which came to my notice, I perceived that it was not less horrible and distressing to the parties concerned in the case of black people than of white ones.*[44]

COMMODORE MATTHEW PERRY

Perry was born in Newport, Rhode Island, and could trace his lineage to Thomas Prence, a co-founder of Eastham, Massachusetts, and Pilgrim Elder William Brewster of *Mayflower* fame. Perry earned the title of commodore in June 1840, when the Secretary of the Navy appointed him commandant of the New York Navy Yard. The United States Navy had

---

43. Daniel Drayton, 137.
44. Daniel Drayton, 196.

no ranks higher than captain until 1857, thus the title of commodore carried considerable weight. Typically, any Navy officer would revert to his permanent rank after a squadron command assignment ended. In practice, commodores maintained regulations that made following their missions difficult. Only slavers with slaves on board could be seized, and the changing of a ship's national identity flag occurred frequently, mostly to confuse witnesses. It seems as if much better odds were afforded to the slave traders. From this time on, America kept a limited number of war vessels off the African coast as a meek sign of warning.

In 1843, Perry took command of the Africa Squadron, whose main duty was to intercept the slave trade under the Webster-Ashburton Treaty, which was intended to end the slave trade. The slave trade route was three thousand miles long. In addition, Southern officers were often in command of these warships, so there was considerable doubt as to their overall effectiveness.

In his wish to end slavery, Perry roamed the seas for years, looking for violators of slave exportation. Unfortunately, there were so many violators with important connections that he eventually saw his role as untenable.

Slave Sympathizers

Some captains were known to be quite sympathetic to the abolitionist cause. They were active public speakers and brave men willing to take a formal stand against the perceived injustice of the day.

LEVI BAKER (1803–1864)

An Opponent of The Slave Inspection Act

A Virginia law passed in 1856 demanded that every ship heading North must be searched for the possibility of runaway slaves. Every inspection carried a fee: five dollars for ordinary vessels and two dollars for coal-carrying boats. If the vessel sailed north without undergoing inspection, the captain was required to pay a fee of $500. If the payment to the court was not addressed, the ship could be seized. This law realized a generous profit for the government, raising $137,000 during its first year of implementation.

The small fee was deemed a nuisance, but most seafaring men agreed to pay the nominal sum to transact business. Captain Levi Baker, however, challenged the constitutionality of this statute. He was a twenty-five-year veteran of sailing through Southern ports. In July 1856, he was the commander and owner of the schooner *N.C. Hall*. He lay at anchor at Hampton, Virginia, with a cargo of corn and fruit bound for New Bedford.

A pilot boat approached and asked Baker his intended direction. Despite the captain's truthful response, no inspection of this vessel ever ensued. Fearing that the fruit had a limited shelf life and seeing a favorable wind emerge, the captain threw caution to the wind and took off to depart. He honestly believed that some other smaller pilot boater would eventually enter his path to conduct the necessary search. No pilot boat was visible, and his cargo was perishable, so he decided to push out to sea.

A month later, the *N.C. Hall* was back in Norfolk with a new captain in charge. Captain Baker was detained in Massachusetts as the vessel's owner. The ship was now in the custody of the state of Virginia, having transgressed the Commonwealth of Virginia's maritime codes. Baker later received permission to return to Virginia to seek his vessel's release. By now, the fines had reached a total of $700. Captain Baker was, above all, a prudent businessman who decided that paying the fee was better than risking the full loss of his ship's cargo valued at over $3,000. He also completed an analysis of the ship's status to determine that keeping the ship away from the sea for too long would most likely result in worms, making the vessel unnavigable.

He took it upon himself to go to every Virginian legal official he could find to obtain a release and pay the fee. No court officer, state representative, or port official would even speak to him. He was even encouraged by some Virginia lawyers, but they had no jurisdiction in the matter. They believed that this law was most likely unconstitutional and should be challenged. Even the state's Governor Wise failed to intervene in the matter.

In effect, he could not recover the ship while Virginia condemned it. It was sold at a public auction for $750. Returning home and feeling dejected, Baker now took on this legal decision as a personal challenge.

He would fight this unjust law on behalf of all the Eastern shippers. He petitioned the Massachusetts legislature to contest this treatment to a higher court. His request was granted, and the state awarded him $2,500 to fight this injustice at the federal level.

However, the sad yet unfortunate truth was that by the time the U.S. Supreme Court was set to hear oral arguments on the case, our nation became embroiled in the Civil War, and there were many more important courts cases demanding their attention. This case was left on the docket but never officially adjudicated. Baker fell victim to the vicissitudes of slavery, federal unrest, and inconsistent maritime practices.

RICHARD DANA (1815–1882)

Author of *Two Years Before the Mast*

Richard Dana was born in Cambridge, Massachusetts, to a well-established colonial family. On his mother's side, Anne Bradstreet arrived on American soil in 1640. Her poetic works were read widely in England as well as the Bay Colony.

Dana began his studies in Cambridge under the tutelage of Samuel Barrett, regarded as a strict instructor. Poet James Russell was his classmate. In addition, Ralph Waldo Emerson, one of Dana's teachers, observed the young man as "being very pleasant yet lacking discipline in his approach." Dana started to attend Harvard but was quickly suspended for a short time in his freshman year for supporting a student protest. Later in his studies, he contracted measles, leading to a case of ophthalmia, a severe eye infection. He left college life. Even though his social status could have resulted in him being assigned a higher station, he signed on as an ordinary seaman on a long sea voyage to build his strength and rebel against his preferential social status. With his wealth, he could have signed up for a classic European jaunt trip, preferred by the upper class.

Dana left Boston on the *Pilgrim*, captained by the stern Frank Thompson, who flogged his men, believing the abuse an acceptable sanction against supposed lazy crewmen. Their trip was primarily a quest for available rawhide in the official Mexican lands known as California in those days. Dana witnessed what he described as "great cruelty" inflicted on the ship's sailors, along with vivid animosity against the Hawaiian people.

To return home quickly, he requested that his return voyage be aboard the *Alert*, bound for Boston. Heading back along the Cape of Good Horn, he described a most compelling image of terrific storms bound within profound beauty. He chronicled vivid descriptions of icebergs, which he believed impossible to give a proper degree of justice to their treachery. Herman Melville liked this passage so much, he once remarked: "But if you want the best idea of Cape Horn, get my friend Dana's unmatchable *Two Years Before the Mast*."[45]

The most incredible part of the book, perhaps, is the weeks and weeks it took to negotiate passage of Cape Horn against ferocious winds and storms, all the while having to race up and down the ice-covered mast rigs to furl and unfurl sails. At one point, Dana describes an infected tooth that swelled up so much he could not work for several days. He then goes on to talk about how scurvy afflicted the crewmen as they rounded the Cape. A memorable detailed picture associated with all Cape Horn crossings was now fully documented.

A few years later, Lincoln appointed Dana as the Massachusetts United States Attorney, and Dana upheld Lincoln's blockade of Southern ports. He had a brilliant legal reputation that grew as he spoke out in favor of granting African Americans voting rights, greater educational opportunities, property ownership options, and even firearm responsibilities.

Future president James Garfield once repeated a direct quote from Dana:

> We have got to choose between two results. With these four million of Negroes within our boundaries, either you must have four million of disfranchised, disarmed, untaught, landless, thriftless, non-producing, non-consuming, degraded men, or else you must have four million of landholding, industrious, arms-bearing, and voting population. Choose between the two! Which will you have?[46]

45. Elias Altman, "The Man Before the Mast," *Lapham's Quarterly* (July 13,2013). https://www.laphams-quarterly.org/roundtable/man-mast (accessed January 19, 2024).
46. Ward M. McAfee, *Religion, Race, and Reconstruction: The Public School in the Politics of the 1870s* (Albany: State University of New York Press, 1998), 11.

We can hear and feel the diametric tensions and opposing sentiments discussed in the day.

Circumstantial Slave Savers

A final group of people connected to maritime life indirectly assisted free slaves. They took positive steps that ultimately resulted in many fruitful results.

JONATHAN BOURNE (1811–1888)
Instrumental to the Presidency of Abraham Lincoln

Bourne's family instilled honesty, integrity, bluntness, and a strong sense of generosity into the young man as a youth. In this section of Sandwich, called Bourne today, the length of time a teacher shared with his students was a direct correlation to the family's financial contributions to the community. In Jonathan's situation, his part of town had the services of an instructor for 113 days a year.

At the age of seventeen, Jonathan divided his time between his studies and serving as a grocery clerk in the largest store of his day. His first-year store duties consisted of basic menial tasks, such as sweeping, waiting on customers, replenishing stock, completing inventory checks, and maintaining the books for his employer, Mr. Webster.

Jonathan managed to save just about every penny he ever earned and quickly saw that greater wealth could be acquired in ways other than being a local farmer or working as a grocery clerk. Analyzing the potentially profitable enterprises of the day, he correctly predicted that whaling would soon become a booming industry. His first investment resulted in purchasing a one-sixteenth share of a whaling ship, the *General Pike*. His return on investment was more than favorable as he realized the immediate growth factor. In the subsequent year, he acquired a one-fourth share of the *Roscoe* for $1,925.

By 1836, he dismissed all aspects of the grocery business and ventured full-time into whaling investment. He acquired a full interest in ten more ships within three more years. Initially, he saw that, for an original investment of $180,450, he could turn a profit of $73,013 annually, which

Jonathan Bourne

equated to a 41-percent rate of return. By 1839, he was well on his way to seeing a profit of over one million dollars per year. He could approach an earning rate of over two million dollars in a good year. He expanded his empire to include a Fire Protection Services division for a short time. Feeling a civic duty, he used his wealth and influence to enter politics as an alderman in New Bedford.

In a well-known family feud with his brother, he struggled in civil court to challenge the distribution of his father's will. Rather than merely squandering funds to a brother he believed was indolent, Jonathan had the courts agree to reduce his brother's annual claims. He then applied these same funds toward other civic projects. The local people admired his inherent instinct for shrewdness and blunt confrontation with facts. His business empire continued to expand. By 1876, he ascended to president of Merchant's Bank, the primary lending institution of its day.

After his wealth was well established, he became a prominent political figure in local and national affairs. Originally named the Whigs, his party affiliation would later change to the National Republican Party, where he was welcomed with open arms. In 1860, he was elected as a Massachusetts delegate to the Presidential Primary Convention. When a close primary contest unfolded between Seward and Lincoln, his influence, personal persuasiveness, and promise of wealthy support carried significant weight into the contest. Today, many pundits agree that his support was perhaps the prime motivation carrying Abraham Lincoln to the presidential nomination. How might the outcome of the Civil War have differed if not for Lincoln's presidential influence?

He later became a central figure in the Western Railroad Movement. His reputation now extended well beyond the Bay State. He was seen as a forceful national figure. He ran for a congressional seat and was elected to the first congressional district in southern Massachusetts. He would eventually retire to the Bourne area of today. His daughter used her wealth to establish parks, libraries, and schools in Bourne. His wealth, compassion, business skills, and complete dedication to community needs were principal reasons that his name arose when this section of Cape Cod pulled away from Sandwich.

SQUIRE ELISHA DOANE (1768–1848)
Shipowner with Hypocritical Actions

Officially, he was not a true seafaring man himself. Nonetheless, Elisha insured more than 125 vessels and cargoes, acting with his sons as partners, and he owned shares of another fifty-five vessels, which ranged from brigs to schooners to packets to whaleships. Is it possible for the same person to be known both for harboring slaves and using them for financial gain in his business? Or can a local tavern owner also head the local temperance society? Elisha Doane was indeed such a man.

Few people in the early 1800s could match the success of young Elisha Doane. He was born into a well-connected family of modest means that was blessed with a solid New England work ethic. He also married into a wealthy family. His bride's father owned a thriving tavern in the heart of Yarmouth, and due to the laws regarding property, he gained the assets of his wife's father and her grandfather, the very first tavern owner during the American Revolution.

Elisha acquired a good fortune in his lifetime. The tavern generated business by virtue of its role as a gathering place for official transactions, militia musters, and auctions of land, vessels, and merchandise. He was seen as an entrepreneur who understood how to leverage indentured servants to full advantage.

He also profited greatly by exploiting distress sales in maritime goods and troubled merchandise. He encouraged New England rum drinkers to frequent his taproom. Whenever customers paid their bills in Spanish dollars, a common practice of the day, Elisha would cash them at Boston banks, where they yielded him a 4-percent premium. It seems as if every activity of Elisha's brought him additional significant income. Every month, he filled an official order for flour used to make wafers, imported sacramental wine for his congregation's use, and sold candles to the Meeting House, where his own son-in-law was the pastor.

His commercial interests were wide and varied. He was a tavern keeper, Justice of the Peace, rope walk owner, shipbuilder, storekeeper, insurer, ship owner, saltworks owner, merchant, fish broker, rum importer, salted fish exporter, landlord, money lender, and mortgagor. He was a master to

Poster drawing of the Drunkards Progress

indentured servants, a gentleman farmer, a dairyman, a church deacon, a politician, a militia officer, an organizer of Yarmouth's first library, a stockholder in Yarmouth's First Bank, and a shareholder in Bass River Bridge. He helped to organize a Harwich factory, a Boston insurance company, the Cape Cod railroad, and ten Boston banks. He also owned five pews in the North Congregational Meeting House, had an interest in Yarmouth Academy, invested in the Boston and Maine Railroad, and was a large holder of New England state bonds.

Indeed, given his innate entrepreneurial talents, it should come as no surprise that Elisha was reputed to be the wealthiest man in Massachusetts—possibly even in the country. In most social circles, he was seen as a just and shrewd businessman. However, the contradictions were many. Elisha Doane owned the town's busiest tavern and often paid his workers in rum in lieu of cash. He then managed to become head of Yarmouth's local Temperance Society chapter. He was also designated as the contact for local runaway slaves but would then engage them in his enterprises, securing them into long-term indentured servant contracts.

CHAPTER ELEVEN

Social Unrest Groups in the 1840s and 1850s

If you think the members of the Abolitionist movement between 1830–1855 were one strong, monolithic group of people, you do not yet have a full picture of the era's social and political turmoil. In her book *American Radicalism*, Holly Jackson paints the picture of a country in a state of constant unrest. At times, splinter groups formed integral parts of a larger vision of social goals for America. On occasion, these same groups would break off as schisms and oppose the other existing movements of the day. There was a constant ebb and flow of social theories floating around that at times advocated ending slavery immediately, yet at other moments, groups might become silent, promoting their own private agenda. Many of these groups were made of diverse philosophies, but all held the constant passion for a strong voice of conscience. These groups competed for attention while often having overlapping memberships. Their degree of engagement plays a significant role in the analysis of a slavery study.

All these movements have the common trait of wanting to push for immediate social reform within the county's current daily infrastructure. The groups united people to a common cause yet further polarized other opposing groups and followers. Often seen as being radical subversives by a subset of the larger society, their support of the freedom for slaves sometimes boosted public opinion yet, in other moments, made the abolitionists appear more radical.

The historic decades prior to the Civil War were rife with social unrest. At times, these various subgroups strongly advocated for immediate antislavery action yet, on other occasions, preferred to support their own beliefs, dividing a newly polarized nation even further.

LUCY STONE
Women's Rights Advocate

The women's suffrage movement has firm roots in Massachusetts. One of the prominent leaders of the movement was Lucy Stone, who dedicated her life to battling inequality. She became the first woman in Massachusetts to earn a college degree, and she challenged gender norms when she wrote her own marriage vows, which reflected her belief in equality, and refused to take her husband's last name.

She was born on August 13, 1818, in rural Massachusetts to Francis and Hannah Matthews Stone. Her parents were farmers with deep roots in New England—her ancestors arrived in 1635 to pursue religious freedom—and her grandfather was a captain in the American Revolution. Stone was raised in the Congregational Church, embracing her father's antislavery zeal.

More esoteric than her brothers, Stone was deeply upset by the inequality that encouraged men to attend college while discouraging women from becoming educated. At the age of sixteen, she worked as a teacher, saving her money to attend college. In 1839, she spent one semester at Mount Holyoke but was forced to return home due to family illness. In 1843, she attended Oberlin College in Ohio. Even a most progressive college such as Oberlin never permitted Stone to develop her public speaking skills. When she graduated in 1847, she declined to write a commencement speech that had to be read by a man. William Lloyd Garrison later hired her as a speechwriter for *The Liberator*.

MARY GOVE NICHOLS
Challenged the Traditional Concept of Marriage

When the "The Free Love Movement" was formed, it was very much a misnamed enterprise. It was a concept that originated in the mid-nineteenth century in England. In this context, Free Love meant an absence of legal ties based on gender rather than any call to promiscuity. It was frequently misunderstood and more frequently charged as evil in the antisocialist press.

The ideals of Free Love were found in one of the earliest American feminists, Mary Gove Nichols. The Goves moved to Lynn, Massachusetts, where Mary ran a private school for girls. In her speeches, she vividly describes four miscarriages. In 1841, she moved back to her family in New Hampshire after leaving her husband, whom she eventually divorced. She dedicated her life to discussing her sexual and emotional abuse. She wanted women to know that they must respect their own bodies and could seek individual careers if they so chose. She also was an advocate for health reform. In 1852, she and her second husband, Thomas Low Nichols, founded a "water-cure" clinic, which was mostly quackery.

GEORGE AND SOPHIA RIPLEY

A Worker-Based Cooperative Farmers Market & Community

The Brook Farm Movement, officially known as the Brook Farm Institute of Agriculture and Education, was a brief attempt at utopian communal living between 1841 and 1847. The farm was established on 175 acres in West Roxbury, Massachusetts, which is now part of Boston. George Ripley, a Unitarian minister and editor of *The Dial*, a popular newspaper of the day, initiated the idea. According to its articles of agreement, Brook Farm was to combine the thinker and the worker, leading to the greatest possible mental freedom.[1]

AMOS BRONSON ALCOTT, RALPH WALDO EMERSON, AND OTHERS

Transcendentalism

The philosophical concept of transcendentalism espoused that man's internal sense of goodness would conquer all. They believed in creating a real-world utopia in which intellectual thought and insight prevailed over reason. Transcendentalism was not a rejection of the Unitarian way of thought but rather a consequence of the Unitarian emphasis on free conscience and intellectual reason. The transcendentalists were not content with the calm mildness and rationality of Unitarianism. Beyond that belief, they longed for a more intense spiritual experience.

Thus, transcendentalism was not a countermovement to Unitarianism but more of a parallel movement stretching to a higher level of spiritual thought. Massachusetts authors led the way with supporters such

---

1. Holly Jackson, *American Radicals: How Nineteenth-Century Protest Shaped the Nation* (New York: Random House, 2019), 191.

as Ralph Waldo Emerson, Henry David Thoreau, and Amos Bronson Alcott. A small transcendental colony existed for years in the town of Harvard, Massachusetts. Bronson Alcott secured several acres of rolling hills ten miles west of Concord along with his famous daughters.

FANNY WRIGHT
The Workers Union Movement

The Fanny Wright Society was another social movement that was widely discussed in its day. Fanny, a Scottish national and philosopher, gave public lectures in the United States, leading to the establishment of Fanny Wright societies. Her thoughts were highly associated with the Working Men's Association, organized in New York City in 1829. She became so well known that her opponents called the party's slate of candidates "the Fanny Wright ticket."

The Workingmen's Party was the first labor-oriented political organization in the country, established in Philadelphia in 1828 and later moved to New York in 1829. The party was born out of the concerns of high-level craftsmen and skilled journeymen relative to their low social and economic status. The "Workies" pressed for universal male voting rights, equal educational opportunities, protection from debtor imprisonment, and greater financial security with shorter hours.

The Philadelphia section of the party agitated for free public education and an end to competition from prison contract labor. Under the leadership of radical Thomas Skidmore, the New York party demanded the ten-hour working day, abolition of imprisonment for debt, and an effective mechanics' lien law for workers in construction. This law would prevent the seizure of a craftsman's tools for a debt. When the New York party came under the leadership of Robert Dale Owen, it added a demand for universal education at public expense. In Massachusetts, this movement counted for one-quarter of all votes in the 1833–1834 elections.

LYMAN BEECHER
The Temperance Movement

In 1810, Calvinist ministers met in a seminary in Massachusetts to write articles on alcohol abstinence to preach to their congregations. The Massachusetts Society for the Suppression of Intemperance (MSSI) was formed in 1813. The organization only accepted men of high social standing and encouraged moderation in alcohol consumption.

In the 1830s, the Temperance Movement was a driving force in political, social, and religious circles. Only a few years later, the movement split between moderates allowing some drinking and radicals demanding total abstinence, as well as a division between voluntarists relying on moral suasion alone and prohibitionists promoting laws to restrict or ban alcohol.

Radicals and prohibitionists dominated most of the largest temperance organizations. Temperance eventually became synonymous with prohibition. In 1838, temperance activists pushed the Massachusetts legislature to pass a law restricting the sale of alcohol in quantities less than fifteen gallons. In the 1840s, numerous states passed laws allowing local voters to determine whether liquor licenses should be issued in their respective towns or counties.

SYLVESTER GRAHAM

Healthy Nourishment and Proper Diet Movement

The concept of the Graham diet and a healthy eating lifestyle became a major issue in the 1830s. Critiques of American food and eating were frequent and loud. This movement is usually associated with Sylvester Graham, the founder of the Diet Reform Movement in the antebellum United States. Graham entered Amherst Academy in his late twenties to become a minister, as his father and grandfather had been. He was forced to withdraw from school a year later due to ridicule and scorn by his fellow students. During the 1830s and 1840s, Ralph Waldo Emerson was described as the "prophet of bran bread," making a name for himself by publishing books on diet and proper living.

Graham developed a system of healthy living that eliminated strong drink and poorly prepared foods. He advocated moderation in all areas of daily life. Graham and his followers posited a strong link between diet, health, and morality, seeing the body as a holistic system that needed to be kept in balance for the individual to maintain physical and spiritual health. Graham gave his name to a movement and a famed "cracker." Those who followed his tenets were known as "Grahamites."

Most Americans today may not know much about Sylvester Graham or realize that they pay him tribute in a small way every time they eat a

Graham cracker, an adulterated form of the bran bread central to Graham's diet system.

Graham's total impact was strongly felt in nineteenth-century America. Thomas Low Nichols, the husband of Mary Gove, was engaged in this cause, claiming that water hydration can solve many medical issues.

CHARLES FOURIER

Fourierist Associations in the United States

This philosophy emerged as a popular attempt at communal life during a short-lived period during the first half of the 1840s. Between 1843 and 1845, more than thirty such "associations," also known as "phalanxes," were established in the United States. Unfortunately, all these communes met with economic failure and rapid abandonment within a comparatively few years. In Massachusetts, there were communes in West Roxbury, Hopedale, and Northampton.

JAMES BIRNEY

The Liberty Party Fostered Antislavery Goals

The Liberty Party was created in 1840 by a scion of abolitionists who believed political action was the best way to further antislavery goals. It lasted until 1848 and stood in opposition to William Lloyd Garrison and his followers, who saw any political activity as both a waste of time and wrong to end slavery.

The party nominated James Birney, a former slaveholder, for president. The party's first national convention took place in Albany, New York, on April 1, 1840, when Birney's nomination was confirmed. This new political group was seen as the death knell for the presidency of Henry Clay. The Liberty Party was the first organized third political party to arise in Massachusetts. It was committed to the eventual demise of slavery.

The Liberty Party supporters fully realized that the abolition of slavery in the South would probably never occur politically or naturally. Nonetheless, the group tried to dramatize antislavery, pressure legislators into taking firmer antislavery positions, and prevent slavery from extending beyond the states where it currently existed into other federal territories.

CHAPTER TWELVE

The Harwich Antislavery Conference of 1848

If you are ever looking for evidence that many Northern citizens, particularly from Cape Cod, were more sympathetic to the slavery movement, we can examine one of the largest and most violent race-based conferences ever held in the United States occurring in Harwich. In 1848, the Antislavery Movement planned a four-day series of intellectual discussions advocating for the immediate end of any form of slavery.

The title of this conference was "The Bulwark of Slavery." The title fit the occasion perfectly. A bulwark can either be defined as a defensive wall or, in nautical terms, as an extension of a ship's side above the level of the deck.

It was rumored that a Harwich sea captain had intentionally and with malice betrayed a runaway slave. While in Norfolk, Virginia, not long before the convention, a slave came on board and asked this captain what he would charge to carry him and another to New York or Boston. The captain made a contract, and the slave paid one hundred dollars in advance. The captain pocketed the cash, then went on shore, betrayed the poor slave, had him arrested, imprisoned, and advertised his presence. The captain then sailed north, bringing the hundred dollars with him along with the twenty-five-dollar reward for catching the runaway. This incensed the abolitionists, who felt the world should know about such perfidy.

The conference's planning committee consisted of the most notable and eloquent speakers of the day who supported the abolitionist cause. William Lloyd Garrison, Parker Pillsbury, Wendell Philips, and Lucy Stone came together to not only voice their perspective on the evil of holding people in captivity, but they also offered their platform to any person who might be holding an opposite view to speak so that the issues could be discerned.

On August 27, 1848, a sweltering Sunday, a crowd of about three thousand people assembled in a grove, likely near the intersection of Bank and Hoyt Streets in Harwich Port, to hear several well-known abolitionists address antislavery.

One of the prevailing thoughts of the abolitionists was that the church itself held a formal bully pulpit that protected the practice of slave ownership. The church often officially declared the concept evil while simultaneously allowing wealthy slave-owning families to run church affairs and stating that a future goal should be under full review while the issue of slavery slowly and deliberately continued.

Taking to the stage, Frederick Douglass remarked on the role of the church:

> *The church is responsible for the persistence of slavery. It has shamelessly given the sanction of religion and the Bible to the whole slave system. They have taught that man may, properly, be a slave; that the relation of master and slave is ordained of God; that to send back an escaped bondman to his master is clearly the duty of all the followers of the Lord Jesus Christ; and this horrible blasphemy is palmed off upon the world for Christianity.*[1]

Two years before the Harwich meeting, the First Congregational Church in Harwich passed a resolution to have "no church fellowship with those who hold or treat their fellow men as chattels or who advocate or approve of the system of human slavery." Since 1830, however, the abolitionist movement had become more militant and aggressive, and some abolitionists saw this resolution as totally unacceptable. In effect, how do you define "fellowship" among church members? Abolitionists claimed the churches used "the do-nothing" or "slow-moving" approach. The words espoused seemed incongruous with the actions of many seafaring men who still profited handsomely from importing rum, selling cotton, and sending lower-grade fish to Southern plantations.

---

1. Frederick Douglass, *Narrative of the Life of Frederick Douglass,* (New York: Dover Publications, 1995), 211.

On that last warm day at the Harwich meeting, the crowd became increasingly restless, concurrent to the speaker's rhetoric, which became increasingly accusatory. During the previous three days, the abolitionists had passed several resolutions, seen by some local citizens as extremely insulting and offensive. There was a mention that organized religion was a lie, that many clergy were unsympathetic to the issue of slavery, and that the government was nothing short of a pack of criminals for their *laissez-faire* attitude. The Constitution was a written covenant associated with death, and the Union offered an agreement with hell itself. Of course, this hyperbolic rhetoric was most dramatic and incited strong feelings from the people attending.

Steven Foster, a staunch abolitionist, added that to vote or hold office and not fight for the immediate dismantling of slavery was a crime scarcely less than blasphemy against the Holy Ghost. On the platform that day with Foster were William Lloyd Garrison, Parker Pillsbury, Wendell Phillips, and Lucy Stone, all fierce abolitionists and accomplished debaters, well able to defend their opinions.

Aroused to indignation, many young men in the audience began to heckle the speakers. The verbal exchanges quickly escalated into a slow boil toward violence. Much later, Parker Pillsbury described what happened next in *Acts of the Anti-Slavery Apostles*.

A diary entry made on that day appears in Benjamin Franklin Robbins's diary, published as *To Always Persevere: A Cape Cod Life*, edited by Marcia J. Monbleau. It states that Braddock Phillips, Nathaniel Chase, Thomas Burgess, Alfred Hunt, Henry Brooks, Joshua Snow, and Captain Stillman Snow and his sons were among those who stormed the platform and pulled down the speakers. Their defenders destroyed the platform itself. In describing the rioters, Robbins added: "The crowd urged, as an excuse, the speakers called them rowdies, but they had not sense enough to know that they proved themselves to be such."[2]

The *Harwich Chronicle* also describes this same set of events in terms of antislavery emotion which this riotous demonstration caused within Cape Cod. The story is repeated from the eyes of the reporter.

2. Frances Geberth, "Bejamin Franklin Robbins: A Life in Harwich," *Wicked Local* (March 21, 2006). https://www.wickedlocal.com/story/archive/206/03/22/benjamin-franklin-robbins-life-in/39373594007/ (accessed February 5, 2023).

The conference occurred in Harwich, Mass, on Sunday, the fourth and last day
of a grand anti-slavery convention, held in a beautiful usually peaceful grove, in
September of the year 1848.

No building on the Cape could have held half of the full audience in physical
attendance. Cape Cod at that time was the birthplace or nursery of more
sea-captains than any other portion, of equal extent, on the whole Atlantic coast.
Many of the most eminent of these seafaring men were early able and faithful
friends and supporters of the anti-slavery enterprise.[3]

But sea captains were not all abolitionists, or else the Harwich Sunday
tumult, in defense of the church as "the bulwark of slavery," would not
have transpired. The constitution of the country, the courts, the political
parties, the commerce, and current trade practices had all been shown to
be conducted in the interest of slavery, yet many negative incidents were
being cited. On this Sunday, the churches and clergy were arraigned as
the bulwark and forlorn hope of the accursed institution. Which brings
us back to the story of the unnamed sea captain and his betrayal of the
slave in favor of double payment.

This quote, made by abolitionist Parker Pillsbury, incited the mob:
"Twenty-five dollars for a deed that no Modoc nor Apache Indian under
heaven would ever have done! In cold, unprovoked blood, never."[4]

Some facts were shared via the unnamed captain himself, early in the
day. In the afternoon, when the crowd was the greatest, a full statement
of the case, in words as fitting, were made. Of course, the effect on the
audience was intense. Depending upon the moral value that different
persons placed on the transaction between the captain and his helpless
victim, the two sides either defended slavery outright or were weak in
fighting for their immediate release.

In the tumult, the captain came to the platform, and not having heard the
full statement, he demanded, in great wrath, who it was that accused him of
stealing! He said somebody had just told him he had been accused of stealing. He
was answered that his name had not been mentioned there; and that nothing
had been said about stealing. He said he had a right to be heard and wished to

---

3. Unnamed Reporter, "The Bulwark Conference in Harwich," *Harwich Chronicle*, August 28, 1848.
4. Benjamin Robbins, August 27, 1848, Diary of Benjamin Robbins, Harwich Historical Society, 6.

be heard. We cheerfully accorded him the platform. He came forward, and in the frankest, blandest manner, stated his own case in his own words. When he concluded, he was invited to a seat on the platform, which he accepted.[5]

Stephen Foster spoke next. He began in quite a conversational tone:

Mr. Chairman, we have now heard from his own mouth, what our friend had to say of the matter in hand. And he confirms every statement of Mr. Pillsbury, excepting one: he has not told us that he is a member in good and regular standing of the Baptist church, as Mr. Pillsbury had assured us, he was. Now I wish to ask him if that is also true.[6]

Pillsbury admitted that with the remainder of his testimony. The journal article goes on to say:

Foster then continued with his argument. And those who ever heard him can more easily imagine than I can describe its power. He easily swayed those hundreds in attendance, yet the captain, who was really on trial himself, listened to every word with respect and attention. He had heard a voice within him, louder, more eloquent than the utterances of Foster, and whose rebuke he could not resist. Anxiety filled the surrounding air.

The mob spirits now rushed for the platform, and with oaths and curses of stunning power, called on the captain to pitch [Foster] down to them. Their numbers seemed legion; and their nature and spirit like that other legion, known of old. The captain mildly replied to them that he wished none of their interference nor defense. He left the platform soon after and moved out of the crowd. Foster then held a long conversation with some Boston abolitionists, who had come down on direct purpose to attend the convention. He very frankly told them that he had no fault to find whatever with our treatment of the matter, nor of him, nor did he ever after offer any complain.[7]

Mr. Foster kept his feet and held the crowd at bay, believing that he showed the local religion to be a falsehood and hypocrisy.

---

5. Benjamin Robbins, August 27, 1848, 8.
6. Benjamin Robbins, August 27, 1848, 10.
7. Benjamin Robbins, August 27, 1848, 14.

A member of the orthodox church, who had just come from his meeting and leaped like a lion on to the platform. His eyes flashed fury if not fire; his teeth and fists were clenched, and he seemed a spirit from the pit, who might have been commissioned to lead its flock to the slaughter.[8]

The church member asked him not to leave or to speak, and paid no respect to precedence or rules. His first note was a shriek, that everything said was a lie.

He was immediately outvoiced by the yelling troop, who leaped like tigers at his heels, and added fearful deeds to his not less fearful words. What became of the platform companions was unclear. The church member was immediately seized, and with kicks, blows, and dilapidated clothing, hurled to the ground.

While they were tearing up the planks, they were uttering most dreadful oaths, and vowing vengeance on the lecturers, should they ever make their appearance there again. The opposition said the abolitionists had assailed their very laws and their religion, which they were going to defend. Other observers would judge what kind of laws and what kind of religion needed such a defense. It was a proud day for antislavery, and one which the Friends would remember with gratitude. The lecturers were not particularly disturbed until all had been said which they wished to say, until every nail was driven in the right place, and then the mob clenched them. They meant their violence for evil, but God meant it for good.

Parker Pillsbury asserted:

. . . the crowd to be like dragon's teeth, which they were then unconsciously sowing, will yet come up, a host of true-hearted anti-slavery men and women, who will redeem Cape Cod from the false religion which now curses and enslaves it. Much praise is due to the friends, who are too numerous to mention, who so nobly stood by those whose lives the hungry mob were seeking. Nor would we fail to make suitable mention of others, who, during the day on Sunday, were active in exciting the mob spirit.[9]

---

8. Benjaming Robbins, August 27, 1848, 21.
9. JJ Bangert, "The Harwich Port Race Riot of 1848," No Place for Hate – Harwich Massachusetts Blog, entry posted Septemeber 5, 2009, http://noplaceforhateharwich.blogspot.com/2009/09/harwich-port-race-riot-of-1848.html (accessed January 30, 2024).

One prominent speaker among them was Henry C. Brooks, of Harwich. Brooks said:

> *The good effect of the mob is already manifest in the increased activity and interest of the friends on the Cape, whose liberal contributions to the cause have been nearly doubled, and who see new reasons for girding themselves to more vigorous effort in behalf of human freedom. And now, wondrous to tell, with such records, the church and clergy claim and boast that they abolished slavery. The real, everlasting truth is, we had almost had to abolish the church before we could reach the dreadful institution at all. We certainly divided if we did not destroy it.*[10]
>
> *At the end of the day, there lay Captain Chase and Captain Smith, of Harwich, both old men, who, with many others, had sprung to the defense of the sea captains. There the two men lay, their faces covered with blood. They were both radical men, only remonstrated with our remorseless assailants. But both would willingly have died in the stead of the captains.*

According to the *Harwich Monitor* truer, nobler men, never lived.[11]

Havoc was soon made of the platform. William Wells Brown, a fugitive slave lecturer, was roughly seized up and pitched over the back of the platform by the infuriated crowd. Mr. Foster was rescued and taken away from danger. His Sunday coat was destroyed from bottom to top, and his body considerably battered and bruised.

A neutral observant to the proceedings, a local Harwich farmer named Benjamin Franklin Robbins, viewed the events. It was his opinion that the accused captain was definitively proven culpable yet wanted to be seen as a respectable citizen. Robbins used the term "mobocrats" to describe the men who stormed the stage. In using this term, he showed his dislike of anarchy, wishing that the discussion could remain civil.

Lucy Stone, noted suffragist and abolitionist, also spoke at the event. She stood with the rest of the committee, ready to accept her fate, but escaped unharmed. She was a recent graduate of Oberlin College at a time when women were banned from admittance to most institutions of

---

10. JJ Bangert, "The Harwich Port Race Riot of 1848."
11. JJ Bangert, "The Harwich Port Race Riot of 1848."

higher education. Stone felt that she had never encountered one group more desperate in determination than at the Harwich conference. The mob stood in defense of the American church.

Church, clergy, and theological seminary, everything, indeed, under ecclesiastical control needed to be directed to immediate freedom. The beliefs of Hon. James G. Birney, who was surely among Lucy Stone's choicest leaders and brightest lights, had his doctrines on trial and used the term, "the bulwark of slavery."

To add to this account of this remarkable scene, perhaps should be subjoined at least an excerpt of the official proceedings of the convention. The following is the final thought of the abolitionists. As an addendum, Parker Pillsbury related an illustrative truth in regard to a Cape Cod sea captain, a member of the Baptist church:

> The Methodist Discipline was provided for 'Separate Colored Conferences'. The Episcopal church shuts out some of its own most worthy ministers from clerical recognition, on account of their color. Nearly all denominations of religionists have either a written or unwritten law to the same effect. In Boston, even, there are Evangelical churches whose pews are positively forbidden by corporate mandate from being sold to any but 'respectable white persons'. Our incorporated cemeteries are often, if not always, deeded in the same manner. Even our humblest village graveyards generally have either a 'negro corner,' or refuse colored corpses altogether; and did our power extend to heaven or hell, we should have complexional salvation and colored damnation.[12]
>
> —Pillsbury letter, The North Star

After the conference, when Pillsbury ascertained that Brown and Foster were safe and that nothing more could be done, he, too, left, taking the public road toward the house of Captain Small, a well-known friend of the oppressed. The mobocrats returned to the grove, howling and yelling in their rage and disappointment that Foster was out of their clutches. When they found that Pillsbury was leaving, the mob followed him, screaming and yelling so loudly, it was heard from more than a mile away.

---

12. *North Star Free Press*, December 5, 1850.

The mob rushed on headlong, and then, though Pillsbury was walking only a short distance in front of them, they turned back to the grove, cursing as they went, and proceeded to vent their rage upon the platform, which they soon demolished.

A further observation on this event was later written by Harwich captain Jonathan Walker in 1843 while he was still imprisoned and awaiting trial for his role in slave trading. It bears directly to the events unfolding here. He kept a journal in which he commented on slavery articles listed in any American paper while he was spending a full year in the custody of a Florida jail.

> *Some editorials of the Barnstable Patriot have gone forth, to prejudice the people's mind against every reasonable measure calculated to aid the abolition of slavery, and to cherish a pro-slavery feeling, and a most unsocial and unchristian spirit. I lament the depravity and lack of dignity which seem to preside over the genius of the editor.*[13]

There is small doubt that using enslaved people to bolster a local or federal economy was the most polarizing issue of the day. In Cape Cod, the pro and anti groups discussing slavery were well established and held firm to their convictions.

The Second Harwich Antislavery Conference of 1860

On September 22, 1860, just before the start of the Civil War, there was another antislavery convention held in Harwich. Captain Gilbert Smith was chosen as chairman. The discussions were loud and passions were as real as ever. The abolitionists felt the oppression of the Fugitive Slave Act in every corner of the country.

People can never be free if an accusation of being a slave enchains them. The enforcement of the Fugitive Slave Act created an intentional police force where every private citizen was guilty of committing a crime by saying nothing if they saw a runaway or by assisting slaves in any capacity to seek shelter. William Lloyd Garrison wanted to go on a formal record denouncing the unjust laws that prevented anyone from responding morally in a civil society.

13. Alvin F. Oickle, 213.

Abolitionists at the second Harwich Cape Cod conference passed five resolutions published in *The Liberator* and used them as a battle cry to fight these injustices as a prelude to war. Garrison claimed the following points must be observed:

1. *That since our first duty in relationship to a sin against God, and a crime against humanity, is the immediate repentance and abandonment of it. Therefore, the main issue of the American Anti-Slavery Society is the natural and exhaustless source of all abominations established and sustained by state law and entrenched within the constitution. Its continued existence is the utter subversion of liberty, law, and religion.*
2. *That the American Union being a confederacy of free and slave states in which the latter are bound to recapture slaves is a bold and impious conspiracy against justice and humanity. We need to raise the war cry of the Abolitionists: "No union with slave holders."*
3. *That while we regard the Republican Party as the outgrowth of having an unholy alliance with slave holders and slave-traders as expounded by Clay and Webster, we renounce their remorseless pledge to keep four million slaves to perish under chains and require that every Northern voter should save his own soul, lifting the oppressive yoke from the bondmen of the south.*
4. *That the continuous use of slave-hunting upon the soil of Massachusetts should be as revolting to the moral sense of people as disgraceful to the high religious character of our ancestors, pledging a law for its immediate prohibition.*
5. *That it is our duty as Americans for us all to work for a proposed law ending the plague of Southern slavery.*[14]

These resolutions inflamed the theme of slavery, leading to an immediate call to action—changes needed to be addressed at once. One explanatory rationale for why this conference was held in Harwich underscores the role that Cape Cod sea captains played in the pro-slavery and antislavery movements. Sailors such as Austin Bearse and Jonathan

---

14. *Harwich Chronicle*, September 24, 1850.

Walker wanted to rescue slaves immediately, while many other captains saw the end of slavery as a definite detriment to the open aspects of positive maritime opportunities.

The crucial role of the Massachusetts people was reinforced in the book, *Massachusetts and the Civil War*. The editors cite many examples of how the Bay State led the way in hastening the advent of war. "Bay Staters wielded an influence over the fate of the nation in the Civil War Era out of proportion to the commonwealth's population and electoral weight to the union."[15]

Antislavery made Massachusetts the headquarters of abolitionism in the country, yet the state also figured prominently in the preservation of the union and was counted significantly in various conservative circles. The schism between a fast-paced freeing of slaves and slower-track efforts reveals how difficult a national compromise was to achieve.

The political divisions were apparent in the words uttered in the Union Club of Boston,[16] first formed by members of the elite Boston gentlemen's club called the Somerset Club. Factions disagreed over whether to support the Union cause during the Civil War or to remain neutral. Different members of the club split along political lines. In response, defectors formed the Union Club, which demanded "unqualified loyalty to the constitution and the Union of our United States, and unwavering support of the Federal Government in effort for the suppression of the rebellion."[17] This ability to forge a common consensus became a model for the country.

Out of many people clamoring for peace, Governor John A. Andrew is credited for his role as a skilled negotiator brokering new alliances. It was Governor Andrew who mobilized the 54th Voluntary Massachusetts Regiment of all Blacks to serve in the Civil War.

15. Matthew Mason, Kathryn P. Viens, and Conrad Edick Wright, eds., *Massachusetts and the Civil War: The Commonwealth and National Disunion* (Boston: University of Massachusetts Press, 2015), 78.

16.

17. The Union Club, "History," The Union Club. https://www.unionclub.org/The_Club/History (accessed March 24, 2023).

CHAPTER THIRTEEN

The Antislavery Movement Originated in Boston

Between 1834 and 1835, the New England Anti-Slavery Society was formed, later changing its name to the Massachusetts Anti-Slavery Society. This was a group of highly socially active, motivated people who aspired to start a new movement designed to win over the moral conscience of the times.

The society employed loyal, confidential workers, gentlemen of capacity, wit, and compassion, who largely contributed to the advancement of the cause. The Massachusetts Anti-Slavery Society's fourth annual meeting was held in January 1836 in Boston. Its scheduled arranged meetings were important enough to be used in the whole of a church or a public hall big enough to accommodate its large membership. Due to safety concerns, they were often forced to meet in smaller rooms on Washington Street, which were used for executive committee meetings and other typical assemblages during the year.

WILLIAM STILL

William Still was a key figure in the antislavery cause. Born in 1821 as a freeman to enslaved parents, William sympathized strongly with the runaway oppressed people. At a young age, he secured a position as an assistant clerk in the Philadelphia Anti-Slavery Society office. He quickly gained literacy skills and was a valuable data gatherer of information on which sea captains were amenable to transporting slaves seeking freedom and which captains could not be trusted. His multiple connections with sailing ships, sea captains, and customs officials earned him the title of "Father of the Underground Railroad."

Still knew the trade routes and ship schedules that opened doors for slaves to book passage to a friendly Northern city. He was perhaps one of the major communicators for the Boston antislavery escape route, becoming the eyes, ears, and even voice of many. Working in concert with people such as John Brown and Harriet Tubman, Still led the struggle for Black freedom, risking his own safety along the way. For him, the success of the Underground Railroad was crucial.

His Railroad system was the cultivation of extensive maritime connections and seafaring treks. Boston, New Bedford, Providence, and Philadelphia were the principal ports involved in runaway escape by sea. Still was in frequent contact with men such as Garrison, Bearse, and Walker to effectuate details and make critical connections.

WILLIAM LLOYD GARRISON

Of course, the leader of the antislavery movement in the country was William Lloyd Garrison, born in Newburyport, Massachusetts. His publication of *The Liberator* was the spark that woke up America. His firm belief that slavery had to end "immediately" was contested by Southerners, politicians, religious leaders, and presidents. He was strident in his belief that slavery was the biggest stain on the American soul.

Garrison led the publication of *The Liberator* and played a major role in organizing a new movement aimed at the complete abolition of slavery in the United States. By January 1832, he had amassed enough supporters to establish the New England Anti-Slavery Society, which grew to have several thousand members by the following summer. In December 1833, abolitionists from ten states came together to form the American Anti-Slavery Society. The New England society was reorganized in 1835 as the Massachusetts Anti-Slavery Society to allow state societies to form in the other New England states. His leadership remained the hub of antislavery agitation throughout the antebellum period. Many of his groups were organized by women who responded to Garrison's appeals for women to actively participate in the abolitionist cause. The largest of these groups was the Boston Female Anti-Slavery Society. They raised funds to support *The Liberator*, published antislavery pamphlets, and conducted antislavery petition drives.

William Lloyd Garrison on Commwealth Avenue, Boston, Massachusetts

The purpose of the American Anti-Slavery Society was to transform the American mindset to the philosophy that "Slaveholding is a heinous crime in the sight of God" and that "duty, safety, and best interests of all concerned, require its *immediate abandonment* without expatriation."[1]

HARRIET BEECHER STOWE

Harriet Beecher Stowe lived in Andover from 1852 to 1864 while her husband Calvin E. Stowe was a professor at the Andover Theological Seminary. Originally, the Stowe house was located on the seminary's property but was moved to 80 Bartlett Street in 1929 when Phillips Academy decided to replace it. This property was so beloved that the couple requested burial rights there.

---

1. Encyclopedia Brittanica, online, s.v. "American Anti-Slavery Society."

Harriet decided to bring *Uncle Tom's Cabin* to life for several reasons. Her father was Lyman Beecher, a devout and pious man. As a child, she was raised in a home with strict religious principles. Her favorite book was *The Pilgrim's Progress*, an analogy of proper Christian life. Her dad would quiz her on various scenes and characters. Her perception of values strongly followed the examples of Jesus Christ.

In the summer of 1849, Harriet's eighteen-month-old son, Samuel Charles, died of cholera. This crushing grief deeply moved her and was blended into *Uncle Tom's Cabin*. Stowe stated it helped her understand the pain that enslaved mothers might feel when their children were stripped away from them.

Another rationale for the story was to highlight the evil that the 1850 Fugitive Slave Act brought to the continuation of enslaved people. Several allegorical passages in the book attempt to draw out the injustices of cruelty to others. Harriet was strongly and deeply upset.[2]

In one section of *Uncle Tom's Cabin*, St. Clare reads the Bible to Tom. The last judgment parable in Matthew 25 tells us that upon our final days, we are judged according to how we treat the poor. In hearing these words, Tom can almost see himself in a mirror. He reflects on how he is treated as a person. How many individuals are living good and respectable lives but not troubling themselves to ask, "How much am I doing to assist my brethren who thirst, are sick, or are in prison?"

Later in the book, Stowe shows how the devil can also quote the good book when Simon Legree demands Tom to whip a fellow slave. Legree says the Bible tells us to obey our master. Tom, however, realizes that this request is taken out of context. If a semi-literate slave can reason so effectively, why then do some feel that the Bible supports the concept of "mastery of people" against the true spirit of Christ, who demands us to love our neighbors as ourselves?

The minute details of life on the plantation were gathered in two ways. The perspective on how slaves felt and viewed their own existence was compared to the witness of a Cape Cod sea captain. Austin Bearse offered a most unusual insight on the whole matter. He started as a slave trader who separated whole families on the slave auction block, but he later converted to the abolitionist cause, saving many souls who yearned

---

2. Nancy Koester, *Harriet Beecher Stowe: A Spiritual Life* (Grand Rapids: Eerdmans Publishing, 2014), 77.

for independence. He witnessed the two sides of the Northern and Southern perceptions and articulated these views in his conversations with Stowe.

Even within the text of *Uncle Tom's Cabin*, there are two competing plot lines.[3] The two plots both begin on a Kentucky farm. In one setting, the poor docile slave is sold to a Southern farmer, taken away from his wife and children to eventually face death at the discretion of a sadistic overseer. In the other setting, Elisa Harris runs to the North with her child, desperately jumping on various ice floes to cross the Ohio River with her husband, who declares, "I want a nation of me own." We surmise that the ultimate happy ending will reside in the voyage

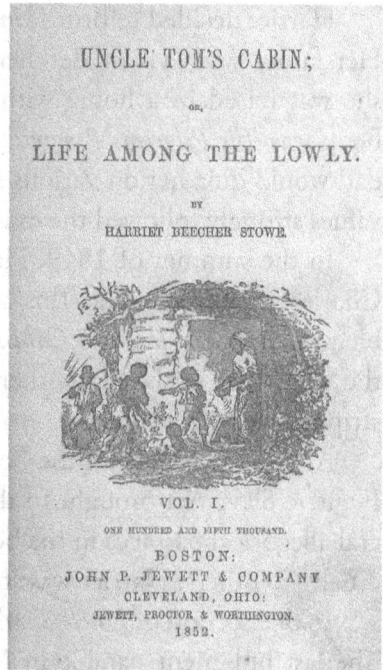

Uncle Tom's Cabin *cover*

to Liberia. The husband states, "The whole continent of Africa opens before us and our children."

Many years after the book's publication, Stowe reflected on the ending and felt she made a major mistake. She believed she gave into the greatest politically expedient response. If the slaves could just agree to leave the continent, all would be well. In fact, having a diversified and integrated nation is by far a morally superior way to go. Nonetheless, the book did achieve its desired goal. The nation was strongly riled and aroused by its content, resulting in being the first book to ever have been banned in several Southern states.

When President Lincoln met Stowe after the Civil War, he declared, "So you're the little woman who wrote the book that made this great war!" Though this comment is often related, the story and the quote are considered by scholars as an apocryphal anecdote, one for which there is no documentable writing by either Lincoln or found by other historians.

---

3. Holly Jackson, 77.

CHAPTER FOURTEEN

Noteworthy Black Slaves Residing in Massachusetts

People are unaware of the many Black slaves coming from Massachusetts who have amazing and inspirational stores. Within this group, there are famed abolitionists, military heroes, defendants accused of witchcraft, celebrated authors, prominent clergymen, and escapees capable of enacting bold and ingenious schemes to gain their freedom. How these escape stories unfolded are worthy of acknowledgment.

TITUBA

The Salem Witch Trials

The first Massachusetts slave to be discussed was the central figure at the start of the Salem Witch Trials. Tituba was one of the first people accused of practicing witchcraft. She was a slave owned by Samuel Parish, living in Salem. Tituba's accuser was her owner's wife, Elizabeth Parish. It is believed that Abigail Williams, a neighbor, saw Tituba practicing some variations of voodoo, which were typical in her former country.

Before any formal accusations were made, Tituba told the local young ladies some lurid tales of black magic and witchcraft. Despite being a Black slave, she was allowed to speak against other white accusers because it was not illegal for slaves to give testimony in court. She became the first person to confess to practicing witchcraft in the village of Salem. In January 1692, after initially denying her involvement in witchcraft, Tituba confessed to making a "witch cake." However, she only confessed to making this cake after her male owner severely beat her.

Tituba also confessed to speaking directly with the devil. In her confession, she stated that the devil ordered her to worship him and then hurt the children of the village. When she was questioned later, she said that she had learned about occult techniques from her mistress in Barbados.

Her testimony made the devil come alive in this pre-colonial village. She later fully recanted her sworn oaths, but by then, it was too late. Between June 1692 and May 1693, twenty-five innocent women, men, and children lost their lives. Tituba's life was spared, but she spent years in a Boston jail. Eventually a benevolent benefactor paid her fines, and she was ordered to return to servitude.

CRISPUS ATTUCKS

Killed at the Boston Massacre

A few days before the Boston Massacre, there was an incident that led up to it. On February 22, 1770, a group of patriots protested at the store of a British loyalist, Theophilus Lillie. Ebenezer Richardson, a customs officer, tried unsuccessfully to break up the assembled crowd. The patriots despised Richardson because he was spying on patriot activities and informing the British. When Richardson tried to rip down one of the patriot's signs, the crowd threw rocks at him, chasing him to his home. Richardson remained in his house as the small mob continued to throw rocks. When he fired his gun into the crowd, he hit Christopher Seider, an eleven-year-old, who died that evening. In the wake of Seider's funeral, several more fights broke out between British soldiers and local city workers.

Eleven days later, Private Hugh White stood outside the Custom House on King Street, protecting the king's treasury. Angry colonists confronted him with verbal insults, and after growing angry in return, White hit a colonist with his bayonet. Now incited, the colonists threw snowballs, ice, and rocks at him. More colonists arrived upon hearing the commotion of White calling for reinforcements. Violence escalated. A voice from the crowd yelled, "Fire." Several British soldiers fired while others followed suit. In all, five colonists were killed: Crispus Attucks, Samuel Gray, James Caldwell, Samuel Maverick, and Patrick Carr.

Crispus Attucks was among the first of the patriots killed by virtue of two musket balls lodged in his chest. He was a sailor of mixed African and Indigenous ancestry. This death of five men at the hands of the 29th Regiment was later called the Boston Massacre. Death instantly transformed Attucks from an anonymous Black sailor in Boston to a martyr for the revolutionary cause.

Not much is known about his life. We know he was a sailor, born in Framingham, Massachusetts. He was most likely a current resident of New Providence in the Bahamas, sailing on a ship destined for North Carolina. His last name, "Attucks," is of Indigenous origin, derived from the Natick word for "deer." The testimony from the British soldiers' trial interchangeably used "mulatto" or "Indian" to describe him, indicating his mixed African and Indigenous roots.

It was common in the colonial era for enslavers to give their slaves an Ancient Roman name. Attucks shared his name, "Crispus," with the son of Emperor Constantine. His name also appears in a 1750 advertisement in the *Boston Gazette* in which William Brown of Framingham called for the return of a twenty-seven-year-old man named "Crispas," described as a six-foot, two-inch "mulatto."[1] This advertisement suggests Attucks was a runaway slave.

On March 5, 1770, witnesses at the trial described Attucks at the front of a group of people armed with clubs, marching toward King Street. He led a crowd, hurling rocks, snowballs, ice, and verbal insults against the British soldiers. British Private Montgomery fired into the crowd along with the other soldiers. Two musket balls ripped through Attucks's chest, killing him instantly. Attucks and Caldwell had no family or connections in Boston, so their bodies lay in state at Faneuil Hall for public viewing.

John Adams, who defended the soldiers in the subsequent trial, described the crowd as aggressors, justifying the killing. He alluded to the jury's prejudices about race and class, describing the crowd as "a motley rabble of saucy boys, Negroes, and mulattos, Irish rabble and outlandish jack tars."[2] In truth, those in the crowd were young, lower-class, Black, Irish, and sailors from out of town. Adams' argument was enough—only Hugh Montgomery and Matthew Kilroy were convicted of manslaughter. The other soldiers were acquitted. It appears as if both

---

1. New England Historical Society, "Christopher Seider: The First Casualty in the American Revolutionary Cause," New England Historical Society, https://newenglandhistoricalsociety.com/christopher-seider-the-first-casualty-in-the-american-revolutionary-cause/ (accessed January 20, 2024).

2. National Park Service, "Crispus Attucks," National Park Service, https://www.nps.gov/people/crispus-attucks.htm (accessed March 12, 2023).

The Boston Massacre

sides of the confrontation acted rashly and without due deliberation. This event surely further sparked the patriot call for liberty.

Town officials buried Attucks and Caldwell in the Granary Building Cemetery. Today, they share one headstone facing Tremont Street.

MARY DUNN (1778–1850)
Underground Railroad Agent

There were many unverified myths and legends about a slave named Mary Dunn who lived in Barnstable County. In fact, she lived in the 6A section very near to where today's Cummaquid Golf Course is located, and a major street still bears her name. She was a free slave who most likely came to Cape Cod from a home in the South. Many people claimed she was a witch with mystical powers. When a Swedish vessel ran aground on Sandy Neck in Sandwich, a few witnesses claimed she was present at the event and that, by sheer force of will, she detoured the ship from a sandy bottom and extricated it to safety.

We know she was of combined Indigenous and Black heritage and asserted ancestry from Western Africa. In 1807, she married a local fisherman. As a team, they tended to the many needs of people from Yarmouth and Dennis. If people needed food, she provided it. She famously produced "yarb beer," a potent and popular beverage enjoyed by many people of Cape Cod.

She was a representative for the Underground Railroad, and when slaves presented themselves as fugitives, she had the knowledge and connections to help them. More than one runaway slave was directed to her home for refreshments and given future directions.

In the summer of 1832, her husband was lost at sea, a frequent situation of the day. They had one daughter, Lucy, who also died at a young age. There is a record in the Barnstable paper of her having paid a fee of one dollar for the rental of a hearse used at her daughter's funeral.

Like many Blacks in the area, she subsisted modestly. She had a modicum of land and grew her own produce, which fed many people. Nonetheless, the county deemed her a pauper, entitling her to wood and some basic supplies. She had the option of living in an almshouse for the needy but was too proud to do so. Plus, her missionary work in the Underground Railroad would have been compromised.

As an enlightened woman, she valued her independence and preferred to fend for herself. This way of thinking led to her demise, as she was caught in a fire which burnt her and her house down to the ground. Women being burnt in their own kitchens was a major cause of mortality in those times.

ELLEN CRAFT (1826–1891)

A Boston Seamstress Who Passed as White

Ellen tried to take advantage of her light-skinned appearance to pass as white while traveling with William, her partner and a fellow slave, from the Deep South by train and boat to reach the North. She dressed as a man since, in that era, it was not at all customary for a white woman to travel alone, especially with a male slave. She faked illness to limit any long conversations with others. She was prevented from learning to read and write under threat of death while she was enslaved, so having the appearance of illness would prevent too much conversation. William pretended to be her personal servant. During that time, slaves frequently accompanied their male masters during travel, so the Crafts did not expect to be questioned.

To her shock, on one occasion, she was temporarily detained for questioning. A train official had demanded proof that William was indeed Ellen's property. Eventually, the two were finally released on the train due to the sympathy of many passengers and the conductor. Their escape is seen as one of the most ingenious plots in fugitive slave history, even more ingenious than that of Henry Box Brown, who once mailed his entire body in a wooden box to his familial connections in Philadelphia.

As a way of hiding in plain sight, the Crafts traveled on first-class trains and stayed in the finest hotels. Ellen was so convincing an actress that she once dined as a guest with a steamboat captain.

To avoid detection, Ellen changed her hair color to resemble that of a white complexion. She wore the appropriate clothing of a young man, traveling in a jacket and trousers that William purchased using his earnings as a cabinetmaker. William cut her hair short to add to her manly appearance. Ellen also practiced male gestures and the normal behaviors of white folks. She wore her right arm in a sling to hide that she could not write.

Ellen and William traveled to nearby Macon for a train to Savanah, Georgia. Although the Crafts had several close calls along the way, they were always successful in avoiding detection. On December 21, they boarded a ship for Philadelphia, where they arrived early Christmas morning.

Shortly after their arrival, abolitionists urged the Crafts to share their escape story in public lectures within abolitionist circles in New England. As part of a campaign to encourage those fleeing from bondage, abolitionists distributed a photograph of Ellen Craft posing in her escape clothes. The Crafts settled in the established free Black community on the north side of Beacon Hill in Boston and married in a Christian ceremony.

Over the next two years, the Crafts publicly recounted their escape and spoke out against slavery in speeches. Because societal demands generally disapproved of women speaking to public audiences of mixed gender, Ellen typically stood on the stage while William told their story. An article published in *The Liberator* on April 27, 1849, reported her addressing an audience of between eight hundred and nine hundred people in Newburyport.

Audiences were intensely curious about the young woman who had been so brave and displayed such confidence in her escape. The Fugitive Slave Act simplified the process by which people might be certified as slaves, requiring little documentation from slave catchers to recapture them or ever claim free Blacks who lacked credentials. Court commissioners appointed to hear such cases were paid more for a positive ruling that a person was indeed a slave.

A month after the new law was in effect, Ellen and William's former owner, Collins, sent two slave catchers, Willis H. Hughes and John Knight, to Boston to capture the Crafts. When the men arrived in Boston, both white and Black Bostonians stood for the Crafts. Boston abolitionists had formed the biracial Boston Vigilance Committee to resist the new slave bill, and its members protected the Crafts by moving them to various "safe houses" until they could leave the country. The two bounty hunters finally gave up and returned to the South.

Collins appealed to President Millard Fillmore, asking him to help regain Collins's "rightful property." Showing his support for slavery, the president agreed that the Crafts should be returned to Collins, and he authorized the use of military force to ensure it.

Fearing possible troubles, the Crafts traveled to England, where Ellen learned to read and write. She published an article that was widely circulated in the abolitionist press in both the United Kingdom and the U.S. in 1852. The press in the U.S. had suggested the Crafts regretted their flight to England. She said:

> So, I write these few lines merely to say that the statement is entirely unfounded, for I have never had the slightest inclination whatever of returning to bondage. God forbid that I should ever be so false to liberty as to prefer slavery in its stead.

In fact, since my escape from slavery, I have gotten much better in every respect than I could have possibly anticipated. I would much rather starve in England, a free woman, than be a slave for the best man that ever breathed upon the American continent.[3]

The Crafts spent nineteen years in England, where they had five children together. Ellen participated in reform organizations such as the London Emancipation Committee, the Women's Suffrage Organization, and the British and Foreign Freedmen's Society.

They earned speaking fees through public lectures about slavery in the U.S. and their escape. William Craft set up a business again, but they still struggled financially. For most of their time in England, the Craft family lived in Hammersmith. Ellen turned their home into a hub of Black activism, inviting fellow Black abolitionists to stay.

After the American Civil War ended, Ellen found her mother in Georgia and paid for her passage to England, where they were reunited. Once in Georgia, she founded a school for slaves to pay for her own freedom.

Ellen authored *Running a Thousand Miles to Freedom*, which became a popular book. The Crafts returned to William's home state of Georgia in 1868, where they started an agricultural school.

Ellen Craft, escaped slave

JOHN MASHOW (1805–1885)

Born a Slave to Become a Master Shipbuilder

The great shipping fleets of Wellfleet in the early 1800s had to be built. One of the least known but perhaps among the prime ship designers of

---

3. Ellen Craft, *The Antislavery Advocate*, December 1852.

this era was John Mashow. He was born in 1805 as a result of the union between a slave and a South Carolina planter. An excellent student who showed promise as an able carpentry worker, he was noticed by John Michaux, a local shipbuilder. He took John into his care, encouraging him to apprentice in the shipyards of South Carolina.

When Mashow's father died in 1815, there was a provision in the planter's will that his adopted son must become a free man upon his death. His next ship tutor had even more of a solid reputation in the maritime world. Laban Thatcher had constructed many coastal vessels used by the Southern fleet. By the age of twenty-seven, his renown as a shipbuilder had reached such a level that he could strike out on his own. His journey to Massachusetts permitted him even more opportunities as the demand for newer, bigger ships was certainly in vogue in that region.

Laban Thatcher was a greatly respected merchant. Much of his work involved building boatyards, ships, and even whole villages. Laban established the quant village of Padanaram (also known as South Dartmouth) as a reference to a biblical figure.

John designed merchant vessels for Thatcher for the next twenty-eight years. When acquiring his new location near New Bedford, he claimed twenty-eight fishing schooners, nineteen whalers, and two sloops as fully completed at his site on the Apponagansett River. Wellfleet sailors requested one-third of these ships. One of John's master ship creations was the *Maria Theresa*, built with Captain George Baker's design input.

One reason fishing became such a profitable industry for Wellfleet sailors was the greater speed and expanded cargo space that a newer, well-designed ship could offer. As a ship architect, John paid great attention to finer lines and sharper bows with a larger sail area. These features contributed to constructing a more competitive, larger, faster schooner that could haul larger commercial products to market. These newly built ships were used for coasting on the eastern shore or hauling oysters to the Boston Market.

As a student of ship architecture, John often first carved a half-model of the schooner's hull. Then he transferred lines from the sections of his model, creating an appropriate mold for shaping each of the vessel's oak frames. His building techniques were both innovative and cost-efficient.

His genius and creative joy brought joy to the owners of the shipbuilding industry. He was in great demand but stayed where he was, often
consulting with Captain George Baker of Wellfleet.[4] His ships were particularly attractive to the Baker family. Records indicate that David Baker
captained the *Baker* while *Maria Theresa* was the pride of George Baker.[5]

In his shipyard, Mashow supervised a crew of sixteen shipwrights and
carpenters. They would lay the keel and bow, cut and raise each frame,
and attach the planking so each ship would be a durable, seaworthy
schooner or whaler.

Mashow's life was profitable, contributing to the rise of the shipping
industry in the Wellfleet region. He became a proud father of five sons
who proudly called themselves whalers. Based on the written acclaim
and notes from the New Bedford Whaling Museum, a ship architect
committee awarded him the title of one of "the most important African
American figures involved in shipbuilding design."

BENJAMIN BOARDLEY (or Bradley) (1836–1902)
First Black Boat Designer of Note

Benjamin Boardley was born into slavery in Anne Arundel, Maryland,
in March 1836. According to the Maryland State Manumission records,
Boardley's owner was John T. Hammond.

As a teenager, Boardley worked at a printing office. He showed ingenuity and strong mechanical skills by the age of sixteen. He built a steam
engine from a gun barrel, pewter, round steel, and various materials. His
master was so impressed, he secured Boardley a position in the Department of Natural and Experimental Philosophy at the Naval Academy at
Annapolis. At Annapolis, Boardley worked as a general helper. According
to the *African Repository* of 1859, he was paid in full for his work, but the
money he made went directly to his master, who allowed Boardley to keep
five dollars a month for himself.[6] As a helper at the Academy, Boardley
helped establish several science experiments involving chemical gases.

Boardley's professors at the Naval Academy were fascinated with him.
Professor Hopkins of the Naval Academy wrote about Boardley's work as

4. Rowland Bowers, "Two Exceptional Men: Fishing Schooners, and Wellfleet," *Fishing Alliance*, May 2018, 12.
5. Skip Finley, "From Slavery to Master Ship Builder and Designer," *Sea History* Vol. 176 (Spring 2021), 23.
6. Allison Rupert, "Benjamin Bradley," *Black Past*, Vol. 6 (February 21, 2009), 11.

a helper, noting that Boardley would set up experiments rapidly. He was a quick learner, declaring that "he always looks for the scientific law by which things act."[7] Professor Hopkins's children taught Boardley how to read, write, and do more complex math, such as algebra and geometry.

With the money he earned from selling the steam engine and the money saved while working at the Academy, he designed a steam engine large enough to run the first mechanical sloop of war, exceeding 16 knots per hour. He sold this model engine to a classmate from the Naval Academy and then used the proceeds to build the "first steam-powered warship." Because he was enslaved, Boardley could not receive a patent for the engine he developed. He could, however, sell the design. He used these profits, plus the money given to him by professors at the Naval Academy, to obtain his freedom at the cost of $1,000. According to Maryland state records, Boardley was manumitted from his owner, John T. Hammond, on September 30, 1859, in Anne Arundel County, Maryland.

The U.S. Naval Academy was temporarily relocated to Newport, Rhode Island, during the Civil War. According to the African Repository for August 1865, Boardley was employed as a freeman at the U.S. Naval Academy.

General view of the Naval Academy, Annapolis, Maryland

---

7. Allison Rupert, 17.

In Newport, Rhode Island, where he worked under the supervision of Professor A.W. Smith, Boardley continued constructing small steam engines and showing his ingenious mechanical skills. He worked as an instructor in the Philosophical Department at the Naval Academy in 1864. He received credit for designing and constructing a "miniature steam engine and boiler using about 6-fly power."[8]

According to the 1900 U.S. Census, Boardley was sixty-four years old and lived in Mashpee, Massachusetts. His occupation was listed as "philosophical lecturer."

COLLINS STEVENSON (1847–1904)
A Black Whaling Captain

Before abolishing slavery in the United States, Black people were denied the right to work in most professions. Even if they made an income, their money went directly to their owner. One clear exception to this rule was in the whaling industry. Although not completely color-blind, what mattered most to whaling shipowners was the sailor's personal ability to handle a sail, toss a harpoon, and work tirelessly on a voyage filled with many dangerous aspects. Whaling was an egalitarian trade that welcomed people of every race, ethnicity, color, and background.

During the 1700s, Indigenous tribe members of the Wampanoags and the Aquinnah comprised most of a whaling crew. European whaling captains typically gave the commands and acquired large shares of wealth. In the 1800s, Black sailors comprised at least one-third of the whaling contingency. Their share of the financial bottom line often was equitably distributed to the whole crew. Throughout the early nineteenth century, whaling, especially the demand for whale oil, remained the third-largest business in Massachusetts and the fifth most profitable business in the country.

Captain Collins Stevenson was a well-established Black whaler. He was born in 1847 in St. Vincent in the West Indies and came to America at the age of eighteen. As a youth, he volunteered enthusiastically as an ordinary sailor, slowly but surely mastering the necessary steps to reach the status of master sailor. He became a shipmaster of the *Carrie D.*

---

8. Allison Rupert, 19.

Knowles at forty-two. Records indicate that when several whaling captains engaged in only a few whaling voyages throughout their careers, Stevenson engaged in at least eighteen different trips.

Immediately after the Civil War, seven Black whaling captains were sailing out of Provincetown. One of the principal owners of whaling ships, including the *Carrie D. Knowles*, was also Black—George A. Knowles. During his tenure as a captain, he brought in whale oil valued today at a rate of $3.1 million. An interesting footnote is that none of the Provincetown whalers were initially born into slavery. They were free men who fought for the privilege of working on a fishing boat on an even basis with other seamen. Stevenson's wealth allowed him to rise to become a lead mason in the King Hiram's Lodge.

In January 1904, Stevenson ventured out on a whaling expedition on the *Carrie D. Knowle*s with a crew of twelve sailors and never returned. His typical fishing trips would last approximately twenty days. While there is still a shroud of mystery as to what truly happened, there are three theories. Two basic ones were common during that time: a terrible storm at sea, or perhaps a ferocious whale capsized the ship. However, a third potential theory has emerged.

An American seaman claimed that this crew was held prisoner in a Venezuelan prison. Senator Henry Cabot Lodge examined this story but could not reach a firm conclusion. It was either a cruel hoax or a true story. One sad consequence of this representation was that the wife of Captain Knowles, Hannah, had definitive plans to remarry. Once she had learned even of the remote possibility that her husband may not have been lost at sea and was still alive, she decided to remain unwed. However, Captain Knowles never returned from his trip, nor did she ever remarry.

SOJOURNER TRUTH
Renowned Speaker

The Northampton Association of Education and Industry (NAEI) was an abolitionist community founded in northern Massachusetts in the 1840s. "The Community" lived by a set of daily morality-based principles, attracting some of the most prominent abolitionists to visit and settle there.

In 1842, ten families banded together to form the NAEI in a sparsely settled section of town (later renamed Florence). They formed "a better and purer form of society."[9] By purchasing a large four-story silk mill and several acres of workable farmland, they encouraged other like-minded families to join them and reside within or near the community. Families who eventually signed on lived on the top two floors of the mill building in a community setting, "sitting at a common table," sharing meals, living quarters, housekeeping, and factory duties.

These members were dedicated reformists who pointed a critical finger at the many in the nation and how they chose to live. The NAEI supported the immediate abolition of slavery and full rights of citizenship for free Black Americans. They enacted full equality in their community life as a model for others. This stance was deemed the most radical for its time. The group attracted several well-known African American speakers to join, such as David Ruggles and Sojourner Truth. Other African American families, many of whom had fled slavery, felt encouraged to settle near the Massachusetts community.

They dedicated themselves to ending slavery in the South and addressing the growing social inequality in the industrial North. The NAEI's 120 members voted to abolish fixed wages within the community. Instead, they instituted a system of profit sharing. The silk business that supported them was meant to provide an alternative to slave-produced cotton fabric. It was run as a worker-owned cooperative, competing with the textile mills in Lowell and the eastern part of the Commonwealth.

Sojourner Truth was originally a slave from New York State. Her rights as chattel property were exchanged by four different owners. She is indeed a unique figure, as she was an antislavery advocate and a feminist seeking the rights of women to be treated equally to men. She never saw these two different issues as being mutually exclusive. One of her famous quotes was "Truth is powerful, and it endures."[10]

Her freedom was finally secured when a Quaker family paid for her freedom. She had sufficient funds to bring a slaveowner to court, challenging his rights to enslave her daughter. Sojourner won that case,

---

9. David Ruggles Center for History and Education, "A Utopian Community in Florence, MA," https://davidrugglescenter.org/northampton-association-education-industry/ (accessed April 14, 2023).
10. David Ruggles Center for History and Education, "A Utopian Community in Florence, MA."

maintaining her rights as a parent. She converted to Methodism and was invited to speak on behalf of other enslaved people. Much of her logic and fundamental reasoning was predicated on religious terms. Whenever the issue of gender superiority arose, she asked an appropriate question: "Where did Jesus come from? Why, Mary, of course."

When Frederick Douglass argued for the Black man to vote, and Elizabeth Cady Stanton protested for the rights of women to cast a ballot, above all people, Sojourner wanted Black women to be free, serving as full-fledged American citizens. Her voice was loud, and her message was clear—Black women warranted being seen and treated equally to any white man. In the 1851 women's convention in Akron, Ohio, she resented the use of the term "the weaker sex" and projected women as the stronger of the two sexes. Her speech, "Ain't I a Woman," was celebrated as a brilliant piece of oratory.

PHILLIS WHEATLEY
Poet Recognized by the Queen

Born in West Africa and sold as an enslaved eight-year-old child to the Wheatley family of Boston, Phillis Wheatley was the first African American to have published a complete book of poetry. She was brought to the United States aboard a vessel captained by Peter Gwinn and owned by Timothy Fitch, an active slave trader in the mid-1700s. She was aptly named Phillis in honor of the ship that brought her to America. The Wheatleys own eighteen-year-old daughter, Mary, was her first instructor. By the age of twelve, Phillis mastered Greek and Latin classics, becoming consumed by ancient poems.

She soon wrote several poems herself. Her first poem, "To the University of Cambridge in New England," displayed elements of Homer and Virgil. Encouraged by Mary to have her poems published, Phillis was brought to London, where she met the Lord Mayor and other British elites. Finally, the Countess of Huntingdon took a strong interest and had her work published. The queen even invited her to present at Buckingham Palace.

Pleased by her success as a writer and being a generous family, the Wheatleys manumitted her. Now the twenty-year-old author could live freely. In 1775, she sent a copy of a poem paying homage to the cause of the American Revolution. It was titled "To his Excellency, George Washington." The general enjoyed the content so much that he invited her to visit his headquarters in Cambridge. This poem was later republished by Thomas Paine in the *Philadelphia Gazette*.

Unfortunately, the two adult members of the Wheatley family died in 1778, and the support for her art was lost. She met a local impoverished Black grocer with whom she had two children. When her husband, John, was brought to a debtor's prison, she had little choice but to work as a scullery maid at a boardinghouse to provide for her children. It was the first time that she was exposed to difficult manual labor. She would die five years later in poverty and was rarely recognized for her achievements.

HENRY BOX BROWN (1815 –1897)

Henry was a slave originally from Virginia who escaped from his master at the age of thirty-three. Being a trained magician, he knew the many secrets that could be hidden in a box. In 1849, he placed himself in a box and mailed himself to friendly connections in Philadelphia, who were pleased to help him. Aspects of his escape were assisted by William Still, who worked as an assistant in the antislavery office for the port of Philadelphia.

Henry Box Brown's exhibition "The Mirror of Slavery" opened in Boston in April 1850. Most of the panels in the maze depicted his own escape and the cruelty of slavery. Brown traveled with the exhibition throughout New England. In August, when the impending passage of the Fugitive Slave Act became a severe danger to his freedom, he became weary and decided to leave his role as a noted abolitionist speaker in the northeast United States. Late in 1850, he took his novel exhibition to Great Britain. Henry Box Brown's "Mirror of Slavery" opened in London shortly thereafter. He lived near London for twenty-five years and gained acclaim with his antislavery panoramas and his magical showman skills.

Brown married and started a family with an English woman, Jane Floyd. Nancy, his original partner, remained in the bonds of slavery. Brown returned to the United States with his English family in 1875 and continued earning a living as an entertainer. He toured and performed as a magician, speaker, and mesmerist, a format akin to hypnosis, lasting until 1889. The last decade of his life, from 1886 to 1897, was spent in Toronto, where he died.

JANE JOHNSON (1820–1872)
A Slave Freed by Abolitionists Moving to Boston

Jane Johnson was a slave whose escape to freedom was the focus of a precedent-setting legal case. Philadelphia abolitionists protected her during her escape in 1855, and she later settled in Boston, where she married. Her son Isaiah served in the Civil War with the 55th Massachusetts Regiment, U.S. Colored Troops.

As a slave in Pennsylvania, she boarded a ferry with her master, Wheeler—one that William Still also boarded. Still told Johnson that she could choose freedom according to Pennsylvania law. While Wheeler and Still were arguing, the owner offered her a promise of freedom, attempting to prevent Johnson from escaping. Five Black dockworkers restrained him while state law was explained to him. William Still quickly escorted Johnson and her children away by a coach, later taking them secretly to his house.

Pennsylvania passed a gradual abolition statute in 1780, which did not free any existing slaves but banned the slave trade in Pennsylvania and freed the children of slaves born after the law was passed once they reached a certain age. Thereafter, Philadelphia became a mecca for free Blacks in America.

Throughout the early 1800s, a steady stream of Black migrants hoping to escape slavery fled into Pennsylvania counties. By 1820, the city's Black population was nearly 11 percent of the total demographics. As the African American population grew, so did a degree of white hostility against them. It is documented that many African Americans were killed in the street and their houses burned during the Flying Horses race riot in Philadelphia in 1834.[11]

Wheeler took the case to court, and Jane Johnson returned from New York to testify during the trial. Her physical appearance created

---

11. Carol Faulkner, *Lucretia Mott's Heresy: Abolition and Women's Rights in Nineteenth-Century America* (Philadelphia: University of Pennsylvania Press, 2011), 65.

Jane Johnson's rescue from a ferry

quite a stir. She entered the court veiled and accompanied by several women abolitionists. They had managed to arrange for local and state officials to protect her.

Johnson made a lengthy statement in court, testifying to her plans to gain freedom on that trip and overturning claims made by Wheeler's attorney. She said, "I went with Still of my own free will."

Due to her testimony, Still and all three of the dockworkers were acquitted. Two dockworkers, John Ballard and William Curtis, were convicted of assault, fined $10, and imprisoned for a week.

It was a legal strategy, using a writ of habeas corpus to imprison a man and return a woman to slavery. Championing the rights of slaveholders to travel to the free states with their slaves despite state laws banning slavery became awkward. Though embedded in convoluted legal speech, the court's decision to imprison Williamson was rooted in the commonplace racist logic of the time.

State and local officials protected Johnson after her brilliant testimony in court freeing slaves. She and her sons soon moved to Boston, where they eventually settled. She married again there.

MARY WALKER

Devoted Mother Seeking Freedom

In 1848, Mary was brought to the Cambridge home of Mildred Cameron, where Mary cared for her medical needs for several years.[12] Mary's skin was so light that she could pass for white. Duncan Cameron, her owner, first perpetuated the ruse that she was not a Black slave but a family member. However, concerned she might flee from his home, Duncan Cameron beat her viciously, knocking out four teeth. After this attack, he could no longer continue with the deception that she was a freed woman.

In time, a pregnant Susan Lesley came to the Boston area, and Mary tended to her needs. Mary was an excellent, obedient servant. She was given the title of the "most tender and judicious nurse one could ever expect" by the Cameron family. She also received a small annual stipend, which she carefully guarded as a vehicle to extradite her children from a North Carolina slave plantation.

Mary's separation from her children caused her great emotional and physical distress. When her situation became known to a mining professor at the University of Pennsylvania, Professor J.P. Lesley, he decided to champion her cause. He wrote a plaintiff plea to the mainstay of the Cameron family, Mildred Cameron, who at the time was one of the richest women in the world. Lesley begged her to consider releasing her children and accept payment for their freedom.

For Peter Lesley, as for many northern citizens, this was a difficult situation. He opposed slavery and wanted to avoid any direct abolitionist involvement. If he came out too strongly opposed to slavery, it could be deleterious to his career and even his personal safety. The severity of the punishments and sanctions for assisting slaves contained in the 1850 Fugitive Slave Act was immense. Many people even slightly sympathetic to the antislavery cause now had to choose which direction they might go.

In the 1850s, many slave catchers traveled to Boston to claim Black slaves to bring back south. Mary was now more concerned than ever. There could never be a complete haven of repose. Nonetheless, friends and mariners associated with the Camerons secured a safe passage north

---

12. Sydney Nathans, *To Free a Family: The Journal of Mary Walker* (Cambridge: Harvard University Press, 2012), 57

and rejoined the mother and children. As long as the wealthy Cameron family lived on Brattle Street in Cambridge, she and her family would finally have the comfort and security of home and haven. The Brattle Street house stayed in the possession of the Walker family until 1912.

FREDERICK DOUGLASS
New Bedford Ship Carpenter

Frederick can claim Massachusetts as his desired home starting in 1837. He was born of the union of an enslaved mother and a European-descended owner. He never experienced full freedom, though he acquired many skills in his young life. His literacy skills grew throughout his adulthood as he met many wealthy abolitionists who saw great potential in him.

By mid-September, he was searching for a platform to demonstrate the many reasons slavery should be abolished. He had heard that New Bedford had a thriving population of free Black people who flourished in their personal behaviors. Having learned the art of caulking a boat at several local ports and being adept in maritime carpentry, he felt comfortable bringing his new wife to a locale where he could now operate as a free man.

Douglass used the term "the Upper-Ground Railroad" to define his escape from slave territory by boat compared to the Underground Railroad. He arrived via steamer to Newport, Rhode Island, then journeyed by stagecoach, moving pennilessly to the whaling city. Once in New Bedford, he arrived at the home of the free black Nathan Johnson, who paid for his ride and provided his first night of shelter. Nathan also suggested that Douglass change his last name, Johnson, as it was the most identifiable name of most Black men.[13] In his recent reading of *The Lady of the Lake*, he claimed the strength of the Highlander clan name of Douglass.

That year, New Bedford had a total population of about twelve thousand people, including one thousand Blacks, with three hundred being free men. The demand for experienced boat builders in this active whaling town was a huge draw for many a runaway. In 1840, the city grossed over seven million dollars in profits from whaling alone, as well as other profitable shipping ventures.

---

13. Kathryn Grover, *The Fugitive's Gibraltar: Escaping Slaves and Abolitionism in New Bedford, Massachusetts* (New Bedford: University of Massachusetts Press, 2001), 180.

Douglass never served as a whaler. He was amazed by the wide variety of career options for Blacks that he witnessed in this city during this time. The population was full of infinite eccentricities, such as wild men coming from the New England Hills and tribal men coming from the most distant ocean islands.

Both Herman Melville and Douglass were in the city from 1840–1841, and there is no record of the two men ever meeting, yet they both waxed on poetically to others about their experiences. Melville focused on the splendor of exciting maritime journeys, while Douglass was struck with the antislavery polemic. Douglass noted that his host, Nathan Johnson, lived in a better house and had more dignity than even poor white people from Baltimore. He was stunned that the Yankee industry could pay such beneficial dividends.

Douglass once knocked on the door of a prosperous house, asking if she needed help storing a recent delivery of coal into a bin. He did the job and was rewarded with two silver dollars for his efforts. He wrote, "My heart swelled. I had no master to take away my work. My hands were my own."

The antislavery movement now had a bright light for its lecture tour and was willing to purchase the freedom for this runaway. It seems ironic to mention, but Douglass earned the right to freely vote in New Bedford with the payment of a one-dollar-and-fifty-cent poll tax while he was living under an assumed name as an illegal fugitive. He later became a speaker, an advocate of human rights, and an esteemed author who would soon prompt many discussions that would greatly change his country.

HARRIET JACOBS

Author of *My Life as a Slave Girl*

Jacobs' owner, Mr. Norcom, frequently sexually harassed her, making Mrs. Norcom jealous. When Jacobs fell in love with a free Black man who wanted to marry her, Norcom quickly intervened and forbade her from even seeing the man she loved. But Jacobs needed protection from Norcom's persistent harassment. Jacobs willingly entered a relationship with a white lawyer, Samuel Sawyer, who came from a privileged white family. Sawyer would become the father of Jacobs's only children, Joseph, born in 1829, and Louisa, born in 1832. Upon learning of Jacobs's pregnancy, Mrs. Norcom misunderstood who the father was. She forbade Jacobs from returning to the house, thus Jacobs lived with her grandmother. Still, Mr. Norcom continued his sexual harassment during his numerous visits there. The new house was only six hundred feet away.

In April 1835, Mr. Norcom moved Jacobs from her grandmother to the plantation of his son. In June 1835, Harriet Jacobs escaped. A white woman, a slaveholder herself, hid Harriet in her house. After a short time, Jacobs had to hide in a swamp near the town, then at last found a small refuge in a "tiny crawlspace" under a garret, where she remained for several years. Infuriated, Mr. Norcom sold Jacobs's children and her brother, John, to a slave trader, demanding they be sold in different states. However, the trader was working for Sawyer and sold all three slaves to him.

In 1842, Jacobs escaped by boat to Philadelphia. After a short stay, she continued to New York City. In 1843, Jacobs heard that Mr. Norcom was on his way to New York to try to force her back into slavery, a legal right at the time. Finally, she arrived at John Willis's home in Boston.

Harriet Jacobs wrote from Boston to her grandmother, asking for her children. This move took Louisa Matilda, Jacobs's daughter, from a house in Brooklyn where she had not been treated much better than a slave.

In Boston, Jacobs took on odd jobs. Her stay there was interrupted by the death of her master, Mary Stace Willis, in March 1845. In a journal written by Harriet, she reflected on the sadness that enslaved Black women felt, often completely physically defenseless and emotionally unequipped if any owner had impure intentions. Her book was circulated widely.

LEONARD ANDREW GRIMES
The Preacher

Leonard Andrew Grimes grew up in Loudoun County, Virginia, before the Civil War. While in his twenties, he witnessed the brutality of slavery on a journey through the South, an experience that radicalized him. When he returned to Virginia, he committed to assisting freedom seekers.

While working as a hackman in the District of Columbia, Grimes discovered that his profession offered the perfect cover for helping fugitives escape Virginia. He helped an unknown number of slaves escape before he was finally arrested and convicted of crimes in 1839. He served two years of hard labor in the Richmond Penitentiary and paid a fine of $100. Upon his release, Grimes and his family settled in New Bedford, Massachusetts, then Boston, where Grimes became minister of the Twelfth Baptist Church.

With legions of self-emancipated slaves among its members, the Twelfth Baptist Church became known as "The Fugitive Slave Church." As a minister, Grimes mobilized the Black community of Boston against the Fugitive Slave Act. He raised funds for fugitive assistance and participated in every significant fugitive slave case, including those of Shadrack Minkins, Thomas Sims, and Anthony Burns. During the Civil War, Grimes joined the Black leaders calling for the enlistment of Black soldiers and was rewarded in 1863 with the creation of the 54th Massachusetts Regiment, one of the war's first African American regiments. The very first all-black unit in the Civil War was the First Kansas Colored Volunteer Infantry Regiment.

MINISTER CHARLES BENNETT RAY

Pastor of The Crosby Congregational Church

Charles Bennett Ray was a journalist, clergyman, and ardent abolitionist. He was born in Falmouth, Massachusetts, on December 25, 1807. In the 1830s, abolitionists sponsored his attendance at Wesleyan Seminary in Wilbraham, Massachusetts, to pursue theology. He continued his studies in Middletown, Connecticut, at Wesleyan University. After the first year, he felt the racial tension building up on campus against him. It was too much to take, so he resigned.

For five years, Ray worked on his grandfather's farm, then he left to pursue boot-making. He opened a boot and shoe store when he arrived in New York City in 1832. Ray then became a Methodist minister. He strongly believed he felt a calling to assist oppressed slaves, so he became a conductor for freedom. Word spread quickly that he was the local contact that would help. In his words: "I would often hear that knock on the door and understood my duty to serve."[14] He was known to have saved hundreds of poor, fleeing slaves, helping them make necessary connections.

---

14. N. Work, "The Life of Charles B. Ray," *Journal of African Studies* 4, no. 4 (2021): 70.

In 1833, Charles Ray joined the American Anti-Slavery Society. He devoted most of his life to the abolitionist movement. In 1837, Ray changed denominations, becoming a congregational minister. A decade later, he joined the ranks of the Vigilance Committee. In one famous situation, he was involved in saving thirteen Black and white men whom legal officials sought. In 1848, Ray rose to the rank of corresponding secretary for the Vigilance Committee, serving actively as a member for fifteen years. He forged a connection between the Boston and New York committees.

In 1837, he assumed pastoral duties at the prestigious, predominately white Crosby Congregational Church in New York City. Seven years after that, he served as the pastor of the Bethesda Congregational Church, another mostly white congregation, for two decades. During this period, he joined the American Missionary Association in spreading the temperance message. He was also a member of the New York Society for the Promotion of Education among Colored Children, and the African Society for Mutual Relief.

In 1838, Ray became the editor of *The Colored American*, the fourth weekly journal published by African Americans. Ray used *The Colored American* to promote the moral, social, and political elevation of the free colored people and the peaceful emancipation of the slaves. Through his paper, Ray supported the newly founded Liberty Party in 1840, the only political party at the time to publicly condemn slavery. Ray died in New York City on August 15, 1886, and was buried in Cypress Hills Cemetery in Brooklyn.

EDMUND KELLY (1818–1894)
National Baptist Leader

Edmund Kelly was the first African American Baptist minister ordained in Tennessee. He escaped to New England in the 1840s but returned to Tennessee after the Civil War. He worked as a preacher and teacher in Columbia, Tennessee, and frequently participated in national Baptist conventions.

Edmund Kelley was born in Columbia, Tennessee, on May 23, 1818, to Edmund Kelly, an emigrant from Ireland, and a slave woman,

Kittie White, who was also from Columbia. His father wished to buy the freedom of his mother and son but could not afford it. When Edmund was six, his mother was sold, yet his sister remained in slavery. In 1833, Kelly was hired by a teacher to run errands and serve as a table waiter. He saw the advantages to an education and secretly traded candy for spelling books and reading lessons. When the mistress discovered Kelly was learning to write, she became upset. However, she allowed it to continue, and Kelly continued to study, although he never attended a formal school.

In April 1837, Kelly was baptized and joined a missionary church in Columbia, then in October, he was ordained by Rev. R. B. C. Harell at the First Baptist Church, an Evangelist church. He was the first Black Baptist preracher ordained in Tennessee when he became preacher at Mt. Lebanon Baptist Church in 1843, which had six members. He is also credited for organizing the First Negro Baptist Church in Columbia in 1843.

Around this time, he escaped from slavery to Massachusetts on the Underground Railroad, then purchased the freedom of his wife and four children for twenty-eight hundred dollars. For this purpose, he collected money in New England as a guest preacher. He then ventured to England, where he decided to purchase his and his family's freedom so they could not be recaptured under the harshness of the Fugitive Slave Act. His children included W. D. Kelly, a member of the 54th Massachusetts Infantry Regiment in the U.S. Civil War. In 1848, he organized the 12th Baptist Church in Boston. Once fully free, Kelly moved to New Bedford, Massachusetts, where he was a leader in his church and the National American Baptist Conventions.

LEONARD BLACK

Author of *The Tortured Life of a Slave Boy*

Leonard Black was born into slavery in 1820 in Maryland, sixty miles south of Baltimore. As a young child, the slaveowner sold his mother in New Orleans. At six years old, he went to work for Mr. Bradford, who separated him from the rest of his family.

No one, who has always enjoyed the right of liberty, can realize the horrors of slavery. To be at the will of another, to be owned like a cow or horse, and

*liable at any moment to the highest bidder, to be transported to a distant part
of the country, leaving the dearest relatives behind; to be, in fine, ground down
mentally and physically by the untold curses of slavery, may be a very pretty thing
to the masters of the peculiar institution, but it is death to the slaves.*[15]

Mrs. Bradford beat Black and made her ten-year-old son spit in his face. When Black couldn't carry a bushel of corn, she hit him with a board, which cut his head so badly it bled more than a quart.[16]

After two years, Mr. Bradford placed Leonard with Mr. Bradford's father, fearing Mrs. Bradford would kill him. As it turned out, Mr. Bradford's father was even worse than Mrs. Bradford. Black used the term "backslider" in reference to the elder Bradford, which meant a "wanderer from God."[17]

Black lived with the senior Bradford for almost eight years. Black was without a hat and pants and had only one pair of shoes and a Lindsey slip. His meals were mere scraps from the table, eaten while standing, and he slept on a piece of carpet by the hearth. One day, when he returned from the cold after fetching wood, he went inside to get warm only to be denied comfort.

Finally, in 1837, Leonard Black escaped to Boston, working odd jobs along the way and evading his captors. Once in Boston, he asked about his brothers. He learned of a George Black, a minister living in Portland, Maine, and Leonard thought the man might be his brother. However, after traveling the distance, Leonard learned that George wasn't his brother, which was a big disappointment. However, George and his family kindly took Leonard in, clothed him, and taught him to read. Leonard found jobs as a farm laborer and as an engineer in a steam factory.

In 1838, he moved back to Boston with George, who became the minister of the African Meeting House on Belknap Street. Leaving his family in Boston, Black moved to Providence, where he lived with Francis Wayland, the president of Brown University. Leonard studied the Bible at the Meetinghouse Street Church. Leonard Black sold his books and worked on a canal boat until an accident almost killed him. In 1847,

---

15. Leonard Black, *The Life and Sufferings of Leonard Black, a Fugitive from* Slavery (New Bedford: New Bedford Press, 1847), 111.
16. Leonard Black, 35.
17. Leonard Black, 143.

he went to New Bedford to dictate his story, published as *The Life and Suffering of Leonard Black*. He preached in Nantucket in the 1850s and returned to Virginia after the war. He died on April 28, 1883, and more than five thousand people attended his memorial service. Every store that employed an African American in that city closed that day.

GEORGE TEAMOH (1818–1887)

From Slave to Congressman

George Teamoh was born enslaved in Norfolk, Virginia. He acquired literacy abilities easily by listening to white children. As a youth, he would sing the alphabet and identify words on handbills and posters. In later years, he found a copy of John T. Walker's *A Critical Pronouncing Dictionary and Expositor of the English Language*, which helped him gain an extensive vocabulary.[18]

Teamoh was justly proud of his hard-won literacy and placed his image on the front cover of six of the eighteen school exercise books he penned. When his skills became known to his neighbors, they were amazed that a Black person could be so eloquent.

Slaveholder Jane Thomas hired out George Teamoh in the 1830s and 1840s as a laborer, caulker, and ship carpenter at the Norfolk Navy Yard. Caulking was strenuous, dirty work, so it became a trade predominantly associated with many African Americans. By the 1840s, the shipyard had fifteen Black and five white caulkers.[19]

When Teamoh first began working at the naval shipyard, white workers were resentful of enslaved labor and fearful that free blacks might inspire some enslaved workers to revolt. A large group of white stone masons had quit their positions in protest, and the shipyard conducted a formal survey to see how best to manage the situation.

The sad result of this study evidenced that the labor supply was both racially insensitive and geared to a predictable profit margin mentality:

> *White laborers cannot, be readily found. If they could be obtained, and when obtained, they will not certainly be procured on terms as advantageous to the*

---

18. George Teamoh, *God Made Man, Man Made the Slave: The Autobiography of George Teamoh*, ed. F.N. Boney, Richard L. Hume, and Rafia Zafar (Macon: Mercer University Press, 1990), 21.
19. George Teamoh, 35.

public, as those now given to blacks. The price of white laborers is from 75-80/
100 per month compared to the blacks paid 62 ½ /100. White laborers do not
perform more labor than the blacks per day. . . . In addition, blacks are not
difficult to govern in the Yard, and I have heard of no insurrectionary, disorderly
or refractory spirits exhibited by them. There are about two hundred and forty-six
blacks employed in the Yard and Dock altogether; of whom one hundred and
thirty-six are in the former and one hundred ten in the latter.[20]

This was a most difficult finding for the white employers to accept.
In his autobiography, Teamoh recalled:

Slavery was so interwoven at that time in the very ligaments of the dock that
to assail it from any quarter was not only a herculean task, but on requiring
great consideration caution and comprehensiveness. At that I was occasionally at
work in the Navy Yard, and with hundreds of others in my condition but felt to
remain there would lead to being worse situated or even sold.[21]

In 1841, Reverend Vernon Eskridge, a Methodist minister and chap-
lain to the Norfolk Navy Yard, married Teamoh to Sallie, an enslaved
woman. In 1853, Teamoh was assigned as a carpenter aboard the merchant ship *Currituck,* bound for Germany. On the return voyage, he
got off in New York, where he hired a lawyer to secure his back pay
and declared himself formally free. He then moved to New Bedford in
December 1853. As a fugitive and freeman, Teamoh received some help
from Underground Railroad agents.

Despite the assistance from others, Teamoh quickly learned "notwithstanding their repeated manifestations of kindness. I was doomed
to share a hard lot in that wealthy city of New Bedford . . . while seeking
employ, I was often shifted from side to side of ware houses groaning
under the weight of life's luxuries in order to catch some warmth from the
sun."[22] Teamoh found that seeking shelter in New Bedford meant living
in a city with many fugitives, all looking for work. He found temporary
work as a caulker but was later laid off. He then shoveled snow despite

---

20. George Teamoh, 48.
21. George Teamoh, 27.
22. George Teamoh, 72.

owning no winter clothes. The increased competition for laboring jobs forced him to relocate to Boston, Massachusetts.

After 1862, Teamoh returned to work as a caulker in the Portsmouth shipyard, rising to become the leader of Portsmouth's African American community while advocating for fair wages for fellow shipyard workers.

Teamoh later jumped into state politics, becoming a delegate at the Virginia Constitutional Convention. He served one term as a state senator during a Reconstructionist Congress (1869–1871) in Virginia. Not only did Teamoh experience the failure of the Reconstructionist government, but he also lost his home in 1871.

In January 1871, Teamoh spoke in favor of an unsuccessful bill designed to outlaw whipping, noting that many former slaves, including himself, had endured such punishments. Moreover, anyone who punished another by whipping, whether white or Black, would have been barred from voting.

In his last two decades, Teamoh concentrated on revising his autobiography. He said he wrote it at "the request of many friends."[23] The manuscript was finally published with the help of his descendants and Mercer University Press. Robert Theamoh, the son of George's brother Thomas Teamoh, became a state senator in the 1894 Massachusetts Assembly.

SERGEANT JAMES HENRY GOODING
One of the First Black Soldiers in the Massachusetts Regiments

In January 1863, President Lincoln asked the Union to create voluntary all-Black regiments. In Massachusetts, Governor John Andrew was one of the first to respond, creating the 54th Massachusetts Voluntary Infantry Regiment. Men from all over New England and beyond heeded the call. Over 180,000 Blacks enlisted nationwide. In Massachusetts, so many enlisted that the 55th Massachusetts Regiment was also formed. Well-known local recruiters included Lewis Hayden and Frederick Douglass. In fact, Frederick's son, Lewis Douglass, was proud to enlist and wear the Union uniform.

Training for the new recruits was initiated at Camp Meigs in Reedville, just outside Boston. James Henry Gooding, an emancipated slave

---

23. George Teamoh, 98.

and former whaler, was among the first men to respond to the call to arms. He was an articulate letter writer who documented the details of the regiment as they moved toward battle. The regiment did more than just operate in the background—they faced battle.

The Charleston, South Carolina, harbor was controlled by a gun battery on Fort Sumter, overseeing the port. The 54th Regiment received orders to seize it. In his letters, Gooding describes the bloody aspects of the fight. In all, 270 men out of the 650-man regiment were either killed, captured, or went missing in action, equaling a casualty rate of 42 percent. The soldiers were not fully successful in their assigned mission but did weaken the fort's overall position.

When Gooding wondered what the basic pay for white soldiers compared to Black soldiers was, he went on to write a letter to Lincoln, asking for better pay for all Black soldiers and questioning the disparity. This issue continued unresolved for decades.

Today, a high-relief bronze monument sculpted by Augustus Saint-Gaudens can be found facing the door of the Massachusetts Capitol, commemorating the brave courage of so many men who faced death to end the practice of slavery.

Robert Gould Shaw Memorial

CHAPTER FIFTEEN

New Bedford: A Safe Harbor for Runaway Slaves in Massachusetts

New Bedford and Cape Cod share many historical and geographical connections. Most of their original economic development was integral to the sea. Farming was never a strong suit, nor was the land conducive to plentiful growth. Even when many large-scale factories emerged in the Northeast, the harbors and the tall ships within them played a major role in sustaining a healthy economy.[1]

Another connecting feature is the type of people who settled here. Many early founders wished to differentiate themselves from the early political systems, holding a different perspective from that of the traditional colonial governor. They were rugged individuals who could take care of themselves.

Specifically, Quakers and some Baptists did not feel comfortable with many of the other local contrasting religious beliefs. Their more radical members abhorred the degree of violence that was incorporated into the slavery system.

Simultaneously, other sea captains believed that giving up on all facets of the slave trade, such as accepting cotton cargo from the South or delivering alewife fish to plantations, would be detrimental. This belief system was demonstrated within the wealthy Rotch family. William Rotch Jr. of New Bedford witnessed the cruel way that his brother John Rotch of Providence dealt with slaves aboard his ship. It was the cruel and inhumane treatment of people, not the oppression itself, that turned many a Quacker against this system.

A final connecting bond was the growth of the whaling industry. In 1835, it was estimated that approximately one-third of all Cape Cod men

1. Grover, *The Fugitive's Gibraltar*, 131.

made their living as whalers.[2] These dates correspond closely with New Bedford's deep engagement with the trade. Whaling captains heavily recruited their crews from the Sandwich Islands or chose deep-skinned Portuguese men who had been whaling for centuries. The whale crews transformed from majority Indigenous to other men of darker skin tones in the 1830s.

These connections show how the welcoming of slaves could easily occur in a large port such as Boston or a neighboring smaller port like New Bedford. On a proportionate basis, more slave escapes led to New Bedford than to Boston.

In 1830, New Bedford had a total population of 7,592 residents. By 1834, the number of Black seamen in the city nearly quadrupled. By 1837, the population and economy had grown so much that New Bedford officially became a city. Its 16,000 residents included 1,047 African Americans, 400 of whom were fugitive slaves. By 1840, the runaway-slave population grew to a much larger number doubling that figure.[3]

There is evidence of numerous runaway slaves directly seeking and obtaining freedom on ships heading from the South to New Bedford. One prime example of an abetting sailor was New Bedford Captain William Taber. There was an advertisement posted in the New Bedford Medley on April 28, 1797, highlighting the degree of deception hidden in the offers to help. Captain Taber felt the obligation to publish the following public announcement at his own expense:

> *To all whom it may concern, know ye that William Taber, commander of the sloop Union, sailed from York River, in Virginia on the 28th of March, bound to New Bedford, I discovered a negro on my ship who had concealed himself, unbeknown to me.*
>
> *It appeared inconsistent for me to return, the wind being ahead. I proceeded on my voyage and landed him in this port. He calls his name James, is about 27-year-old, and says he belongs to Mr. Shacleford, a planter, in Kings County, Virginia. Any person who claims him will know by this information where he is—for which purpose it is made public by this information where he is and*

2. Grover, *The Fugitive's Gibraltar*, 152.
3. Grover, *The Fugitive's Gibraltar*, 201.

every legal method has been taken to prevent the owner losing his property, in my power.
—William Taber, 1797 Public Notice – New Bedford Paper, 1797[4]

The reason for this announcement was far from having the Black man apprehended. Taber used the notice to absolve himself of any wrongdoing. The law at the time was complicated. Massachusetts no longer legally allowed slaves to be brought to the Commonwealth, yet the federal standard also applied under the Fugitive Slave Act. The skipper had the onus to return the property. This statement washed his hand of all criminality. In these early days, the slave catchers were slightly less vigorous in their approach and the rewards were smaller. Taber told the world where to find them. A few decades later, this ploy would never have worked, as all slaves would be consistently hunted down by professional slave catchers who roamed the land and sea, hungry for the money and the mission.

More than likely, the captain fully knew of the stowaway on board, giving full support for his release. William Taber was both a strong antislavery advocate as well as a mariner who desired to see his homeport replete with free people willing to work hard. Many of the freed slaves arriving in New Bedford either already had some maritime skills or could be easily trained.

Another example of a pro-slavery Westport sea captain was Thomas Wainer, a mulatto and a business partner of Paul Cuffee. Wainer was a frequent master of the *Ranger*, a seventy-ton schooner, and other smaller vessels that ran out of Westport, carrying cargo as far south as Savannah, Georgia. His all-Black crew raised many an eyebrow when they picked up their load of wheat or corn. On a voyage on April 8, 1799, Samuel Sloane, the owner of a runaway slave from Maryland's Eastern Shore, felt convinced that Wainer was involved in the escape. The document below asked for the return of his property.

Notice of Samuel Sloane, Somerset Co. Maryland

---

4. Timothy D. Walker, "Sailing to Freedom: Maritime Dimensions of the Underground Railroad," *Sea History Magazine*, 175 (Summer 2021): 22-23.

Run away from the subscriber, living in Somerset Maryland, a Negro man named HARRY, about 23 years old of a dark complexion, with thick lips and full eyes. Harry has a notable scar on one of his ancles, occasioned by a burn, also is marked on the calf of one of his legs by the bite of a dog and may perhaps bear on the back of his neck some marks of a blister plaster, applied to it while sick.

Harry is supposed to be carried off by a certain Thomas Wainer of Westport, Massachusetts, a Mulatto who traded here and cleared out as captain of a small vessel from Westport, whither I suppose him to have gone.

Negro Lucy, wife of said Harry, and the property of William Tingle, is said to be with him and in a state of pregnancy. Whoever delivers the said Harry to me, shall receive forty dollars and in proportion is secured in any jail of the United States, so that I get him.

—Kings Ferry, Maryland[5]

The semantics in the wording highlight a few salient issues. First, the description of the blister plaster suggests that kindness was shown to the slave. This action seemed to upset the owner. The use of the phrase "is carried off" is certainly vague and does not indicate any direct evidence of the captain's guilt. Nonetheless, it is most obvious that the owner wanted his property to be returned and the accused captain to be placed in jail. The insistence of prosecution coming under the application of the Fugitive Slave Act is a way to redress the wrongs suffered by the supplicant.

The caulking skills of Black workers led to animosity with whites in New Bedford. People who had the skill and ability to keep boats afloat were in high demand in the early 1800s. The East Coast clamored for men who could upgrade all kinds of maritime equipment, secure a watertight boat, make resistant barrels, produce weather-calibrated sails, and perform maritime carpentry. New Bedford was no exception. This type of training was specifically called for in whalers, brigs, sloops, and other vessels coming into and out of New Bedford Harbor. Let us examine the process of waterproofing or caulking as used in the Great Era of Sail. Perhaps the most proficient and greatest number of caulkers were slaves

---

5. Staff Writer, "SouthCoast an early destination for fugitive slaves," *The Standard-Times*, February 1, 1998, *https://www.southcoasttoday.com/story/news/1998/02/02/southcoast-early-destination-for-fugitive/50586658007/* (accessed December 13, 2023).

who acquired this art in ports like Baltimore, Portsmouth (Virginia), and Wilmington (North Carolina).

On ships, tar and pitch mixed with whale blubber were the most common sealing method of the time. Wooden boats were made water-resistant by putting tar in the hull. The pitch or tar sealed the wooden boards of the ship together, keeping water out and allowing the boat to float. Traditional caulking on wooden boats used cotton and oakum (hemp fiber soaked in pine tar). These fibers were driven into the wedge-shaped seam between planks using a caulking mallet and a broad chisel-like tool called a caulking iron.[6]

To caulk a large-scale vessel, four or five strands of cotton and oakum were driven into the seam using a beetle, an instrument resembling a huge sledgehammer, and hawing irons, the larger versions of caulking irons. One person held the iron, while another person wielded the beetle.

A fortuitous match existed between the skills acquired by many runaway slaves from Virginia and the Carolinas and the destination to which they arrived. Skilled, maritime-trained slaves were the most likely to run away. Many slaves were highly adept at ropemaking, sail weaving, caulking a boat, loading cargo, coopering a barrel, or forging a strong steel anchor. These men were a desperately needed commodity in any shipyard. Nonetheless, a small conflict arose when these new workers reached shore. Some white caulkers felt uncomfortable working with Blacks. They resented their skill and actual appointment to caulking tasks, taking jobs away from whites.

Most of these more complex tasks were valued and compensated in a hierarchical structure. The white men and even some of the free Blacks were engaged in these specified tasks for years and did not wish to relinquish these higher-paying jobs to the new arrivals. As a result, despite the ability to do much more intricate labor, skilled slaves were typically given the most menial, low-paying assignments. Frederick Douglass experienced this type of prejudice while seeking some caulking jobs at the New Bedford piers.

In 1838, Frederick Douglass, twenty years old and with two escape attempts, was working as a caulker, pounding hemp into the seams of

6. Grover, *The Fugitive's Gibraltar*, 61.

wooden ships and pouring hot pitch to make them waterproof. However, some of the dock workers in Massachusetts were not particularly enthused about having Douglass working with them. He certainly could do ordinary shipping tasks like mundane carpentry or basic clean-up, but the more skilled laborers closed their ranks, not wishing to work alongside Douglass. Douglass now realized that there were different strata of society, some of whom were not welcoming to Black slaves.

Some abolitionists in the North saw Douglass as an equal. Other Northerners wanted to see all Blacks free but perhaps not fully integrated, while still others held a vast array of contrasting, biased opinions. Douglass pondered that if a man could not reach his full potential, he saw a distinct limit to one's freedom.[7]

One of the earliest antislavery organizations originated in New Bedford. In 1826, the Massachusetts General Colored Association started contributing financial support to *The Liberator*, pushing for immediate freedom from slavery. William Vincent was appointed as New Bedford's newspaper agent. Vincent was among several men of color operating a boardinghouse for Black mariners. In his home, he had twenty-three residents of varying ages. In most cases, he secured protection papers, keeping them safe. Fleeing slaves felt comfortable making plans to arrive in this Massachusetts city.

---

7. Frederick Douglass, 93.

CHAPTER SIXTEEN

Captains of Color

While we commence to analyze the connection of whaling to the concept of slavery, a blended, intricate image unfolds for the many documented whalers of color. We know the point of origin from where these types of captains started their quest. Sag Harbor (Long Island), Nantucket, New Bedford, and Provincetown formed the center of the whaling industry. We know who set out to sea. The captains and crews were a combination of people who, at appearance levels, never would seem to bond well together to pursue a dangerous mission.

On the decks of the whalers, we can find slaves, slavers, Indigenous men, abolitionists, Quakers, pirates, criminals, men of faith, investors, and figures of great daring. The rationale for the whaling trade was obvious—a significant accumulation of wealth was there for the taking. Whaling was the third highest source of American economy for many years.

The Wampanoags were among the first demographics from the New England shores to reach the large mammals. Aquinnahs from Martha's Vineyard realized the value that whales represented. They celebrated whaling in a quasi-religious experience, the sacred "Powdawe." They placed their small, tribal dugouts against the largest creatures of the sea. When the Indigenous vessels returned to the local village, tribe members celebrated with loud chanting and dance rituals. There is little doubt that precolonial mariners acquired a certain degree of their skill for whaling by speaking with Indigenous people and replicating their methods.

Many factors led to people of color gravitating to the whaling business. Free Black men had limited options. In most other professions, a career ladder never appeared. Escaped slaves lucky enough to make it to a safe port, like New Bedford, could be employed immediately with the added incentive of being at sea for long periods to avoid their potential capture. Whaling opened the door to career advancement.

Slaves and descendants of slaves often worked at the docks, acquiring maritime skills. Indigenous people could earn a small salary through manual labor, which assisted their families. People from the West Indies could move away from the oppressive conditions of their former plantations. Cape Verdeans could flee from the drought-induced devastation of their homeland. All in all, for several decades, crewmen of color consistently comprised at least 30 percent of the whaling workforce.[1] When the prejudice of white dock workers took hold, it steered more free slaves and runaways away from dock work to seek out long-voyage whalers as a potential source of employment.

There is a traceable cycle of when different men of color engaged in this endeavor.[2] Prior to the American Revolution, it was common to see about one-third of Indigenous people, Black slaves, and mixed-race sailors owned by New England merchants assigned to whaling ships. When slaves sailed on whalers, they were required to relinquish any salary to their masters. Decades later, when the profits from whaling greatly increased, the use of Indigenous people dropped significantly in favor of more Europeans as compared to racially diverse people. One solution for people of color struggling to find work was to have captains of color become the masters, employing those they deemed the best fit. Driven by desperation, Cape Verdeans were dying in large numbers in their own homeland in the 1830s. Many of them emigrated to Massachusetts to seek whaling and other jobs.

One family, originally from Martha's Vineyard, started operating nearer the New Bedford area in Dartmouth, Massachusetts. They assumed a major role in the whaling industry. The Cuffees moved their major base of operation to a homeport, keeping many people of color and mixed-Indigenous origin employed.

The whaling industry ran in American history, most prominently from 1720 to 1860. For more than two-thirds of the era, legal justification for slavery was basically the law of the land. The Cuffees took hold of a well-established national need, acquiring more whale oil. The

---

1. Skip Finley, *Whaling Captains of Color: America's First Meritocracy* (Annapolis: Naval Institute Press, 2020), 67.
2. Skip Finley, *Whaling* Captains, 88.

whaling business itself was in sharp decline by the end of the Civil War. It then was transported away from New Bedford and headed toward the tip of Cape Cod to Provincetown. Most of the Northern states, from Massachusetts to New Jersey, were the principal home of the whaling industry. From 1775 to 1790, there was an aggregate growth of 3,723 slaves within our new nation.

States	1775 # of slaves	1790 # of slaves	Number of Major Whaling Sea Ports
Massachusetts, Connecticut, Rhode Island, New York, New Hampshire, Pennsylvania, Delaware, and New Jersey	7,700	11,423 (Note that Massachusetts lists "0" as its number for legal reasons.)	Massachusetts: 41 Connecticut: 10 Rhode Island and New York: 8 each New Hampshire, Pennsylvania, Delaware, and New Jersey: 1 each

Finley, *Whaling Captains of Colors*, Index, 201.

A whaling ship is an excellent vehicle for carrying slaves due to its physical structure and total size. The width and depth of the ship's lower decks were designed to carry many rows of oil barrels and other kinds of heavy merchandise. This factor was evident when Paul Cuffee considered the American Colonization Society. Cuffee was seen as the major hero who could execute bringing slaves to a separate kingdom in Sierra Leone. In truth, after conducting an initial study, he never used whaleboats for this purpose.

Whaling was quite arduous work, requiring precision and months of training. Just considering size and financial scope alone, in 1854, a whaling vessel typically earned $160,000 for the year. The ship could accommodate as many as eight hundred slaves per voyage. In total, whaling ships could have transported eight hundred enslaved bodies at the going rate of $250 per slave. Their profit could be as high as $200,000 in just one voyage, if ever used for that purpose.[3]

Most whaling captains were either Quakers, who denounced slaveholding, or were Black themselves, abhorring the thought of supporting human chattel. By 1783, throughout Massachusetts and especially in Nantucket and Cape Cod, where many Quakers lived, freeing slaves

---

3. Skip Finley, *Whaling Captains*, 256.

became the norm and not the exception. Both Nantucket and Province-town would become the home for many Black seamen seeking to reach the exalted status of becoming whaling captains.

In 1772, Prince Boston was freed from slavery and allowed to keep his full share of maritime profits. In 1822, Absalom Boston took command of the whaler the *Industry*. One year later, Peter Green took command of the whaler *John Adams*. In 1836, Edward Pompey was in charge of the *Rising States* and took an all-Black crew as his mates, with a Black owner sponsoring the voyage. In the same year, Samuel W. Harris, a Black whaler, became captain of the *Phoebe*.

In his book, *Whaling Captains of Color*, Skip Finley identifies seventy-five whaling ports of historical record, and tells of their length of time associated with whaling attempts at each port. Of the seventy-five possible ports, forty of them were from Massachusetts, showing that the Bay State holds a unique position in whaling history.

Forty of the Seventy American Whaling Ports, all from Massachusetts

#	First Year	Port	Last Year	Total Years of Service
1	1791	New Bedford MA	1928	137
2	1784	Boston, MA	1901	117
3	1821	Provincetown, MA	1920	99
4	1785	Dartmouth, MA	1877	92
5	1785	Newburyport, MA	1868	83
6	1785	Wellfleet, MA	1867	82
7	1788	Nantucket, MA	1868	80
8	1816	Edgartown MA	1894	78
9	1839	Somerset, MA	1912	73
10	1811	Westport, MA	1879	68
11	1815	Fairhaven, MA	1876	61
12	1785	Plymouth, MA	1845	60
13	1794	Wareham, MA	1853	59
14	1788	Gloucester, MA	1841	52
15	1818	Salem, MA	1868	50
16	1786	Bristol, MA	1827	41
17	1820	Falmouth, MA	1859	39

#	First Year	Port	Last Year	Total Years of Service
18	1832	Fall River, MA	1860	28
19	1840	Sippican, MA	1865	25
20	1816	Rochester, MA	1840	25
21	1849	Beverly, MA	1873	24
22	1830	Lynn, MA	1853	23
23	1841	Mattapoiset, MA	1864	23
24	1867	Marion, MA	1885	18
25	1822	Marblehead, MA	1833	11
26	1851	Orleans, MA	1861	10
27	1841	New Suffolk, MA	1850	9
28	1851	Sandwich MA	1859	8
29	1833	Dorchester, MA	1837	4
30	1841	Freetown, MA	1844	3
31	1847	Yarmouth, MA	1849	2
32	1785	Hingham, MA	1785	1
33	1786	Braintree, MA	1786	1
34	1789	Cape Cod, MA (unspecified)	1789	1
35.	1841	Buckport, MA	1841	1
36	1841	Duxbury, MA	1841	1
37	1846	Barnstable MA	1846	1
38	1848	Chilmark, MA	1848	1
39	1849	Quincy, MA	1849	1
40	1850	Truro, MA	1851	1

Adopted from Finley, *Whaling Captains of Color*, 211-212.

Some observations we can discern about the whaling ports:

1. Of the seventy cited whaling ports in our country, forty are directly from the Cape Cod region or a close environment.

2. Based on the longevity of trips, the longest-serving ports are New Bedford, Boston, Provincetown, Dartmouth, Newburyport, Wellfleet, Nantucket, Edgartown, Somerset, and Westport.

3. Due to Quaker influence, many Black captains and seamen made up a disproportionately high level of influence and participation on these voyages.

4. Between all the Cape Cod and nearby towns represented here, sailors in dozens of ports were sympathetic, offering slaves safe harbor and a place to obtain work.

5. Many towns attempted to profit from whaling but gave up these efforts quickly, demonstrating the difficulty of the task.

RICHARD JOHNSON
A Whaler and Slave Saver

Still another connection to Paul Cuffee was Richard Johnson. In 1815, he married Ruth Howard, the widow of Paul's son-in-law. Richard was a shrewd businessman who owned no less than four whaling ships. At a time when most Black entrepreneurs had significant challenges obtaining the funds needed to start a new business, Richard was viewed as a man of sterling integrity who always knew how much to value cargo in proportion to earning a healthy profit for both buyer and seller. As a young man, Richard fought for the American cause during the War of 1812 and was captured, spending months in a British prison. Some American captive seamen in this war were offered the option of whaling for Great Britain in lieu of jail, but most rejected assisting the British cause.

Upon his release, Richard returned to Dartmouth and joined the whaling community. As he obtained his new ships, he frequently used Black sea captains to master them. With the ship *Industry*, he hired Absalom Boston from Nantucket to take the wheel. For the *Rising States*, he used Edward J. Pompey and William Cuffee. The vessel *Francis* and the whaler *Washington* had various Black crewmen and captains.

Although no evidence is found, there is a strong indication that Johnson used both his whalers and his captains to assist escaped slaves in finding their way North. In his book, *Rise to Be a People: A Biography of Paul Cuffee*, Lamont D. Thomas states, "Mr. Johnson was always ready to extend the hand of relief to his enslaved countrymen, and no one was ever more ready to assist, according to his own ability, in the elevation of his people."[4] Thomas later became the New Bedford editor for William Garrison's *The Liberator*, for which he gathered much respect among all races of people.

---

4. Lamont D. Thomas, *Rise to Be a People: A Biography of Paul Cuffee* (Urbanna-Champaign: University of Illinois Press, 1971), 179.

Of course, Black captains and crews faced enormous peril when they sailed into southern ports. Not only did the Fugitive Slave Act put them at great risk, but individual states could also write legislation that benefited them. By 1822, three Southern states passed the Negro Seamen Acts, which ordered the arrest or detainment of Black seamen and passengers arriving at their posts to identify runaway slaves.

Due to the heavy influence and wealth of the Cuffee family, merchants from Boston who supported the use of Black sailors petitioned Congress to ban these types of laws and restrictions. The words of Garrison's *Liberator* took on the cause and were successfully argued in a North Carolina court that, at a minimum, Black sailors should be allowed to stay on board the ship while in port rather than being placed in a prison during the duration of the ship's visit at the dock.

It seems most appropriate that the last successful American whaling expedition left from New Bedford in 1925, captained by an Azorean master with a mostly Black crew. The *John R. Manta* returned with three hundred barrels of sperm oil valued at five thousand dollars per barrel.

As a collective family unit, the Cuffees, Wainers, and Cooks amassed a substantive fortune as Black sea captains in America prior to the Civil War. They dared to take leadership positions that delved into a perilous and competitive business yet, if done well, could be extremely profitable. There are four key takeaways from their accomplishments:

1. The success of Black whaling captains could be seen as a source of great pride among slaves and fellow sea captains.
2. Blacks represented themselves and the whole of maritime trade honorably and professionally.
3. The respect afforded to these men by public officials was enormous during a turbulent time in our nation's history, often asking for help or advice.
4. Although no formal evidence exists to support it, one might suggest that slaves seeking freedom may have been in contact with people connected to the Cuffees, asking them to consider safe passage to the North.

CHAPTER SEVENTEEN

The Maritime Escape Route

In history books, the social movement that brought most runway slaves to liberty is known as the Underground Railroad. Frederick Douglass referred to it as "the Above-Ground Railroad" based on his experiences, principally seeing the ships that either unknowingly held stowaways or made intentional plans to do so. Based on their convictions, sea captains either accepted or rejected attempts to convey escaped Black slaves northward.

In a detailed study on abolitionist practices, Timothy Walker analyzed the integral role that many seamen played in facilitating an escape strategy in his book *Sailing to Freedom: Maritime Dimensions of the Underground Railroad*. Derived from the literature and the research cited in many accounts, personal descriptors for runaway slaves might pop up as simply "the Maritime Escape Route." In the first leg of the trip, runaways would go to a major maritime hub. In many cases, New Bedford, Boston, or Westport are the preferred landing spots. Once safely in Massachusetts, arrangements were made to arrive in safer locales.[1]

Rather than facing miles of arduous walking, engaging in dangerous confrontations with slave catchers, exposing oneself to perilous road hazards, spending potential months on the lam, and carrying significant money for bribery, a journey on a ship was the more efficient and possibly more reasonable way to go.

A sea voyage might be obtained as a daring, risky attempt by the slave to go into a hidden compartment on a boat, or it could be bartered openly with a captain or a crew member. It could be even simpler if the runaway knew with certainty that the captain heading to a safe harbor

---

1. Timothy D. Walker, ed. *Sailing to Freedom: Maritime Dimensions of the Underground Railroad* (Boston and Amherst: University of Massachusetts Press, 2021): 175.

was sympathetic to the cause of freeing slaves. Once arriving on a dock, if an immediate position aboard a sea vessel was open, it may be an attractive consideration for both the slave and captain to consider. If the sea was not the chosen profession, connections were made inland through the connecting options available to the Underground Railroad.

Several pieces of evidence support the nautical solution. First, we have the words spoken by the captains themselves. Captain Daniel Drayton, who died in penury in New Bedford, wrote in his memoir about how frequently runaways approached him.

> *No sooner, indeed, does a vessel, known to be from the North, anchor in any of these waters in the Chesapeake Bay, and the slaves are pretty adroit at ascertaining where a vessel comes from, than she is boarded, if she remains any length of time, and especially overnight, by more or less of them, in hopes of obtaining a passage in her to a land of freedom.*[2]

Another piece of evidence is the strong desire for slaves to seek employment near a harbor. They sought work as coopers, longshoremen, caulkers, sail weavers, and boat repairmen. Many Southern states passed laws prohibiting slaves from toiling near a seagoing vessel.

Other states, such as Virginia, passed a law requiring the official inspection of all cargo ships, which came with a fee. In addition, posters, flyers, and newspapers printed advertisements for the return of runaways, principally in major cities with large ports. Conversely, abolitionists printed posters in wharves, docks, and harbors that warned runaways to be careful. Below is an example of a warning to all people of color, announcing a pressing new act passed by the mayor of Boston:

CAUTION !!!!!!!

COLORED PEOPLE

OF BOSTON, ONE AND ALL

YOU ARE HEREBY RESPCTFULLY CAUTIONED AND

ADVISED TO AVOID CONVERSING WITH THE

WATCHMEN AND POLICE OFFICERS OF BOSTON.

---

2. Drayton, 72.

For since, the recent order of the Mayor & Aldermen,
they are empowered to act as
KIDNAPPERS and SLAVE CATCHERS

And they have already actually employed in Kidnapping, Catching, and Keeping Slaves. Therefore, if you value your Liberty, and the Welfare of the Fugitives among you, SHUN them in every possible manner, as so many Hounds on the track of the most unfortunate of your race.

Keep a Sharp Look Out for kidnappers, and have TOP EYE open
April 14, 1851[3]

3. Jamie Lamont Lathan, "New Format, Same Old Story?: An Analysis of Traditional and Digital U.S. History Textbook Accounts of Slavery" (PhD diss., University of North Carolina, 2013), 94.

Bibliography

Bangs, Benjamin. *Benjamin Bangs Journal, 1763-1765*. Massachusetts Historical Society. https://www.masshist.org/collection-guides/search/results?guide_type=& terms=Benjamin+Bangs (accessed April 5, 2023).

Beagle, Jonathan M. "Remembering Peter Faneuil: Yankees, Huguenots, and Ethnicity in Boston, 1743–1900." *The New England Quarterly* 75, no. 3 (September 2002): 388-414.

Bearse, Austin. *Reminisces of the Fugitive-Slave Law Days in Boston*. Boston: Warren Richardson, 1880.

Bendini, Silvio. *The Christopher Columbus Encyclopedia*. Vol. 2. Smithsonian Museum Press, 1991.

Bigelow, Francis Hill. *Historic Silver of the Colonies and Its Makers*. New York: Kissinger Publishers, 2005.

Black, Leonard. *The Life and Sufferings of Leonard Black, a Fugitive from Slavery*. New Bedford: New Bedford Press, 1847.

Blight, David. *Frederick Douglass: Prophet of Freedom*. New York: Simon and Schuster Press, 2018.

Bowers, Rowland. "Two Exceptional Men, Fishing Schooners and Wellfleet." *Fishing Alliance*. May 2018.

Brandt, Nat. *In the Shadow of the Civil War: Passmore Williamson and the Rescue of Jane Johnson*. Columbia: University of South Carolina Press, 2007.

Cave, Alfred A. *The Pequot War*. Boston and Amherst: University of Massachusetts Press, 2009.

Chervinsky, Lindsay. *The Enslave Household of John Quincy Adams*. Washington, D.C.: Washington Historical Society, 2018.

Chapman, Maria Weston, ed. *The Non-Resistant*. Weymouth: The Non-Reistance Society, 1840.

Clausewitz, Carl von. "Notes from the Dutch Reformed Church." In *Original Narratives of Early American History*, PAGE RANGE. Londong: Forgotten Books, 2008.

Cobb, Elijah. *Memoirs of a Cape Cod Skipper*. New Haven: Yale University Press, 1925.

Coll, Thrush. *Indigenous London: Native Travelers at the Heart of the Empire*. New Haven: Yale University Press, 2016.

David Ruggles Center for History and Education. "A Utopian Community in Florence, MA." https://davidrugglescenter.org/northampton-association-education-industry/ (accessed April 14, 2023).

de Crevecoeur, J. Hector St. John. *Letters of an American Farmer: A View of Early America*. The Avalon Project Press, 1782. https://avalon.law.yale.edu/subject_menus/letters.asp (accessed June 17, 2023).

Diemer, Andrew K. *Vigilance: The Life of William Still, Father of the Underground Railroad*. New York: Alfred A. Knopf, 2022.

Deyo, Simeon L. *History of Barnstable County, Massachusetts*. Barnstable: Higginson Book Company, 1890.

Dow, George Francis. *Slave Ships and Slaving*. Cambridge: Cornell Maritime Press Inc. and Marine Research Society, 1927.

Douglass, Frederick. *Narrative of the Life of Frederick Douglass*. New York: Dover, 1845.

Drayton, Daniel. *Personal Memoirs of Daniel Drayton*. Ann Arbor: University of Michigan Press, 2005.

DuBois, W. E. B. "The Suppression of the African Slave-Trade to the United States of America, 1638–1870." PhD diss., Harvard University, 1896.

Carol Faulkner. *Lucretia Mott's Heresy: Abolition and Women's Rights in Nineteenth-Century America*. Philadelphia: University of Pennsylvania Press, 2011.

Finley, Skip. *Whaling Captains of Color: America's First Meritocracy*. Annapolis: Naval Institute Press, 2020.

Finkelman, Paul. *Slavery in the Courtroom: An Annotated Bibliography of American Cases*. Washington, D.C.: Library of Congress Publication, 1985.

Galenson, David. *White Servitude in Colonial America: An Economic Analysis*. Cambridge: Cambridge University Press, 1971.

Gallay, Alan, ed. *Indian Slavery in Colonial America*. Lincoln: University of Nebraska, 2009.

Graham-Pye, Susanna. "Harwich's Heated Reckoning." *Capecodlife.com*, November/December 2022. https://capecodlife.com/harwichs-heated-reckoning/ (accessed on January 14, 2023).

Grover, Kathryn. *The Fugitive's Gibraltar: Escaping Slaves and Abolitionism in New Bedford, Massachusetts*. New Bedford: The University of Massachusetts Press, 2001.

Harris, Sheldon H. *Paul Cuffe: Black America and the African Return*. New York: Simon and Schuster, 1972.

Jackson, Holly. *American Radicals, How Nineteenth-Century Protest Shaped the Nation*. New York: Random House Press, 2019.

Johnson, Claudia Durst. *Daily Life in Colonial New England*, 2nd ed. Santa Barbara: Greenwood Press, 2017.

Keith, George. "An Exhortation and Caution to Friends concerning Buying or Keeping Negroes." *Pennsylvania Magazine of History*, 1889.

Koester, Nancy. *Harriet Beecher Stowe: A Spiritual Life*. Grand Rapids: Eerdmans Publishing, 2014.

Larsen, Julia. "The Life of Charles B. Ray (1870–1886)." Blackpast, entry posted June 30, 2008, https://www.blackpast.org/african-american-history/ray-charles-b-1807-1886/ (accessed July 17, 2023).

Lepore, Jill. *The Name of War: King Philip's War and the Origins of American Identity*. New York: Vintage Books, 1999.

MacLeod, Jessie. "Ona Judge: A George Washington Slave." The George Washington Presidential Library. https://www.mountvernon.org/library/digitalhistory/digital-encyclopedia/article/ona-judge/ (accessed June 14, 2023).

Maltz, Earl. *Dred Scott and the Politics of Slavery.* Lawrence: Kansas University Press, 2007.

Manegold, C. S. *Ten Hills Farm, The Forgotten History of Slavery in the North.* Princeton" Princeton University Press, 2011.

Mason, Matthew, Kathryn P. Viens, and Conrad Edick Wright, eds. *Massachusetts and the Civil War: The Commonwealth and National Disunion.* Boston: University of Massachusetts Press, 2015.

Medford Historical Society. "Excerpts from Letters to his Ship Captains." Medford Historical Society. https://medfordhistorical.org/medford-history/africa-to-medford/timothy-fitch/ (Accessed November 12, 2023).

Medford Historical Society. "From Africa to Medford: The Untold Story." Medford Historical Society. https://medfordhistorical.orgmedford-history/africa-to-medford/ (accessed December 14, 2023).

Melish, Joann Pope. *Disowning Slavery: Gradual Emancipation and "Race" in New England, 1780–1860.* Ithaca: Cornell University Press, 2000.

Morgan, Edmund S. *American Heroes: Profiles of Men and Women Who Shaped Early America.* New York: W. W. Norton & Company, 2009.

Nathans, Sydney. *To Free a Family: The Journal of Mary Walker.* Cambridge: Harvard University Press, 2012.

National Park Service. "Abolitionism in Boston Harbor." *Boston Harbor Exhibit,* 2023.

National Park Service. "Exploits of Captain Drayton in Boston Harbor." National Park Service. www.nps.gov/boha (accessed January 12, 2023).

Newell, Margaret Ellen. *Brethren by Nature: New England Indians, Colonists, and the Origins of American Slavery.* Ithaca: Cornell University Press, 2015.

Nicholas, Mark A. "Mashpee Wampanoags, Fishery, and the Financial Impact of the Community." *Journal of the American Indian* (Summer 2022): 31-38.

Oates, Stephen B. *The Approaching Fury, Voices of the 1820–1861.* New York: Harper-Collins, 1998.

Oickle, Alvin F. *The Man with the Branded Hand: The Life of Jonathan Walker, Abolitionist.* Yardley: Westholme Publications, 2011.

Paul, Joel Richard. *Indivisible: Daniel Webster and the Birth of American Naturalism.* New York: Riverhead Books, 2022.

Peterson, Mark. *The City-State of Boston: The Rise and Fall of an Atlantic Power, 1630–1865.* Princeton: Princeton University Press, 2019.

PBS. "This Far by Faith: 1526-1775, from Africa to America." The Faith Project Incorporated. https://www.pbs.org/thisfarbyfaith/journey_1/p_3.html (accessed May 10, 2023).

Rediker, Marcus. *The Fearless Benjamin Lay: The Quaker Dwarf Who Became theFirst Revolutionary Abolitionist.* Pittsburgh: Penguin Books, 2010.

Reséndez, Andrés. *The Other Slavery: The Uncovered Story of Indian Enslavement in America.* Boston: Houghton Mifflin, 2016.

Sheidley, Nat. *Revolutionary Spaces.* Faneuil Hall: Museum Exhibit, 2020.

Shrewsbury Historical Society. "Captain Josiah Richardson." Shrewsbury Historical Society. https://www.shrewsburyhistoricalsociety.org/josiah-richardson (accessed December 2, 2022).

Sherwood, Henry Noble. "Paul Cuffe." *The Journal of Negro History* 8, no. 2 (April 1923): 153-161.

Sterne, Emma. *The History of the Amistad.* Garden City: Dover Evergreen Classics, 2021.

Teamoh, George. *God Made Man, Man Made the Slave: The Autobiography of George Teamoh.* Edited by F.N. Boney, Richard L. Hume, and Rafia Zafar. Macon: Mercer University Press, 1990.

Thomas, Lamont. *Rise to Be a People: A Biography of Paul Cuffe.* Urabana-Champaign: University of Illinois Press, 1971.

Walker, Timothy D., ed. *Sailing to Freedom: Maritime Dimensions of the Underground Railroad.* Boston and Amherst: University of Massachusetts Press, 2021.

Walker, Timothy D. "Sailing to Freedom: Maritime Dimensions of the Underground Railroad." *Sea History Magazine* 175 (Summer 2021): 20-23.

Warren, Wendy Anne. "'The Cause of Her Grief': The Rape of a Slave in Early New England." *The Journal of American History* 93, no. 4 (March 2007): 1031-1049.

Warren, Wendy. *New England Bound: Slavery and Colonialization in Early America.* New York: Liveright Publishing Corporation, 2016.

Washburn, Emory. *Slavery as it Once Prevailed in Massachusetts.* Boston: John Wilson and Son Press, 1869.

Wilson, Henry. *The History of the Rise and Fall of the Slave Power in America V2.* Boston: Houghton Mifflin, 1872.

Work. N. "The Life of Charles B. Ray." *Journal of African Studies* 4, no. 4 (2021): 361-371.

Zacks, Richard. *The Pirate Hunter: The True Story of Captain Kidd.* New York: Hyperion, 2002.

About the Author

Dr. Michael Pregot has spent a long career in public education. He has served as a world language teacher, school principal, district-wide superintendent, college professor, and coordinator of an Educational Leadership Program at the graduate level. He has owned his home on Cape Cod for twenty years, becoming enamored with Cape Cod maritime stories and history along the way.

||||||||||||||||||||||||||||||||

www.ingramcontent.com/pod-product-compliance
Lightning Source LLC
Chambersburg PA
CBHW011159090426
42740CB00020B/3409